KU-312-867

The Mistresses of Henry VIII

KELLY HART

The History Press

Kelly Hart is an English historian who currently lives in Glasgow, Scotland. She works as a teacher and author and specialises in studying women of the Tudor period. This is her first book. She is currently writing *The Seventh Wife*, a biography of Katherine Willoughby, duchess of Suffolk.

To my husband, Andrew Gatenby

HOUNSLOW LIBRARIES	
HOU	
C0000 002 465 683	
Askews	18-Nov-2009
942.052	£12.99

First published 2009

The History Press
The Mill, Brimscombe Port
Stroud, Gloucestershire, GL5 2QG
www.thehistorypress.co.uk

© Kelly Hart, 2009

The right of Kelly Hart to be identified as the Author
of this work has been asserted in accordance with the
Copyrights, Designs and Patents Act 1988.

All rights reserved. No part of this book may be reprinted
or reproduced or utilised in any form or by any electronic,
mechanical or other means, now known or hereafter invented,
including photocopying and recording, or in any information
storage or retrieval system, without the permission in writing
from the Publishers.

British Library Cataloguing in Publication Data.
A catalogue record for this book is available from the British Library.

ISBN 978 0 7524 4835 0 (hardback)
ISBN 978 0 7524 5496 2 (trade paperback)

Typesetting and origination by The History Press
Printed in Malta

Contents

Chronology

1509: On St. George's Day, Henry was officially proclaimed King Henry VIII. He was described as '*a youngling, he cares for nothing but girls and hunting*'. Within weeks, the new seventeen-year-old king had married his brother's widow, the pretty twenty-three-year-old Princess Katherine of Aragon. Henry seemed enamoured with his new wife.

1510: The first rumours surfaced of Henry's affairs with other women; in this year a scandal arose from his affair with Lady Anne Stafford, the married sister of the Duke of Buckingham. This relationship may have continued over the next three years.

1513: Henry invaded France and spent time at Margaret of Austria's court, much of it in the company of Étiennette de la Baume.

1514: There were the first suggestions of affairs with Bessie Blount, Elizabeth Carew and Jane Popincourt. Cracks were beginning to show in the royal marriage and there were the first rumours of an annulment.

1516: Jane Popincourt, with a generous leaving present from Henry, returned to France to join her former lover, the duc de Longueville. Katherine of Aragon finally gave birth to a child who would survive to adulthood, Princess Mary.

1517: Around this year, Henry began an affair with his wife's young maid of honour, Bessie Blount.

1519: Bessie gave birth to Henry's only (acknowledged) illegitimate child, Henry Fitzroy.

1522: A marriage was arranged for Bessie Blount, which probably marked the end of her affair with the king. There were rumours she was replaced by '*Mistress Parker*'. Around this time, he became involved with another lady-in-waiting, Mary Boleyn.

1524: Mary Boleyn gave birth to a daughter, Catherine Carey.

1525: Henry ceased to cohabit with his wife, Katherine of Aragon, who was then thought to be beyond childbearing.
His relationship with Mary Boleyn came to an end.
Henry gave his illegitimate son, Henry Fitzroy, several titles, including duke of Richmond and Somerset. There were rumours from then on that Fitzroy was being groomed as the next king of England.

1526: Mary Boleyn gave birth to a son, Henry Carey, who was later rumoured to be the king's child. The King declared his love for Mary's sister, Anne.

1527: Henry proposed to Anne Boleyn and initiated annulment proceedings to rid himself of the ageing Queen Katherine.
Cardinal Wolsey, the King's chief minister, initiated ecclesiastical proceedings against Henry's ex-mistress, Lady Anne Stafford, for adultery with Henry's close friend, Sir William Compton.

1532: Around December, Anne Boleyn became pregnant by Henry.

1533: Henry married Anne in a secret ceremony, although his first marriage had not yet been annulled.
Princess Elizabeth was born in September.

1534: The first rumours began of Henry's infidelity with a '*very handsome young lady*' at court. She was said to be popular with the conservative faction and corresponding with Henry's daughter Mary.

1535: Henry embarked on a six-month affair with Anne Boleyn's cousin, Mary Shelton.

1536: Henry attempted to make another maid of honour, Jane Seymour, his mistress. She refused unless he could offer her marriage. Queen Anne was arrested for treason, incest and adultery and executed. Eleven days later, Henry married Jane.
It was reported that Henry regretted his marriage to Jane once he had seen two new ladies at court.
Henry's illegitimate son, the duke of Richmond, died aged seventeen, leaving Henry inconsolable.

1537: Queen Jane died giving birth to the future Edward VI. There were no further rumours of Henry having extramarital affairs, except those which led to marriage. He was forty-six years old.

1538: Henry began looking for a fourth wife. Mary Skipwith and Mary Shelton were considered to be contenders, as well as several princesses.

1540: Henry married Anne of Cleves, but was unwilling to consummate the union. After six months, the marriage was annulled and he wed Anne's teenage maid of honour, Catherine Howard.

1542: Catherine Howard was executed for adultery. Henry was rumoured to be considering Elizabeth Brooke or Anne Bassett as her replacement.

1543: Henry married Katheryn Parr.

1546: Henry agreed that Queen Katheryn should be arrested for heresy, although he later changed his mind. It was rumoured that Henry wished to replace Katheryn with her close friend, Katherine Willoughby, duchess of Suffolk.

1547: There was an attempt to make Lady Mary Howard – the king's daughter-in-law – his mistress, so she could then control Henry and Prince Edward. Those involved in this scheme were sentenced to be executed.
Henry VIII died and was buried, as he had instructed, next to Jane Seymour, his *true wife*.

Pastime with good company,
I love, and shall until I die.
Grudge who will, but none deny,
So God be pleased, thus live will I.
For my pastance:
Hunt, sing, and dance,
My heart is set!
All goodly sport,
For my comfort,
Who shall me let?

Youth must have some dalliance,
Of good or ill some pastance.
Company methinks them best,
All thoughts and fancies to digest.
For idleness,
Is chief mistress
Of vices all:
Then who can say,
But mirth and play,
Is best of all?

Company with honesty,
Is virtue, vice to flee.
Company is good and ill,
But every man has his free will.
The best ensue,
The worst eschew,
My mind shall be:
Virtue to use,
Vice to refuse,
Thus shall I use me!

Written by Henry VIII

Introduction

Henry and His Women

He was Bluff King Hal; big, handsome, victor of the jousts and all a sovereign should be. He was a fat tyrant, irritably shouting at and striking his servants, turning the established Church on its head in his lust for women and wealth. He was a man who married six times but claimed only two had been legally binding; he has fascinated generations since, and has attracted the attention of numerous talented researchers. In this book, I have pieced together all the information on his mistresses, his wives and the women he pursued. Here, we will look at the ladies who attracted the man who could have had anyone – the cream of Tudor society. And they were every bit as intriguing as the man himself.

His most famous mistresses, Bessie Blount, the mother of his son, and Mary Boleyn, the sister of Anne, are well-covered in this book, as well as many women who here emerge from the shadows: Lady Anne Stafford, sister of the first peer of the realm and Henry's second cousin; Jane Popincourt, his sisters' French tutor; Mary Shelton, a poet and cousin of the Boleyn sisters; Elizabeth Amadas, a '*witch and prophetess*'[1]; and Elizabeth Brooke, whose husband had left her because of her adultery. There was also the beautiful Étiennette, who enchanted Henry while he was at war in France, the popular maid of honour Anne Bassett, Henry's daughter-in-law, Mary Howard, duchess of Richmond, as well as women he kept in secret houses and the wives of two of his close friends.

People assume that a man who had six wives must have had six hundred lovers and imagine Henry was a consummate philanderer, chasing every female he saw. But Henry was essentially a one-woman man; he had many lovers but was usually faithful to each in turn. In the sixteenth century, it was a common belief that gout, constipation and a red face could be caused by too much sex – Henry appeared to have all of these symptoms. This was why rumours about syphilis took root; people believed that Henry had been so promiscuous, he *must* have caught it. The reality was quite different.

Henry VIII deserves to be one of England's best-known kings. He founded the Church of England, radically changing the course of English history and the culture of the nation, and he cemented the union of England and Wales, which stands to this day. He can make a good claim to the title 'Father of the English Navy' and he consolidated and strengthened English rule in Ireland – by the end of his reign he had become 'King of Ireland' instead of the 'Lord' his predecessors had used. But Henry's fame does not lie with these considerable achievements – he is well-known because of his unconventional attitude to women. His determination to give some of his lovers everything they wanted – even the crown off his wife's head, or his wife's head itself – has secured his place in history.

It is unsurprising that Henry had many lovers as most noble families wanted one of their women to attract the king's attention, and they were paraded before him in their costliest clothes and elaborate jewellery. Many of them never washed, had wooden teeth, bad breath and body odour, but they doused themselves in perfume, trowelled on the make-up with a rabbit's foot and fluttered their eyelashes at the omnipotent monarch, and sometimes they were successful in attracting him. Families could receive great benefits from a member of their family being in the king's bed. His queens watched their ladies-in-waiting carefully, ensuring they dressed conservatively and spent much of their day on their knees praying, embroidering – anything his wife could think of to keep her ladies from becoming a threat; but Henry's queens had to learn to turn a blind eye to his philandering. Nearly all of his affairs were with ladies-in-waiting, who spent most of their time with Henry's wife, creating an awkward atmosphere in the queen's apartments.

The younger Henry seemed to prefer women to girls, choosing females in their mid to late twenties, although several teenage maids of honour also became the objects of his affection. Yet he does not seem to have had an exact type, which made it difficult for the courtiers to second-guess his feelings and so influence him through their female relatives. Feisty, submissive, beautiful, plain, intellectual and illiterate are all terms that have been used to describe one or more of Henry's lovers. Yet there was one clear theme from his thirties onwards – he seemed to choose the opposite of the last woman he had fallen for. Henry was considered a demigod by his subjects, so each woman he chose was someone who had managed to stand out in a crowd of stunning ladies. Looking good was not enough (indeed, many of Henry's lovers were considered plain); she had to have something extra special to keep the King's interest.

Henry has been portrayed as a man who did not overwhelm his lovers with generosity, but those who he really loved were well looked after. Bessie Blount became the first royal mistress in centuries whose bastard quickly received a title – and her son was given a double dukedom, making the six-year-old the foremost nobleman in the realm. There is convincing evidence that Henry VIII intended to make their son his heir – elevating Mistress Blount to mother of the king. And if Henry had not fallen in love with Anne Boleyn – or if she had been prepared to accept the usual role of mistress – then England might still be a Catholic country and the Anglican Church never have come into existence, in England or across the world. He was prepared to do whatever it took to have her, with far-reaching consequences.

Henry's wives reflected and, to some extent, influenced his politics, and so did his mistresses. In France, to be the king's mistress was not a secret affair; it was a recognised position at court, coming with its own apartments, power and privileges. Only one of his lovers was given something of the role she would have expected in France, and this was Anne Boleyn, an exceptional woman by any standards, whose spectacular rise to power was matched only by her dramatic fall. Most princes were notorious for their liaisons, but for Henry these were private relationships not to be displayed to the world, and he would not have given a political position to a woman just because she was attractive. Yet he was very susceptible to subtle influence from his paramours, as his courtiers well knew and an intelligent woman could exploit.

Henry was quite a catch – he was widely considered to be handsome and charming, the life and soul of the pageant, the feast and the hunt, with his boyish charm and boundless energy. It is hard to trust contemporary descriptions of kings – people were invariably dazzled by the splendour of the monarch's clothes, jewellery and entourage, and so all royalty were described as extremely attractive and incredibly intelligent. But there is no doubt that Henry VIII deserved most of the accolades he received.

Thomas More described him as a man who made each person he spoke to believe that he or she alone had the King's '*special favour*'.[2] Yet he was a complex character, full of contradictions. Henry was very learned, spoke several languages and wrote books on theology, but he was also an athlete who excelled in all sports. His people loved him although he could be an insecure egomaniac; vain, manipulative and with a talent for self-delusion. As his reign progressed, these were the character traits that came to the fore, and ladies had far more to gain and far more to lose from attracting his attention.

The dominant females in Henry's childhood would have had a profound influence on his attitude to women. His mother, Elizabeth of York, and his strong-willed paternal grandmother, Margaret Beaufort, were his female role models – and they could not have been more different. Margaret Beaufort's royal blood had meant she was always in danger. The heiress of the Lancastrian dynasty was the guiding hand in plotting for her only son, Henry VII, to become king of England and she was the force behind the throne throughout his reign. She lived for religion, scholarship and her family; her experiences made her a character of steel. And it was Margaret Beaufort who had the most contact with, and control over, her young grandson, Henry.

Yet it is likely that Henry saw the ideal woman as similar to his mother – submissive. Elizabeth of York was reportedly docile and gentle, the very image of the perfect sixteenth-century woman. As the heiress of the Yorkist kings, she had a better claim to the throne than her Lancastrian husband, but did not seek power or influence in her own right. Henry VIII's only lover who truly fitted this description, Jane Seymour, is the one he chose to be buried with. Henry may have considered it no coincidence that this was the wife God chose to give a male child to, the wife who was all a Christian lady should be. Yet this was not the type of woman who often attracted him; his romantic choices usually veered between flirty, frivolous girls and formidable, intelligent women who were more than a match for him.

Henry did not follow conventions when it came to love, although in every other way he was a very traditional man. Marrying for love was considered eccentric, even insane, but for Henry it helped usher in an era of English nationalist feeling with an English Church and a succession of English queens. Marrying one of his own subjects was a revolutionary idea, but it did not start a revolution in people's attitudes to marriage; most still chose dynastic and financial considerations over mere emotional factors.

Five times Henry married women because he was attracted to them, and only one of these was a foreign princess with influence and a decent dowry. His choices did not usher in acceptance of divorce either – they just meant that the archbishop of Canterbury occasionally authorised an annulment, rather than the Pope, and these were still very difficult to obtain.

His wives have emerged in book after book as six very different women, portrayed as feminist icons of the Tudor age. Bessie Blount, Mary Boleyn, Mary Shelton, Anne Stafford, Jane Popincourt and Elizabeth Amadas, as well as his other mistresses, deserve to have their amazing life stories told, just as Henry and his wives have; I aim here to rescue them from obscurity. The sixteenth century was a time of profound change in religion and society right across Europe – and some of Henry's lovers were involved in influencing these events. For the first time, the information on Henry's mistresses has been gathered together in one book and we can see the women behind the smokescreen. You know about Henry's queens – now it is time to read about Henry's queans.[*]

---

[*] Quean: an overly forward woman; hussy.

Chapter 1

The Teenage King

'Company with honesty
is virtue – and vice to flee ...'

Henry VII had been seen by his people as a miser, and had died an old man without the magnetism and charisma, the common touch, that his son seemed to have been born with. The nation rejoiced at the sight of Henry VIII, a magnificent, fun-loving giant, who was determined to spend his inheritance on lavish displays of power and prosperity. Young Henry had become the only hope of the Tudor dynasty after the death of his brother, Prince Arthur, in 1502, and so his father had mollycoddled him, preventing him from mixing freely with the court or participating in the dangerous sports to which he would dedicate much of his adult life. The Spanish envoy, Don Gutierre Gomez de Fuensalida, wrote that the young Henry was 'locked away like a woman ... he is so subjugated that he does not speak a word except in response to what the King asks him'.[1] Unlike many kings, Henry may not have had a mistress before he ascended the throne.

Once king, Henry began to make up for lost time, and was 'never still or quiet'.[2] He was now revelling in his new-found freedom, and as his courtiers knew, this was likely to include spending time with beautiful women; many of the nobles would have been competing to find him a mistress. One courtier, George Cavendish, described Henry at his accession as 'young, lusty and courageous'.[3] Thomas More wrote that: 'Among a thousand noble companions, the King stands out the tallest, and his strength fits his majestic body. There is fiery power in his eyes, beauty in his face, and the colour of twin roses in his cheeks.'[4] And with his crown, as well as his personal attributes, many ladies would have been very attracted to the teenage king.

According to the French ambassador, in 1509: 'Henry is a youngling, he cares for nothing but girls and hunting'.[5] His councillors could deal with the rest. The young king quickly became the centre of a group of young and hedonistic men, all of whom were anxious to keep him amused. He spent little time with his aged councillors and began to favour those who had not served his cautious father. However, matters of state did not weigh heavily on Henry's young mind; he wished to pursue women, to entertain and to be entertained, to bring back the glamour and excitement that the court had lacked during his father's reign.

But there was one important issue for Henry to resolve. He was betrothed to Princess Eleanor of Austria, but announced that his father had begged him to marry Princess Katherine of Aragon instead. Henry had previously been affianced to Katherine, but this had been set aside because the alliance was no longer so advantageous to the English, and her father had not paid her dowry in full. The betrothal had easily been declared void, after genuine concern from ecclesiastics, including William Warham, archbishop of Canterbury, over the legality of any marriage between Henry and Katherine. This was because she had been, for five months, the wife of Henry's brother. Even though she insisted the marriage had never been consummated, this still made her Henry's sister under church laws, and as such he could not marry her. A papal dispensation had allayed most people's concerns, but this affinity was still an easy ground on which to end the engagement – and later the marriage.

Declaring that it had been his father's dying wish was one way to placate the rejected Princess Eleanor and her powerful family, but the marriage was probably Henry's decision alone. It was a choice based on politics and attraction; it certainly caused great relief and joy to Katherine and her servants. It was a show of England's might that Henry was married to a daughter of the Catholic king. Princess Eleanor would have been as good a match, but Katherine and Henry had met at court many times and, throughout her widowhood, Katherine had clung to the belief that Henry would marry her if he was allowed to. The Spanish ambassador saw 'no likelihood of it'[6] but Katherine was proved right. Now the chivalrous knight had rescued the damsel in distress.

The Infanta Katherine had been in England, impoverished and excluded, for over six years waiting to see if the king would marry her, caught between the tight-fistedness of her father and of her father-in-law. She had been kept deliberately short of clothes, of the servants that were considered essential to the dignity of a daughter of Spain, of money to pay the servants she did have. She was now the queen and she and the nobility were exultant. It had been six years since there had been a queen of England, and so there had been few women at court. Now Henry was in charge of his own destiny – and many young women were arriving, excited to become ladies-in-waiting, and ready to serve their queen – and their king.

Katherine was a popular choice as queen, with the courtiers, the common people and with the king. She was strong-willed but deferred to her husband; she was astute and had been trained from birth to play the role of queen consort. She set about befriending the highest nobles in the land, defusing some of the annoyance felt at court that the king befriended any man who amused him, and she chose as her motto: 'Humble and loyal'. The twenty-three-year-old princess was considered attractive; she was very short, and had fair skin, which may have come from her English heritage. She had long, auburn hair, and she often wore it loose. She was slightly plump, which was considered both attractive and a sign of fertility, the most important attribute a queen could have.

Isabella and Ferdinand had five children who survived to adulthood, so the English hoped that Katherine would be as fertile as the mother she resembled in many other ways. Fertility in a wife was so important that it was endlessly speculated about, with all the court trying to work out from the woman's mother and grandmothers if she was likely to be a good breeder. Yet Katherine does not seem to have always taken care of herself. Even from early on in Henry's reign, Katherine's fasting was very committed, with Luis Caroz, the Spanish ambassador, reporting that it was causing irregular periods.[7] Courtiers would repeat Henry's private information to foreign ambassadors, even regarding the queen's menstrual cycles, to help ascertain if she was pregnant or likely to become so.

On 11 June 1509, fifty days after Henry VII's death, Henry and Katherine were married and they had a spectacular joint coronation. Henry wrote to his father-in-law that 'My wife and I be in good and perfect love as any two creatures can be'.[8] This appears to have been more than mere flattery, but any passion from Henry's side seems to have evaporated within the first five years of marriage. Yet chivalry, admiration, friendship and respect for her lineage remained. Katherine was a significant influence on Henry, particularly in the early years of their marriage, although his respect for her opinions was partly based on the usefulness of the alliance between England and Spain. Katherine was devoted, from the very beginning of her marriage, to the young man who had rescued her after six years of insult and deprivation. Her obvious attachment to her husband was touching and pleased the court.

Katherine has been described as Henry's first love; she was certainly the first woman he publicly displayed affection for. Her good looks and exotic appeal may have encouraged Henry to marry her without worrying about the rest of the dowry or the theological objections to marrying one's brother's widow. Henry is said to have bragged openly at court about how his wife had been a virgin on their wedding night, which later he dismissed as 'spoke in jest, as a man jesting and feasting says many things which are not true'.[9] Doubts about their marriage would come later, when Katherine was older and unattractive.

The royal couple enjoyed hawking, riding, dancing and all the other festivities of the court. After being in limbo for so long, Queen Katherine must have been euphoric, and pleasing this young woman would have appealed greatly to Henry. Katherine was probably the only one, other than his sisters, who could really understand Henry's childhood and his responsibilities, as she had also been born and raised to rule. She admired, studied and patronised the work of English humanists and encouraged Henry to do the same, as well as helping many foreigners come to England to spread their knowledge and to study further. She was one of the most highly educated young women of her age, and, like Henry, had been educated in the humanist tradition. Erasmus, the leading humanist scholar of his age, thought Henry very learned, but Katherine of Aragon even more so. They seemed a good match.

In 1511, at the christening of their son Prince Henry, who lived for only seven weeks, Henry wore clothes embroidered with the letters H and K entwined on them. At some earlier jousts, Henry wore Katherine's initials on his sleeve. This was unusual; princes did not usually choose their wives to pay court to. Henry did far more than was expected of a royal husband to show affection for his wife. The king seems to have been genuinely enamoured; in the books the entertainment costs were repeatedly written down as 'for the Queen's pleasure' and 'for a gladness to the Queen's grace'.[10] He valued her opinions on everything from music to politics.

Their lives were a constant round of entertainments and the ladies were the centre of court life, of the dances and the masques. As a person's rank was judged by how many servants he or she had, a queen had to have a plethora of attendants. Noble blood was not always enough to get them a place at court – Henry VIII demanded that all his wife's ladies be 'fair'[11] and that they had to be dressed splendidly, at their own considerable cost. Ladies-in-waiting spent most of their time with the queen; but, as Katherine would learn, many of them also spent time with the king.

It has often been asserted that Henry was faithful to Katherine until he was first linked to Bessie Blount, five years into his reign. In reality, Henry was involved with other women from the very beginning of his first marriage. He seems to have been attracted to Katherine at first – a bonus for an arranged marriage – but there were many other tempting offers for the teenage king. And within a year of marriage, the whole court was aware of who the king's lover was. And his wife was devastated by his betrayal.

Henry's desire for Lady Anne Stafford caused a scandal that reverberated around Europe. In May 1510, only a year into his marriage and while the devoted Queen Katherine was pregnant, Henry strayed. Anne Stafford was a dangerous choice – she was the sister of the premier peer of England, Henry's second cousin, and a married woman. Edward, duke of Buckingham, was outraged that his sister could demean the family by becoming the mistress of any man, even a king. Descended from Edward III several times over, the Staffords were suspected of considering themselves more royal than the Tudors.

Most families would have been pleased that the king had chosen their relative. The personal was truly the political under Henry VIII, and so the courtiers tried to excel at the pastimes he enjoyed, and went to extreme lengths to gain his friendship. Court was all about trying to get the ear of the king; it was natural that to spend nights next to that ear would be an advantage much sought after. Mistresses provided sex and companionship for their lover, but they were also useful to other courtiers, as being close to the king's favourite meant being close to the king himself. A mistress would often distribute patronage or even head factions. This is why families were often happy for their relatives to commit adultery if it was with the king – it provided the whole clan with access to power. Unfortunately for Henry, the duke of Buckingham did not see it that way.

In 1503, it had looked likely that Henry VII would die without an adult heir; his son was then only twelve years old. As Henry VII claimed the crown more through conquest than through bloodline, this did not bode well for the future of the Tudor dynasty. People began to speak of offering the throne to the duke of Buckingham, or perhaps Edmund de la Pole, if the King died, but 'none of them spoke of my lord prince'.[12] Knowing this would have left Henry VIII very wary of these noble families of royal lineage. If Henry VII had died then, it is likely that the Lady Anne Stafford would have become a princess and young Henry would have mysteriously died, or at best been driven into exile. It is little wonder that, only seven years later, the duke of Buckingham thought his sister too good to be the mistress of a Tudor.

The Staffords were the most aristocratic family in the country. In the fifteenth century, when the mighty Howards were yet to have a member rise even to the position of baron, the Staffords were a well-established ducal family. Anne Stafford was descended from Edward III through three lines, and she was Henry's cousin several times over. Her family had a much simpler and less disputed lineage than that of the Tudors. A Lord Stafford was called to Parliament in 1299 – the Tudors were unheard of until two centuries later. But Buckingham failed to realise that times had changed – without the support of the king of England, all his titles, his impressive ancestry, meant nothing.

With Anne Stafford, as with his other mistresses, Henry tried to conceal his affairs from the queen and his court. He had very little privacy, just like all other Englishmen of his era. He was not alone when he went to sleep, dressed or when he went to the toilet – even ordering a plate of food involved an elaborate procedure, with strict etiquette to be observed. His father had created a separate area, the Privy Chamber, where entry was heavily restricted and those servants who were allowed access were selected most carefully. Here he had his bedroom and private rooms, his library, his own gardens. This gave the monarch an air of unavailability that made contact with the king all the more sought-after.

Henry VIII took this one step further and built more rooms within his palaces to separate himself. This meant he could be more discreet as to whose company he kept than could most courtiers and kings. Francis I of France had only three rooms to himself. Yet secrets were still extremely difficult to keep at Henry's court, with everyone living in such close proximity to one other. It was then that friends such as William Compton were useful, as they could arrange for the king to meet women in their London residences or houses near to whichever palace the king was then residing in.

If the king wished to spend the night with his wife, there was a ceremonial aspect to it; he would be dressed in his night robe and led by his gentlemen of the chamber and other servants to his wife's apartments. He would usually have sent a message that he would soon be arriving, or occasionally he would appear unannounced. His grooms would accompany him down the passageway connecting his apartments to his wife's and then some would wait outside to accompany him on his return and to guard him. Before they left the room, they would have to check for intruders by thrusting their swords beneath the mattress and into any other potential hiding place. His sexual visits to his wife were governed by etiquette based on years of tradition but a similar procedure must have been required for when he saw his mistresses, for there was the constant danger of assassination. Henry's two uncles, known to history as the Princes in the Tower, had 'disappeared' and his maternal grandfather had tried to have Henry's father murdered on a number of occasions. It was unthinkable for the king to be left entirely alone.

As soon as the queen had received the message that he wished to spend the night, her ladies-in-waiting would have begun to prepare her for bed. They would have undressed her, helped her into her nightclothes, taken off her headdress and combed her hair. Then her attendants would disappear and the two would be left alone. The lady who would usually sleep at the bottom of the queen's bed would discreetly absent herself. The ladies-in-waiting would all therefore have been aware how often Henry was visiting his wife at night. Anne Stafford would have regularly prepared Queen Katherine for bed with the king, with both women fully aware of the other's relationship with him.

The duke of Buckingham was informed, allegedly by his sister Lady Elizabeth Stafford, of Anne's affair and he went to investigate.

Whilst the Duke was in the private apartments of his sister,* who was suspected with the King, Compton came there to talk with her, saw the

---

* Chapuys does not state which of the Stafford sisters Henry was involved with. Several factors point to Anne, particularly that she later lived openly in adultery with William Compton; there is no recorded stain on Elizabeth Stafford's reputation. The confusion over which Stafford sister was involved led some to believe that he was pursuing both sisters – the original source is clear that it was only one of them.

Duke, who intercepted him, quarrelled with him, and the end of it is that he [Compton] was reproached in many very hard words. The King was so offended at this that he reprimanded the Duke angrily. The same night, the Duke left the palace, and did not return for some days. At the same time, the husband of that lady went away, carried her off and placed her in a convent sixty miles from here, that no one may see her.

The King, having understood that all this proceeds from [Elizabeth Stafford], the day after she [Anne] was gone, [he] turned her [sister] out of the palace, and her husband with her. Believing that there were other women in the employment of the favourite such as go about the palace insidiously spying out every unwatched movement in order to tell the Queen, the King would have liked to turn them all out, only that it has appeared to him too great a scandal. Afterwards, almost all the Court knew that the Queen had been vexed with the King, and the King with her, and that the storm went on between them.[13]

To offend the monarch was a dangerous move, but Buckingham seemed unconcerned. He had never been a close friend of Henry's, but he had now made an enemy of the king. Henry, as Buckingham would discover, was not a man who forgave easily. As the first duke in the realm, Buckingham does not seem not to have felt the need to stoop to the sycophancy lower courtiers indulged Henry with. Many people believed that the king would not strike so high in the nobility, unless it was for far more than careless words. But this was not the medieval era, when the king had been the first among equals and his nobility were omnipotent within their local areas. The Tudors had changed this – now the king was the absolute ruler, and woe betide *any* subject who forgot this, peer or peasant.

Both Buckingham and his sister Elizabeth, Lady Fitzwalter, were close friends of Queen Katherine, and it was probably one of them who told the queen. Katherine was heavily pregnant and it was therefore dangerous for her to suffer emotional trauma. The unborn heir was of paramount importance to the Tudor dynasty and Henry was fuming that the hysteria over this incident may have endangered the pregnancy. Contemporary wisdom held that sex during pregnancy was both immoral and risky to the baby; therefore it is not surprising that it was at this time, a year into his marriage, that we first hear of the nineteen-year-old king taking a mistress. Anne's siblings' interference and his wife's overreaction had resulted in this unnecessary and embarrassing scene.

Lord George Hastings, Anne's husband, was in a very difficult position. He had several titles – he was the 3rd Baron Hastings, the 4th Baron de Moleyns, the 5th Baron Hungerford and the 6th Baron Botreaux. But if his grandfather had not been attainted and executed by Richard III, George would have also been an earl. He was determined to regain the earldom of Hastings, and so by carrying his wife off to a convent, he was taking a risk. But he not only had to keep the king onside; he had also to appease Buckingham, his powerful brother-in-law.

Along with Anne's brother, Henry Stafford, Lord Hastings was part of the king's inner circle of friends. This was a position he would have been intent on retaining. Henry Stafford had been given the title 'earl of Wiltshire' around 1510; this may well have been connected to the king's relationship with Anne. It had been in his family for the last two generations but Stafford was not automatically entitled to it. After his death, the earldom was given to the father of Henry's then-mistress, Mary Boleyn, who also had a slim claim to it. Henry was showing himself as a king who was remarkably generous to his friends.

An interesting part of this story is the reaction of the queen. She was 'vexed with the King' and 'almost all the court knew ... the storm [that] went on between them'.[14] Katherine should have been aware that husbands, especially royal ones, were unlikely to be faithful, but she was devastated. Her mother, Queen Isabella, had been unhappy about her husband's infidelities but accepted them, as queens had little other option. According to the records, Katherine wept and ranted at her embarrassed husband; but she learnt her lesson. As far as we are aware, she did not berate the king again for his love affairs – until his mistress, Anne Boleyn, tried to obtain a position above what his other lovers had accepted.

Kings were rarely faithful, especially as their marriages were principally arranged for dynastic purposes and for the furtherance of their foreign policy. Several kings, including Henry's father, Henry VII, are thought to have had no mistresses at all; but this was unusual and rarely admired. Few lauded his fidelity to his wife, considering it suspect in a man who could have any woman he wanted. People expected a powerful man to have many mistresses and the king should not let down his public. Many subjects lived vicariously through tales of the king and his court.

In 1521 Wolsey and Henry were handed their opportunity to bring down the belligerent duke of Buckingham. One of the duke's employees wrote to Wolsey, alleging that Buckingham had bragged of an astrologer's prediction that he would become King of England. To even discuss the king's death was high treason, and the duke seemed to be wishing for it. Buckingham apparently made this worse by adding that he believed most people would support his accession, rather than Henry's daughter or any of the Tudor line. He was also said to have hinted that he would overthrow Henry in battle and discussed how his father had planned to assassinate Richard III.

The duke had shown a lack of judgement on a number of occasions since he had stormed out of the court in anger at Henry's affair with Anne. He had arranged the marriage of his son to Ursula Pole, whose grandfather had been Edward IV's brother – and no rumours of illegitimacy damaged his claim to the throne as they did for Edward IV and Henry VIII's other royal ancestors. It was risky for an aristocrat to acquire this much royal blood, but Buckingham, like all at court, wanted his children to make advantageous marriages – this was not proof of treacherous intent. Buckingham has been described as pompous, but at a time when pride in one's lineage was considered only proper, he had reason to be arrogant. Anne Stafford does not seem to have shared her brother's egotism about their ancestry – her later relationship with the low-born Compton confirmed that.

A man of Buckingham's influence and birth was a potential danger to the king. Even in September 1519, the Venetian ambassador wrote that 'were the King to die without heirs male, he [Buckingham] might easily obtain the crown'.[15] If Henry had a legitimate son, the duke's arrogance and bloodline might not have been such a threat, but after twelve years of marriage, it was clear that a healthy boy may never arrive. It is likely that the lack of a male heir was at least one of the reasons that Henry felt the need to have Buckingham executed. The Tudor dynasty, especially Henry's young daughter, needed to be protected; the Staffords had become a serious threat.

Buckingham was beheaded on 17 May 1521 for treason. It had been a long time since a nobleman of his stature had been executed and it served as a reminder that none were safe if they thought themselves above the king. On Buckingham's arrest, Henry took the opportunity to curtail the power of some of those connected to him, whether they had been implicated in this case or not. Anne does not seem to have been included in this 'purge'. Whether he had been truly angered by his wife's affair or not, Lord Hastings had managed to retain his position. The king created Hastings the earl of Huntingdon in 1529,[16] and in 1538 he was described as a man 'of great power' although also of 'little discretion and less experience'.[17] Whether Anne was close to her brother or not, his execution must have shocked her to the core and brought back painful memories of the family's troubles after her father was executed on Richard III's orders. That her ex-lover was the protagonist in her brother's downfall would surely have upset her further.

Buckingham's arrest and execution were met with widespread disbelief across Europe. When Charles V heard, he wrote to his aunt, Katherine of Aragon: 'Then the butcher's dog has pulled down the fairest buck in Christendom.' Although many people blamed Thomas Wolsey, the king's low-born chief minister, Henry was fully behind this arrest. Reports from foreign courts show that it was a widespread belief that Henry's attack on a Stafford could start a civil war. The English knew better, Henry was in full control of the country – and who could they now replace him with?

By this point, Anne's affair with the king, which had ended around eight years before, was probably just a distant memory to her and her family. She was busy producing a child a year for her husband, who had quickly allowed her to rejoin court life. She had little chance of persuading the king to spare her brother, especially as the evidence, whether fabricated or not, was enough to show that Buckingham could be a serious menace. We have no evidence to show that the man who was probably by then Anne's lover – William Compton – spoke up for her brother either, although he was a close friend of Henry's and had significant influence over him. He probably knew the king too well to try to change his mind once it had been made up; he also did not want to associate himself with the traitor. Even Buckingham's sons-in-law gave evidence against him. Compton was one of those who benefited financially from the redistribution of Buckingham's lands; he received Maxtoke Castle in Leicestershire from the attainder.

Her husband evidently forgave her, but this was not the end of Anne's infidelity. Few women could risk being brazen in their adultery, but women near the top of the social hierarchy, such as Anne Bourchier and Elisabeth Brooke, could afford to follow their hearts. By 1522 Anne was in a committed relationship, so serious that her lover had made extensive provision for her in his will. And this relationship was with Sir William Compton, who was not only a close friend of the king's, but is also thought to have been his go-between during Anne's relationship with Henry. Compton was said to have helped organise the king's rendezvous with several lovers. Compton was the Gentleman of the Stool – Henry's closest attendant, who accompanied him even to the toilet – and was given a huge number of offices and favours during Henry's reign.

In 1527, seventeen years after her affair with Henry, Cardinal Wolsey tried to prosecute Anne and Compton for adultery through the ecclesiastical courts. The cardinal would not have dared do this if Compton and Anne had still been in such high favour with the king. However, they denied the charge; Compton took the sacrament and swore on it that Anne was not his lover.[18] But when he died the following year, his will showed that he had left money for masses to be said for her soul every day, and he left her the profits from some of his lands in Leicestershire.[19] His will had been written in March 1522 and he did not change it before he died in 1528, indicating that they had been in a serious relationship for at least six years, and probably far longer.

It was still risky for a woman to be the mistress of a man, even of a king. English women, especially noblewomen, were less restricted than elsewhere, which shocked many visitors. But this does not mean that they had much freedom by modern standards. They were still expected to marry and have children; they still stood a good chance of dying while doing so. Sex outside marriage was illegal and the penalty was to be flogged and made to walk barefoot through the streets, a punishment that was dished out to Jane Shore, Edward IV's mistress, twenty-six years before Henry's reign began.

Jane was convicted of harlotry by Richard III, soon after her lover's death. She was made to walk barefoot in front of a cross, carrying a taper and dressed only in her petticoat through the streets of London. She was ogled by large crowds, who had gathered to see the late king's mistress near-naked, and she was then imprisoned in Ludgate. Despite widespread infidelity, England was still a country where people lived in terror of Hell. '*Thou shalt not commit adultery*' was a Commandment and even at court they were aware of the potential consequences of disobeying these teachings.

After the execution of her brother, Anne remained at court. Buckingham's son recovered some of his father's less significant titles, but not until Edward VI's reign. The Staffords were damaged – and Lady Anne Stafford's affair with Henry VIII may have started the resentment that led to the fall of the whole family. But despite Buckingham's demise, being a Stafford still gave her high status at court. She became a countess and her relatives remained in many influential positions. But her family never regained their previous influence and status.

From the late 1530s, Anne was a servant of Henry's daughter, Mary. Anne died in 1544 and was buried in Stoke Poges, Buckinghamshire. At the time of her death, Henry was married to his sixth wife – a very different man to the teenager who had flattered her with his attentions. Hastings had died a few months earlier. Their offspring carved out successful careers at court during the reigns of Henry's three children.

We have no evidence as to when this affair ended. There is one source that reveals much about Henry's love life – the list of his New Year's presents. For New Year 1513, the king gave Anne Stafford 30 oz of silver gilt, his third most expensive present that year out of the many he gave.[20] This suggests that the affair may have resumed when Anne returned to court from the convent and lasted another three years. There is little other explanation as to why she would have been so high on his list. The only evidence of their affair is from 1510, but we have nothing to tell us if removing her from court ended their relationship. His wife and her husband and brother may have been furious at first, but if Henry had wished to continue the liaison, he would have done so.

Circa 1514, Anne gave birth to her son, Francis Hastings, later the 2nd earl of Huntingdon, and then had seven more children who survived childhood. It is surprising that there is no record of her conceiving during her first five years of marriage. It may be that she was not living with her husband for at least part of this time, or simply that any children did not survive. Her relationship with the king may have finished around 1514, although there has never been a suggestion that Francis Hastings was Henry's son. Yet as Anne was unfaithful throughout much of her marriage, and Hastings knew this and yet acknowledged *all* her children as his own, there is a reasonable chance that there was at least one cuckoo in his nest, whether the king's or Compton's.

We know Henry was involved with Anne in 1510, but for the next three years, there is no record of Henry having a mistress. He gave every outward impression of being enamoured with his own wife, something that pleased the country greatly. The lovers' knots displayed around the palaces, with H's and K's, or H's and C's entwined; receiving envoys in the queen's apartments and allowing her to act as an unofficial Spanish ambassador; publicly showing his respect for her opinion and lineage; this was far more than most kings did for their wives. Henry was a romantic idealist, and Katherine of Aragon knew how to make him feel like a chivalric knight. But however good a husband he appeared, he was probably still regularly unfaithful.

Chapter 2

A French Affair

'Youth will needs have dalliance,
Of good or ill some pastance ...'

But it was not only Henry's relationships that were being debated. Caroz, the Spanish ambassador, wrote to Katherine of Aragon's father to express his concern about her close relationship with her Spanish confessor. Another Spanish ambassador, Fuensalida, considered Fray Diego Fernandez a troublemaker. The confessor was extremely controlling of Katherine and her household, demanding her obedience in all things, particularly before her marriage. Yet there is no reason to suspect that Katherine's reliance on Fray Diego was indicative of a sexual relationship, despite the concerns of some of Katherine's servants and the ambassadors. It would be almost unthinkable that a woman of Katherine's character would indulge in an affair.

Yet for a princess, it was not simply the truth, but how it appeared to others that was important. Katherine described Fray Diego as *'the best that ever woman in my position had'*.[1] Her behaviour with him was more indiscreet than the friendships Anne Boleyn would have. In an age where men went into the priesthood as often for a good career as out of piety, spending large amounts of time alone with a man – and being affectionate towards him in public – was dangerous behaviour for any lady. Fray Diego was not leading a celibate life in England, and had acquired a reputation as a womaniser. However, Henry must have been unconcerned; Diego did not return to Spain until around five years later.

Henry soon found other mistresses, although most of them were probably short term. In 1513 he was consumed by the idea of war and decided it was time to conquer France. He had been King of England for four years and was determined to assert his authority on the international stage. Since 1337, when Edward III had laid his claim to the French throne, each king of England had also styled himself 'King of France'. France was far too large for Henry VIII's medium-sized army to conquer, but he was determined to prove himself in battle. His wife was back home sewing flags for the war effort, running the country and worrying about the danger he was in – while he was careering around the French countryside and entertaining local ladies.

From the beginning it was clear that the enterprise was doomed and Henry would be betrayed by his allies. The Holy Roman Emperor, Maximilian, and Henry's father-in-law, Ferdinand of Aragon, were wily old men – Ferdinand had been praised by Machiavelli himself for his cunning. They wanted the King of England to cause problems in France, but they were not interested in seeing him become the ruler of two powerful kingdoms. Henry was still young and naive and they guessed that a *show* of support, and the provision of some entertainments – including attractive women – would distract the young king until it was too late.

While he was away, Henry appointed Katherine 'Governor of the Realm', giving her all the authority of the king himself. She was kept busy arranging a campaign against the Scots, who had predictably invaded the north of England while the English army was stretched elsewhere. The queen was left in charge of a council that had never taken orders from a woman before and she coped admirably. Once a week she sent Henry a letter, informing him of important matters of state but also showing the genuine concern one would expect from a devoted wife whose husband was at war; she declared that she could be 'never in rest until I see letters from you' and begged Wolsey to remind Henry to 'avoid all manner of dangers'.[2] Henry did not respond himself, but asked Wolsey to write the replies.

Henry's army swiftly conquered their first target, the city of Thérouanne. For a month after this, the weather was too bad for an assault on the next city, Tournai. Henry spent this time building relations with the premier family of Europe and ensuring he mixed business with pleasure. He spent his time with Maximilian, the Holy Roman Emperor, the Emperor's sister Margaret, Regent of the Netherlands, and Margaret's court, impressing them with his jousting, archery, dancing and mastery of several musical instruments. Among Margaret's maids of honour were a Flemish woman named Étiennette de la Baume and a twelve-year-old English girl called Anne Boleyn.

A month later Henry conquered Tournai, an important city which bordered the emperor's territories and was a major route for transferring goods across Europe – and all without Henry ever personally fighting a Frenchman. After a couple of months, Henry's army achieved the victory he craved – the Battle of the Spurs, during which the English chased after French soldiers who were under instruction not to fight. It was stretching the truth to label it a battle, but Henry's army captured some French nobles and sent them back to England to be held for a ransom. The only time this whole adventure was dampened was when Henry's close friends, Sir Edward Howard and Sir Thomas Knyvett, were killed in a skirmish at sea. The English army had conquered only two significant French towns in an otherwise embarrassingly fruitless campaign, although Henry had shown that he could be a player on the European stage. Queen Katherine was far more successful – the English response to the Scottish invasion had resulted in the death of King James IV and half his noblemen, preventing Scotland from threatening English security for a generation.

The French king had paid little heed to this incursion and after Henry took Tournai, Louis simply paid him to leave. Ferdinand had already signed a peace treaty with France, as had Maximilian; Henry was only informed after the event. Henry returned home to a hero's welcome which was somewhat overshadowed by his wife's achievements during his absence. When he was reunited with his wife, 'it was such a loving meeting that every creature rejoiced'.[3] Yet Henry was furious with Katherine for encouraging him to rely on her double-dealing father, and their relationship never quite recovered from this humiliation.

The following year, Henry received a letter from Étiennette and it is from this that we know of Henry's brief relationship with her. She was a noblewoman, the daughter of Marc de la Baume, Lord of Châteauvillan, and she was not the only de la Baume in history to attract the attention of a king; in the next century, her kinswoman Louise-Françoise de la Baume became the *maîtresse-en-titre* of King Louis XIV of France. Étiennette seems to have attracted Henry soon after his arrival in Lille. She wrote to Henry because she was about to get married, and he had apparently promised her ten thousand crowns as a wedding present – perhaps as compensation for her lost virtue. In August 1514 Étiennette became the third wife of the elderly Jean Neufchatel, seigneur de Marnay. We have no indication of her age, but her husband was sixty-two, which is perhaps why the marriage was childless.

She sent the letter to Henry with 'a bird and some roots of great value, belonging to this country'. She first reminded him who she was:

> When Madame [Margaret of Austria] went to see the Emperor, her father and you at Lille, you named me your page "*et n'avoie autrement nom de par et dautre chouses*" and when we parted at Tournai you told me, when I married, to let you know and it should be worth to me 10,000 crowns or rather angels. As it has now pleased my father "*me marier*", I send bearer, an old servant of my grandfather, to remind you … *la plus que* your very humble servant, E. la Baume.[4]

We do not know if he kept his promise. She also wrote to Henry of how: 'you spoke many pretty things to me'.[5] Henry was by now being regularly linked to other women.

By 1514, cracks were beginning to show in the royal marriage. In this year, Henry, 'for love of a lady, clad himself and the court in mourning',[6] possibly on hearing that Étiennette was getting married, but probably in connection to a woman at the English court. The infidelities continued, but his strong relationship with his wife had only been damaged, not destroyed. The trickery of her father had dented Henry's trust in her, and around this time rumours started that Henry was planning to annul his marriage after five years. It was reported in Rome that: 'The King of England means to repudiate his present wife because he is unable to have children by her, and intends to marry a daughter of the French duke of Bourbon.'[7] The next month there were similar rumours in England.[8] We must be careful not to let hindsight guide our conclusions on this possibility; Katherine was pregnant at this time, so it is highly improbable.

In the Tower of London it is still possible to see Henry's armour from 1514, showing love knots with 'H' and 'K' decorating the metal. The King had been riding into the jousts as 'Sir Loyal Heart', paying tribute to the lady he was 'serving' in the sense of courtly love – his wife. Their initials and even their images were entwined on candlesticks, cups, basins and salt cellars.[9] But during 1514 Katherine lost much of her political influence to Thomas Wolsey, and her place in Henry's heart to a succession of her own ladies-in-waiting. She was now twenty-eight and had endured several traumatic pregnancies and births, which would have taken their toll on her figure; her foreign connections had helped Henry little and she was no longer the grateful young woman who lived to please her husband. The royal couple were drifting apart.

Around this time, the Venetian ambassador described Queen Katherine as 'rather ugly than otherwise'. Other sources report similar unflattering comments and Katherine had recently given birth to her third child – by the end of Henry's affair with Bessie, she had given birth to six children and probably also suffered miscarriages. Her hair was turning from the red which had attracted so much admiration to a dull brown. Around 1518, Katherine is thought to have begun to wear a hair shirt, which would not have made her more attractive to Henry. All her praying had not helped her, but she turned more and more to her religion as Henry turned away from her. It was only as their marriage progressed that their differences, in age and personality, made themselves obvious.

It was understandable that a king who could have anything he wanted should decide to take a mistress from one of the many young, beautiful women at the court. Most of their families would have considered this an honour – although not all, as Henry had discovered. The king was a very attractive man, so many women would have been drawn to him. Despite these affairs, Henry and Katherine continued to have a relatively happy marriage. They had much in common: music and masquerades, scholarship and theology.

Peter Martyr, writing from the Spanish court, reported that, in 1514, Henry had blamed his wife for Ferdinand's duplicity and had boasted to her that he had been unfaithful; this was said to have upset her so much she miscarried.[10] This may or may not have been true – we do not know Martyr's sources – but it indicates that Henry's infidelity was well known. Henry may have become angry with his wife as it became increasingly clear that she would not bear him a son, but after only five years, he was probably frustrated, but still hopeful. In 1514, along with the rumours of annulment and adultery, Henry was linked to three ladies-in-waiting. The first was Jane Popincourt, an older woman; the other two, Elizabeth Blount and Elizabeth Carew, were aged around fourteen.

Henry seems to have been particularly attracted to French women. As well as Étiennette de la Baume in Lille, and later the Francophile Boleyn sisters, Henry allegedly had an affair with Mademoiselle Jane Popincourt.

During the Christmas festivities of 1514, Katherine was heavily pregnant and therefore could not participate in the dancing and entertainment. Tradition dictated that Henry ask the next highest-ranking lady to dance – his sister, Mary, or in her absence, a duchess. Instead, for the Twelfth Night masque at Eltham Palace, Henry chose Bessie Blount and Jane Popincourt, low-ranking young women, as his partners.

Jane, also referred to as Jeanne or Joan, was one of the few women Henry had regular contact with during his mollycoddled childhood. It is unclear when she arrived in England, but by 1498 she was tutoring Henry's sisters in French, and she may have occasionally taught the young Henry as well. She would have helped the two princesses, Margaret and Mary, improve their French conversational skills and their understanding of French culture, which was important as it was likely that either Margaret or Mary would marry a French prince. In 1502, when Henry was eleven, Jane Popincourt became a maid of honour to his mother, Elizabeth of York, and then to Katherine of Aragon on Henry's accession.

Jane was, like Anne Stafford, older than Henry. She must have been at least fourteen when she secured a position as the princesses' tutor and was probably older. This makes her at least thirty in 1514; at least seven years older than the king. To be unmarried at this age was unusual. And like many woman who had been at court a long time, she did not have an unblemished reputation. Jane had been involved in a scandal four months before she was first linked to the king.

During Henry's invasion of France the year before, there had been only one battle for Henry to celebrate – the Battle of the Spurs. During this skirmish, Henry's men captured Louis, duc de Longueville, a member of the extremely powerful Orléans family. Lord Longueville was a charming courtier, and although he was kept in England as a hostage, he was treated more as a guest and as an extra ambassador for France. The English had been allied to Maximilian and Ferdinand, but Henry made it clear to Longueville that he would prefer to work with the French. Longueville negotiated the continuation of France's annual bribe to England, to stop English kings challenging for the crown of France, and helped arrange the marriage of Henry's sister to the King of France at the same time. And he also began an affair with his compatriot, Jane Popincourt.

Jane had, by then, been in England for at least sixteen years and had become close to the royal family. She seems to have been not only a tutor to Henry's sister, Princess Mary, but also a close friend. In September 1514, Jane was chosen to be a maid of honour to Mary when she married Louis XII. Here was an opportunity for Jane to return to her native land as a confidante of the new Queen of France. Apparently this

> was at the suit and desire of my lord Longueville, as he told me and my fellows before; for he told him that the Queen loved and trusted her above all the gentlewomen that she had about her.[11]

The marriage was not a prospect to delight the heart of a young, beautiful and headstrong eighteen-year-old princess. King Louis may have been very popular with the French people, but the fifty-two-year-old man looked much older than his years, was not in good health and had already been married twice. Mary had been betrothed to Charles, the heir to Spain and the likely successor to the Holy Roman Empire, and was therefore the future ruler of half of Europe. Charles' chin was so deformed that he could not chew his food properly and he was obsessed with clocks; nevertheless, he was young. Mary would have appreciated all the friends she could get when she began her marriage.

Jane would have been a useful ally for the new queen to have at the French court, as she could pass on to her important information and help the English ladies with any linguistic or cultural difficulties. Unfortunately, when Louis saw Mademoiselle Popincourt's name on the list of those to attend his virgin bride, he was horrified. He declared that: 'As you love me, speak of her no more. I would she were burned!'[12] Mary was said to have been very upset by this. To be considered too immoral for the French court was quite an indictment – the relaxed French attitude to adultery and sexuality would horrify and intrigue much of Europe for generations. But Louis XII wanted his court to be virtuous.

Henry's affair with Jane probably began after Longueville left in the autumn of 1514. Like many of Henry's mistresses she had no faction, no power and so was not a threat to anyone at court. She did not even have powerful relatives at court, who might sweep her off to a nunnery as Anne Stafford's husband had – and she did not have a good reputation to protect. She was first linked to Henry three months after Longueville's departure, and her relationship with the French nobleman appears to have been common knowledge. We hear little more of Jane until she left England in May 1516. Henry gave her £100 when she returned to France[13] and she soon renewed her affair with the duc de Longueville.

There is no contemporary record of an affair between Henry VIII and Jane Popincourt, but there is circumstantial evidence. It rests on the king choosing her to dance with him in 1514, her willingness to embark on an affair with Longueville, and her large leaving gift; these could all be irrelevant. She had no significant influence, and therefore was of little interest to the ambassadors whose reports we rely on for information about Henry's love life. However, it does seem likely; by tradition, he should have chosen to dance with the highest-ranking lady present, and his choices of Bessie Blount and Jane Popincourt, neither of whom could be argued to fit this criteria, is significant. Jane also, in personality and age, matches the type of woman the king seemed to prefer at this stage of his life.

Chapter 3

The Beauty of Her Time

'The best I sue,
The worst eschew …'

At some point between 1514 and 1518, Henry became attracted to another of his wife's maids of honour. Elizabeth Blount, commonly known as Bessie, was around thirteen when she was first linked to the king. She seems to have been the mistress he esteemed the most – probably for the same reason that, as the years went by, Jane Seymour was elevated onto a higher and higher pedestal in Henry's mind. Bessie gave him the only present a sixteenth-century monarch truly wanted – a healthy son. And had this son lived past his teenage years, there is a substantial chance that he would have become King Henry IX.

Bessie first came to court in March 1512 when she was aged around eleven. Her family were not aristocratic but were members of the gentry, who, with the right opportunity and some talent, had earned a place at court. Bessie became only the second person in the family to acquire a title. However, the Blounts of Kinlet could trace their lineage back to the fourteenth century and Bessie's mother, Katherine Peshall, was the heiress to Knightly. The Peshalls had supported the unknown Henry Tudor against King Richard III, which had been an asset during the reign of Henry VII.

Bessie's parents were given a good opportunity for advancement in 1501, when Arthur, Prince of Wales, and his young wife, Katherine of Aragon, arrived to set up their own court in Ludlow as titular heads of the government in Wales. The Blounts were based in nearby Shropshire. Bessie's parents were probably interviewed when the case was being drawn up that Katherine of Aragon and Arthur Tudor had consummated their short marriage. It may not have been as prestigious as to serve at the court in England, but to be lady-in-waiting to the young Spanish princess was perhaps more exciting than to serve the ageing queen, Elizabeth of York. As King Henry VII aged, so the Blounts were ingratiating themselves with the king and queen to be; their future looked bright. John and Katherine Blount would have hoped to increase their young family's fortunes – then tragedy struck.

In 1502 Prince Arthur died, leaving his brother, eleven-year-old Henry, as the heir apparent and Katherine of Aragon as an unwanted widow. The Blounts' chance for advancement seemed to have come to nothing. The court at Ludlow was disbanded, and all the attendants, including the Blounts, had to petition anyone of influence for a place at court or else return to the countryside. And it was around this time that Bessie was born.

Their main patrons were a distant branch of the family tree, the Mountjoy Blounts, who were far more prosperous and better connected. William, Baron Mountjoy, became Queen Katherine's chamberlain and a close friend of the king, the queen and Sir Thomas More – it was probably Mountjoy who secured a place as maid of honour for Bessie and helped her parents obtain positions on the periphery of the court. Her father, John Blount, became a well-respected knight at the courts of both Henry VII and Henry VIII and had been involved in the 'invasion' of France in 1513. He was a yeoman of the guard, part of the king's private bodyguard. To gain this position one was expected to be a good soldier, quick-witted and a good archer. Men were also chosen for their height and good looks, traits Bessie may have inherited. John Blount was a loyal servant, but not a shining light of the court.

When Bessie first went to court, she was a lower member, one of the dozens of hangers-on hoping for an official position. In 1514, when she was blossoming into a young woman, Bessie became Queen Katherine's maid of honour. It was a far cry from rural Shropshire and Lincolnshire, where Bessie had grown up with her many siblings. To be chosen out of the five Blount sisters she must have possessed all the qualities that were expected of a lady at court – beauty, grace and good manners. She must also have impressed twenty-nine-year-old Queen Katherine, who personally approved which ladies would serve her.

The court was an exciting place to be. A Venetian visitor wrote that

> The wealth and civilisation of the world are here and those who call the English barbarians appear to me to render themselves such. I here perceive very elegant manners, extreme decorum and great politeness, and amongst other things there is this invincible King, whose acquirements and qualities are so many and so excellent, that I consider him to excel all who ever wore a crown.[1]

And Bessie was to spend her time around this magnificent monarch.

Serving the queen was one way to be presented to all the noble families, in the hope of making the best possible marriage, and competition was fierce. Many, if not most, of the women who served at court were given their position because their families had tirelessly petitioned on their behalf. Their relatives had usually presented the king and queen with expensive gifts and, more importantly, had served the king loyally for a number of years. Not every woman from a gentry family could gain a place – only the most attractive and intelligent were sent. Bessie's family would have been hoping that her position at court was the pathway to an impressive marriage for her – as, in time, it was.

She would have been educated to be a good courtier from birth. A lady would be expected to play a musical instrument, dance, sing and perform for others. Bessie was described as a talented singer and dancer, who excelled '*in all goodly pastimes*'.[2] As the queen's attendant, she would sew garments for masquerades or for the poor, spend her time in prayer and at mass; when England went to war, she would sew flags, standards and badges for the men. She had menial tasks to complete every day, but this was not considered beneath her dignity as she was serving the royal family. Besides, the chores took up little of the day. This service simply reinforced the social order.

From Henry's reign onwards, the ladies also often read books, especially on religion or those by classical writers – the only books that women were permitted by society to read, lest their brains become corrupted. Women were more easily tempted by the Devil and so had to be carefully protected. These activities also prevented the young maids of honour from spending their whole time gossiping and discussing their love affairs; after all, their reputations reflected on their queen's. Many ladies-in-waiting could not read or write well but Bessie seems to have been well-educated – she owned poetry books in both Latin and English.[3]

By 1513, when Bessie became a maid of honour to Katherine of Aragon, her parents must have been thinking about marriage for their twelve-year-old daughter – after all, her parents had been aged seven and ten at their wedding. Bessie had little money but some good connections and was an attractive girl. The only potential problem was that Bessie's paternal grandfather was rumoured to have been insane, which could cast doubt on the sanity of any children from the family.

Bessie Blount earned 100s a year when she was first appointed maid of honour.[4] Before she left for court, her family would have ensured that she had a wardrobe full of garments far more expensive than her meagre salary would allow. She would serve the queen's dinner but might also be invited to go hunting and hawking with the royal couple, star in the masquerades, cheer the participants at competitions and attend numerous feasts and festivities. The ladies might gamble at cards, deliver messages for the queen or start a flirtation with one of the king's men; their precise role depended on the present queen, but they were always at the centre of court life.

Love affairs were rife at court. Even having to share bedrooms did not stop them, though there was little chance liaisons would escape becoming public knowledge. Very few people slept alone in their own bed – even the king had a man sleeping on the floor next to his bed, or even in the bed with him, although this was for security. Each aristocrat had their own mini-court on their estates with their own gentlemen and ladies-in-waiting, those who did not quite have the contacts to get into the king's court. These youths were as under-employed as the king's attendants, with similar results.

In October 1514, the duke of Suffolk, who had recently married Henry's sister, Mary, was away from court; this was two months before Bessie was first linked to the king. Suffolk wrote to his brother-in-law: 'I beseech your grace to tell Mistress Blount and Mistress Carew the next time I write to them or send them tokens, they shall write to me or send me tokens again.'[5] This can only have been courtly love; Suffolk is unlikely to have been asking for Henry's help in committing adultery, two months after marrying the king's sister. Some historians have interpreted this letter to mean that Henry was having affairs with both women at the same time, or that Henry was involved with Bessie while Suffolk was pursuing Mistress Carew. It is likely that it was Suffolk who was pursuing both girls, but in the courtly love sense; he was still trying to win over his new brother-in-law. There is nothing else to suggest that Bessie Blount had an affair with Suffolk before she moved on to the king. This letter indicates that Bessie was not Henry's mistress at this point, as the duke of Suffolk is unlikely to have 'served' a lady whom the king was also paying court to, but Henry and Bessie clearly knew each other on informal terms.

The sending of tokens – small personal gifts such as a brooch or a brace-let, to remember the person by – was an essential part of the tradition of courtly love. Henry enjoyed these French and Burgundian customs, and they were popular in England. A suitor would give a woman gifts and atten-tion, claiming to be her loyal servant. He may have written a piece of music or a romantic poem for her. The man would act as if he was desperately in love with the lady, yet knew she was too good for him to ever obtain.

This was a way for men and women to be made to feel attractive, in a time when people could rarely choose to marry for love. Men could get this attention elsewhere, usually from women of lower status, but women could not risk the scandal, to themselves or to their families, of being caught committing adultery. Before marriage, it was usually only if she gained a promiscuous reputation or became pregnant that a scandal would result. After marriage, it was a very different matter. A woman could put the whole ancient (or not so) lineage of her husband's family at risk if he had not fathered her children.

Courtly love was not about sex, but about emotions and romance. In a harsh world, where life expectancy was short, marrying for money and status was considered the only sane option. Yet there needed to be some way of meeting people's emotional needs, without risking adultery and disgrace. Courtly love was considered love in its purest, most romantic form, unsul-lied by sex. It gave a set of rules and regulations through which the courtiers could show affection, attraction and adoration in a socially acceptable way. It was an important part of life for a courtier.

Elizabeth Bryan was soon to marry Nicholas Carew and may have taken his name on their betrothal; it is more likely that it was she who was men-tioned in the letter than one of Carew's four sisters or a kinswoman of his. Elizabeth Carew's mother was Margaret Bryan, the half-sister of Elizabeth Boleyn, the mother of two of Henry's lovers, Mary and Anne. She was around the same age as Bessie, a maid of honour and considered very attrac-tive. If the 'Mistress Carew' was Elizabeth, then there are other sources to link her to Henry. He gave her extravagant gifts, including the 'many beauti-ful diamonds and pearls and innumerable jewels' which were said to be part of the queen's collection.[6] Records show that the king gave Lady Carew extremely expensive gifts for New Year and on the birth of her son. But this may have been because she was the wife of such a close friend, although Henry was not usually so generous to his friends' wives.

Sir Nicholas Carew had been brought up with Henry; if Henry or Suffolk had been having an affair with Elizabeth, would Carew have cared? He was rumoured to have been involved in helping arrange rendezvouses for the king with women at his house – this may have included with his own wife. There is no suggestion that their marriage was a love match and he would have understood the benefits that pleasing the king could bring him. Elizabeth Carew may or may not have been his mistress, but the other woman mentioned in Suffolk's letter – Mistress Blount – certainly was. What is unclear is when their relationship started.

Bessie was first linked to Henry when he chose her as his dancing partner at the Twelfth Night celebrations in 1514.[7] Henry was then twenty-three and she was around thirteen. In an age where poor diet delayed the onset of puberty, this was very young, but not considered too young for a relationship with a man. There was concern that having sex at an early age could cause illness or even death, but when life expectancy was so low anyway many were prepared to take risks. The first sign that Bessie's family had come into more favour was in July 1514, when her father was unusually given more than £146, two years' worth of advance wages as one of the king's spears.[8]

At this time, Katherine was recovering from another labour, another dead child. She miscarried again in 1515, then conceived soon afterwards and gave birth to Princess Mary in 1516. Katherine had two more pregnancies in 1517 and 1518, both of which ended in miscarriage. Henry was clearly still doing his duty, but his wife would have been pregnant and therefore sexually unavailable most of this time. Katherine also 'suffered from leucorrhoea, a particularly unpleasant and odorous infection that sometimes followed on the heels of childbirth'.[9] This could not have made her attractive to Henry.

In April 1515, the king was described as: 'the handsomest potentate I ever set eyes on; above the usual height, with an extremely fine calf to his leg, his complexion very fair and bright with auburn hair combed straight and short in the French fashion, and a round face so very beautiful that it would become a pretty woman.'[10] Bessie may have felt herself to be the luckiest woman at court when he showed an interest in her. She was considered very attractive herself, being described as 'eloquent, gracious and beautiful'.[11] She 'was thought, for her rare ornaments of nature, and education, to be the beauty and mistress-piece of her time'.[12] A contemporary described 'that intire affection past betwixt them, as at last she bore him a son'.[13]

'At last' is an indication that Lord Herbert thought their relationship had been a long-term one. Unfortunately, we do not have a portrait of Bessie; the only possible depiction of her is from a brass in St Mary and All Saints Church, South Kyme.

Bessie appeared in court masques regularly until October 1518. After this we have no record of her participating in the entertainments. It is likely that this was, at least initially, because of her pregnancy. Bessie conceived around August 1518 – while Katherine was six months pregnant. Katherine gave birth to a stillborn daughter; it was to be her last pregnancy. The queen probably knew of her maid of honour's growing belly, which must have devastated her – especially when Bessie gave birth to a healthy baby boy.

Bessie left court in 1519 and went to stay in a house called Jericho in Blackmore, Essex, which the king had leased. Henry's closest servants were warned 'not to enquire where the King is or goeth, be it early or late', and not to indulge in 'talking of the King's pastime' or his 'late or early going to bed'.[14] Henry made frequent and secretive visits there and around this time he had Newhall Boreham built nearby.[15] Bessie may not have been the only woman to have spent time with Henry at Jericho over the years.

In spring 1519, Bessie gave birth to Henry Fitzroy, the king's son, at some time between April and June. King Henry was happy to acknowledge the boy, although his existence was not widely known until six years later. He was given the Anglo-Norman surname 'Fitzroy' meaning 'son of the king' which had been used by several kings of England for their illegitimate children. Cardinal Wolsey, who had bastards of his own, was appointed Fitzroy's godfather. A healthy boy was a sign of the king's virility; it was clear now that the lack of a strong son could be blamed on his wife.

Extra-marital relationships could be a way to escape the responsibilities of always acting as a king was expected to; with his mistress he had a chance to lead a somewhat normal family life, and with a woman he had chosen himself. These early days with baby Henry Fitzroy, in an informal household where mother, father and baby could spend time together, was a luxury not afforded to legitimate royal children, who were whisked away from their parents soon after the birth. Henry had an opportunity, in Jericho and his other hideaways, to spend time with women without the extensive etiquette that was expected of him at court. Here, he could relax. Here, he could enjoy spending time with his newborn son. He was probably closer to Henry Fitzroy than to his three legitimate children, and the two spent a large amount of time together.

A bastard was also a useful diplomatic tool. Kings were often happier to rely on them than on their other children or their councillors. Illegitimate offspring could not usurp their father's position as a legitimate heir could, as they depended wholly on their father's goodwill. This made them far more trustworthy than others at court. Henry used both his children to his advantage in 1525, appointing the nine-year-old Princess Mary as titular head of the government of Wales, and appointing the six-year-old duke of Richmond to a similar position in the north of England. This could have been a stepping stone to setting a historical precedent: either by creating Mary his heir and the future first queen regnant of England, or by making his illegitimate son the next king.

There is no evidence that Bessie's relationship with the king continued after Fitzroy's birth, but the delay in finding her a husband suggests that it did. We do not know when Bessie's relationship with Henry ended, but we can make a guess. When a mistress married a courtier, it was usually a sign that the relationship was over. Bessie probably married Gilbert Tailboys in 1522, when Henry Fitzroy was three years old, and this is likely to have marked the end of her affair with the king. The first mention of Bessie as Lady Tailboys is from this year, when Henry granted the couple some land.

Their eldest daughter, Elizabeth, is described as twenty-two years old in 1542. If this was accurate, Bessie's daughter would have been conceived in 1519 or 1520. However, this is the only evidence that the Tailboys married soon after Henry Fitzroy's birth. It is from 1522 onwards that Henry began making grants to the married couple. In April 1522 a lucrative wardship was given to Lord Tailboys[16] followed by the manor of Rokeby, Warwickshire, which had belonged to the attainted Buckingham.[17] Although Bessie did come back to court, it was not as a maid of honour to Queen Katherine. This may have been Henry's attempt to appease his wife.

Bessie's husband was Gilbert Tailboys; as the heir to a barony, he was Bessie's social superior, and his family had connections with the Staffords. Nevertheless, he was the son of a madman, and there was a stigma attached to that. A woman of Bessie's birth and personal attributes might have achieved as good a marriage by herself; yet it was still a step up the social ladder. Tailboys was a member of Wolsey's household and the cardinal may have been involved in arranging the match. Henry does seem to have had his hand in it, as the marriage settlement put all property and income from Bessie to remain with her if her husband died, and then go to *her* heirs – it did not, as it often would, go to the Tailboys family on her death.[18] This would not have been as good a deal as the Tailboys might have hoped for. Bessie's worth to the family relied on a three-year-old boy surviving to adulthood.

In 1522, the year Bessie married, Henry allegedly spoke to the Bishop of Lincoln about the possibility of annulling his own marriage. Katherine had not been pregnant for three years, and it was becoming increasingly clear that her childbearing days were over. She was now thirty-seven years old and she seemed to have already gone through menopause. Although there was still a *small* chance that Katherine would have more children, Henry Fitzroy was by then a healthy three-year-old; there is a chance that the king was considering legitimising a union with Bessie. This is pure speculation, but an interesting possibility. Whatever Henry's intentions, the response from the bishop was presumably that an annulment would be impossible. There were no further reports of Henry wishing to annul his marriage until five years later.

Henry's next mistress was allegedly 'Mistress Parker'.[19] It has been suggested that this was Arabella Parker, a merchant's wife, or Margery Parker, a member of Princess Mary's household. It could possibly have referred to Anne Boleyn's sister-in-law, Jane Parker, or one of her close relatives; we can only speculate. Whether this particular rumour was true or not, we know that another lady-in-waiting soon became the king's lover: 1522 was the year Bessie married, and it was also the year that Sir William Carey, the husband of Mary Boleyn, began to get grants from the king.

Chapter 4

The Boleyn Girls

'So God be pleased, this life will I
For my pastance,
Hunt, sing and dance,
My heart is set ...'

The story of Mademoiselle Boleyn returning from the French court and falling in love with King Henry, a liaison lasting for about four years, sounds familiar. Some historians in the early twentieth century thought that it was simply a rumour that Henry had relationships with both Boleyn sisters, but the evidence is clear: Henry VIII was involved with Mary Boleyn. The fact that the two sisters were the antithesis of each other makes the story all the more intriguing.

One source of evidence that Mary Boleyn was Henry's mistress is Cardinal Pole's article, 'On the Unity of the Church', which was printed in 1538. Here Pole states that Henry had conducted an affair with Anne's sister. Pole was Henry's cousin, and a fierce opponent of the Reformation. But he was unlikely to be spreading false rumours – in this article, originally written during Anne Boleyn's reign, he was trying to persuade Henry, not insult him. A friar called Peto had apparently told George Throckmorton that the king had affairs with both Mary Boleyn and her mother before he pursued Anne. Pole does not seem to have taken the rumour about Anne's mother seriously.

Yet there is nothing to indicate that Charles V raised this as an objection to Henry marrying Anne Boleyn, despite this placing Anne in the same position as Katherine of Aragon under ecclesiastical law – as Henry's sister. If the emperor did know, he also knew that the Pope would not care. Katherine was the sister of Charles's mother, who he had locked in an asylum so that he could inherit the kingdom of Spain while she was still alive. He was hardly likely to risk that kingdom to defend Aunt Katherine, who he had only met twice. In 1527 Henry sent the Pope a letter asking for a dispensation to marry a woman whose close relative he had committed adultery with. This makes his relationship with Mary clear; as do his words, when told of the rumours that he had been the lover of both Anne's sister and mother: 'Never with the mother.'[1]

Some Victorian historians doubted that Henry ever had an affair with Mary because it was not mentioned by Katherine of Aragon in the annulment proceedings. But Katherine was blinkered when it came to her marriage. She was a daughter of Spain – she was not going to acknowledge that Anne Boleyn, the daughter of a viscount, was a rival to her. She always argued the case as it was presented to her, by insisting that she had not consummated her marriage to Prince Arthur and that the Pope had given a valid dispensation for her to marry Henry. We have no record of her openly referring to Anne; she probably thought it beneath her to be discussing Henry's mistresses. The reason he couldn't marry Anne was because he was already married to *her*; everything else was irrelevant.

Mary and Anne Boleyn were probably both born at the smaller family residence of Blickling Hall in Norfolk rather than the more impressive Hever Castle in Kent. The church in Blickling, fifteen miles north of Norwich, still has some references to the Boleyns. Matthew Parker, the family chaplain and later the archbishop of Canterbury, described Anne as his 'countryman'. In the sixteenth century, he would have meant that she was from the same area of England as he was – Norfolk.[2]

The Boleyns could trace their lineage back to the thirteenth century. Their family were originally tenant farmers from Norfolk. In 1457 Mary's ancestor, Sir Geoffrey Boleyn, was lord mayor of London – an important position, but not an aristocratic one. Sir Geoffrey wed Anne, the heiress of Lord Hastings, and through her the family acquired both Hever Castle and Blickling Hall. Their son was knighted by Richard III and made a baron by Henry VII. He married very well, to Margaret, the daughter of Thomas Butler, earl of Ormonde, who had no sons and plenty of assets. Their eldest child was Thomas Boleyn, Mary's father.

There has been much discussion about which of the Boleyn sisters was the elder. Thomas and Elizabeth Boleyn married around 1498 and Mary was probably their first child, born the next year, with Anne born in 1501. George was probably born around 1504. Although two contemporary sources suggest 1507 as the year of Anne's birth, later research disputes this. There are many pieces of circumstantial evidence for the earlier years of birth. Mary had apparently acquired a reputation for being sexually available in France by 1519; it would seem correct to say she was about twenty when she left there. And if Anne was born in 1501, she would have been twelve when she left England, the minimum age to serve as a maid of honour to Margaret of Austria and then Queen Claude of France.

Therefore, Mary was about twenty-one when she married and twenty-three when she was having an affair with King Henry, having already developed a reputation in France. Anne was back in England by 1522 and so would have been about twenty-one then herself, and around twenty-four or twenty-five when she caught the king's eye. This is unusually old to be unmarried considering her connections, but there would have been many noblewomen in her position. If the later birth dates are correct, Mary would have been aged around twelve when she married William Carey – having already acquired a reputation at the French court and having had relationships with both the King of France and the King of England.

Some historians argue that Mary was the younger, but this is unlikely as Mary was married first – this might have been the case if she were the younger daughter, but it would have been very unusual. The sixteenth century was not a time when even people themselves were sure of their own age – it simply did not matter. There is one piece of compelling evidence that Mary was the elder of the Boleyn sisters. Her son, Lord Hunsdon, stated that Mary was the elder when he was petitioning for the earldom of Ormonde to be returned to the family. Lord Hunsdon, like all noblemen of the time, would have been well aware in what order siblings within his family had been born and therefore what he may be entitled to.

As George Boleyn had died without offspring, the title should have gone to the heir of the elder sister. If that was Anne, then the earldom and its assets belonged to the heir of *Anne* Boleyn – Elizabeth I, the monarch Lord Hunsdon was hoping would grant him the earldom! Queen Elizabeth would have known whether her mother was the elder or not, and a mistake on Lord Hunsdon's part here could have led to accusations of trying to defraud the queen. Hunsdon must have been one hundred per cent sure Mary was the elder to petition for the title.

Thomas Boleyn was a younger son, who was perceptive enough to marry into the Howards, one of the premier families in England, while they were temporarily out of favour. He married Elizabeth Howard, the daughter of the earl of Surrey. Surrey's father, John, 1st duke of Norfolk, had died fighting for Richard III against Henry VII, ushering in difficult times for the once-mighty family. At the time of Thomas's marriage, his father-in-law had been attainted and so was not then an earl; he also had twenty-three children to provide for. It was therefore an equal match. Within two decades, Elizabeth's brother was a duke and her family were back in their prime.

Mary Boleyn's mother, Elizabeth, was a lady-in-waiting to Katherine of Aragon from 1509. There is every chance that she was as attractive as her three charming children, but she does not seem to have shared their strong personalities – we know practically nothing about the woman whose daughter and granddaughter became queens of England. It is surprising that we hear so little of Elizabeth in the stories of her successful and diligent husband and her three flamboyant and scandal-prone offspring. She was at court and is mentioned as Anne's main chaperone throughout the six years before Henry married Anne. Yet, we have no insight into her character; she is simply mentioned as being at Anne's side.

Thomas was well-educated and considered the best French speaker at Henry's court. He also spoke Latin well and was interested in humanism. He started to work his way up in the service of Henry VII and became one of the king's council. He attended the wedding of Katherine and Arthur; in 1503 he was one of those chosen to accompany Princess Margaret on her journey north to marry the King of Scotland. He was 'squire of the body' by 1509 and was made a Knight of the Bath, alongside many others, to celebrate Henry's accession to the throne. This gave him access to the king, which was all-important at court.

Thomas Boleyn was also involved in the court's social life, the hunting, hawking, fancy dress and bowls; he was said to be an excellent jouster[3] and Henry admired men for their sporting prowess. He worked hard and was intelligent and discreet enough to be appointed ambassador to the Netherlands, France and Spain. In 1530 Henry said that there was no negotiator as skilled as Boleyn.[4] Added to this, Erasmus described Boleyn as 'outstandingly learned'.[5] Boleyn was also said to have a furious temper, which his daughter, Anne, seems to have inherited. On the death of Wolsey, Thomas Boleyn held a feast, with entertainments showing the cardinal on his way to Hell.[6]

The Boleyn children were all given the best possible education. George became an accomplished poet and charming courtier, and Anne fascinated many with her quick wit, although Mary appears to have had little interest in intellectual accomplishments. The Boleyns helped train their children for court from the beginning, teaching them to become fluent in French, to join in the popular games and sports, to dance and sing well and to behave as etiquette dictated. The Boleyn sisters were effectively sent to the Continent as a finishing school, to continue their education academically and in court pursuits – their mistakes would occur elsewhere, then they would dazzle the English court on arrival. It seems to have been a successful strategy. And they both attracted admiration, in France and England. Sir Thomas Boleyn seems to have had little difficulty obtaining places at court for all his offspring.

In October 1514 a woman whom Henry loved greatly, his sister Princess Mary, went to France to marry King Louis XII. Mary Boleyn, now aged around fifteen, was appointed as one of the maids of honour. Louis sent several ladies home soon after the wedding, but Mary and Anne Boleyn were both kept on as her attendants.[7] Queen Mary was certainly not happy about Louis' choice of whom among her ladies-in-waiting to retain – the younger, prettier and more pliable of the bunch. This was an important opportunity for the sisters, but one not without its risks. The French court was considered a place of loose morals and Francis, the heir to the throne, was at the very centre of its myriad improprieties. Paris was aped throughout Europe; its clothing, dances and entertainments were the most stylish, sophisticated and glamorous in Christendom. But according to Monsieur de Brantôme: 'Rarely did any maid or wife leave the court chaste.'

Francis did not keep his love life private and discreet, before or after he became king, as his English counterpart did. A contemporary wrote: 'Alexander the Great saw women when there was no business to be looked after. Francis I looks after business when there are no women.'[8] This was Mary and Anne Boleyn's first experience of court and where they first got their impressions of kings and infidelity. Louis XII seemed to adore his new bride, but he was increasingly unwell and absent from the entertainments being held in the queen's honour.

In January 1515, three months after their arrival, Louis died. The English attendants were then unsure of their future. Mary and Anne would have been waiting around, listening to all the gossip – it is unlikely that they would have been allowed to attend Queen Mary while she was being isolated to check if she was pregnant. The French needed people around the potentially pregnant queen who were completely loyal to the crown of France; if Mary had conceived, then her unborn child, if a boy, was the King of France. Once it was discovered that the queen was not pregnant, she returned home, but the Boleyn girls were allowed to stay on at court.

Mary Boleyn was developing a reputation for promiscuity, according to Ridolfo Pio, the papal nuncio in France. He later described her as '*a very great wanton with a most infamous reputation*' while at the French court.[9] As ambassador to France from 1518 to 1521, Thomas Boleyn had many contacts at the French court and would have been informed of Mary's extracurricular activities. He would have seen firsthand how his younger daughter Anne was fitting in as if she were a French noblewoman. Thomas Boleyn had asked Anne to be '*a woman of good reputation*'[10] at the Burgundian court – perhaps he should have warned his elder daughter more. Mary's reputation did not discourage Francis I, or several of his friends, from having affairs with her. King Francis is said to have described her as a 'hackney' whom all could ride.[11] At the French court, there would have been considerable competition for such a title; Mary must have been extremely free with her favours to deserve it. This was Mary's first experience as a maid of honour, enjoying what most highborn girls dreamed of – she clearly made the most of the freedom she finally had.

When Henry VIII came to the throne, his good looks, charisma and common touch were praised in eulogies across Europe. He was young where the Emperor Maximilian and Louis XII were old, he was generous and extrovert, the opposite of his cautious father. Then, in 1515, a new king ascended the French throne. Francis I was younger than Henry and from the entertainments at the Field of the Cloth of Gold, where Henry insisted on wrestling Francis, Henry showed his obsession with being better than Francis at everything.

Henry was very competitive, especially as Francis was challenging Henry's position as the most dashing prince in Christendom. Before the kings had met, Henry asked Pasqualigo, the Venetian ambassador, many questions about King Francis. Henry asked:

'The King of France, is he as tall as I am?'

The ambassador replied that they were about the same height.

'Is he as stout?' asked Henry; no, he was not.

'What sort of legs has he?' Thin legs. The King of England then told Pasqualigo to look at his thigh, shouting that he 'also has a good calf to his leg'. It is therefore interesting to imagine whether Henry quizzed his new mistress about how he compared to his rival, as she had been in the bed of both kings.

In England, Mary's father could keep a close eye on her – and try to salvage her damaged reputation. Here he might arrange a valuable marriage, securing for the Boleyns the place in the upper echelons of society to which they aspired. She had been given an advanced and varied education for the time, inspired by the new humanist movement, and she had learnt her trade as a courtier in the most sophisticated court in Christendom. In 1520, probably before her relationship with the king, Mary married Sir William Carey.[12] William was the son of Thomas Carey of Chilton and Margaret Spencer. Like many at court he was descended from the fecund Edward III; his mother was a cousin of Margaret Beaufort, Henry VII's mother. Nevertheless, the second son of a gentry family was not who Thomas Boleyn would have been hoping his daughter would marry.

As the daughter of a man who was the heir to the earldom of Ormonde, and of a woman whose brother was the duke of Norfolk, Mary was a catch. Sir William Carey was a friend of the king, member of the Privy Chamber and a patron of the arts, introducing the Dutch artist, Lucas van Horenbolte to England. But the match was probably slightly beneath her; because of her birth and beauty, the Boleyns could have arranged a better marriage.

The main reason that historians suspect Henry's affair with Mary began in 1520 is the haste with which Mary's wedding seems to have been organised. Thomas Boleyn arrived in England only a week before the wedding, but he may have been conducting marriage negotiations through relatives or by letter. Carey's father was out of the country and did not return for the wedding, but in an age where travelling was hazardous and time-consuming, this does not indicate a lack of consent. The king was the guest of honour, but he often attended the weddings of his courtiers; they involved the feasting, dancing and jovial atmosphere that he enjoyed so much. Henry gave the young couple 6s 8d, his usual wedding gift. These items of circumstantial evidence can be pieced together to indicate that this marriage was a cover for Mary's relationship with the king, but it is unconvincing. Henry had not arranged a marriage for Bessie Blount until after their affair ended and he knew the potential dangers of being involved with a married woman.

So if the affair did begin in 1522, when the king began to give grants of land to the couple, why did Mary marry William Carey when she could have aimed higher? Although there may have been an alliance needed between the families, there is no hint of it. The answer may be found in the character of the bride; Mary could have been considered 'soiled goods' because of her behaviour in France. With many other English women in Paris at that time, it is likely that her reputation travelled across the Channel. A promiscuous woman would not be accepted by many men's families – how could they know that the heirs she produced were really her husband's children? Thomas Boleyn may have thought it was important to marry her off quickly, before she could cause any more scandal.

The only other likely explanation is that they married for love. There is no evidence for this, but because William Carey died soon after the Boleyns came to prominence, we know little about him or his relationship with his wife. Mary would have gained admirers as soon as she arrived at court, and may have fallen in love with one of them and wished to marry. Marriage was probably the safest option for her: she was stubbornly committed to following her heart. But there is no evidence that the marriage was arranged to cover an affair with Henry.

Although the king may have noticed the pretty newcomer when she arrived at court, all the evidence suggests that their relationship only became amorous around 1522. William Carey had been getting fifty marks a year from the king but this was increased by the generous grants, such as the keepership of Beaulieu and a wardship. Grants from Henry VIII to William Carey were regular between February 1522 and May 1526, two months after the birth of Mary's son, Henry Carey.[13] They were presumably in exchange for Carey's compliance in the affair.

Henry had chosen the right man to cuckold, as Carey's prospects relied on him being one of several young men whose high jinks amused the king and all knew the king's affection to be changeable. Not all husbands were so compliant. A century later, Louis XIV of France had to deal with the irate duc de Montespan, who removed the gates to his château, declaring that his cuckold's horns were too high for him to travel through them. Lord Hastings had carried his wife off to a convent when he discovered that she was having an affair with King Henry; his other known mistresses had been unmarried. Henry was not a man to shrug off scandal, so it would have been deeply embarrassing for him if William Carey had caused a fuss.

The first mention of Mary at the English court was in 1520, at her wedding. Pretty and experienced, with a hint of French glamour, Mary would have attracted attention immediately on her arrival at the English court. She may have enjoyed her time in France, but England was where she was expected to find a husband and settle down. London may not then have had the glamour of Paris, but the young king was trying to change that.

As Bessie Blount began her married life, Mary Boleyn became more prominent in the masques at court and she would have been a part of all the court festivities, enjoying the feasting, the dances and the music. Henry's wife was now prematurely aged and his mistress of several years had been discarded; Mary was in a powerful position. We have no evidence of her exercising patronage, although her father and husband were well-rewarded by their king during these four years. Nevertheless, although Mary probably did not exploit her position, she would have become an important person at court. She was not ambitious – this may have been one of the traits Henry liked about Mary; she would probably have been an easygoing mistress, making Henry feel strong and important – the opposite to the effect her sister had on him.

Any woman would have been flattered to be chosen by Henry out of the hundreds around court. He was a handsome and charming young man and his crown just added to his other attractions. Lacking both the willpower and the chastity of her younger sister, Mary began a relationship with the king. She appears to have been a woman who lived for the moment and dived head first into love affairs.

Mary was probably genuinely attracted to Henry. She does not seem to have cunningly kept him interested in order to promote her family or earn expensive trinkets for herself; after her sister became queen she had many chances for advancement, and threw them all away for love. At this time, Henry was a man who women would have desired whether he was a sovereign or a servant. There is no reason to suspect that this was not an authentic and passionate relationship between two young and attractive people – unlike some of the king's later liaisons.

In March 1522 there was a masquerade called the *Assault on the Castle of Virtue*, or the *Château Vert*. It was performed in front of most of the court, and the king's partner was Mary. Each woman represented a good feminine quality; Anne Boleyn, who was new to the court, was appointed as 'Perseverance', with the king's sister, Mary, as 'Beauty' and Mary Boleyn as 'Kindness'. It seems that much thought was put into the names, as these aliases reflect what we know of all three women. During this masque, Anne met her sister's lover, perhaps for the first time in an informal setting.

The English court was not as outrageous as that of France, but there was bawdiness. Women took part in banter using sexual innuendoes but they had to be careful not to talk as if they had actually indulged in these practices. Although premarital sex, even for women, was not a complete disgrace at Henry's court, it could be if one was caught – especially if the woman became pregnant. For married women like Mary Boleyn it was extremely dangerous, as a cuckolded husband could make life hell – unless it was the king whose eye she had caught.

Throughout the 1520s Henry often visited Penshurst Place, which was both conveniently near to Hever and managed by Thomas Boleyn. The first definite documented evidence of Henry's relationship with Mary is from 1523, when Henry owned a ship named the *Mary Boleyn*.[14] This may have been bought from Thomas Boleyn and thus already named. If it was not, then the use of *Boleyn* rather than *Carey* in the ship's name may be significant. One of the pieces of 'evidence' used against the Protestant martyr, Anne Askew, twenty years later, was that she continued to use her maiden name after her marriage. The use of Mary's maiden may name indicate that Henry saw Mary as an unmarried woman. Henry was never a man who liked to share his women; and it is likely that the Careys' marriage was in name only while she was being courted by the king.

William Carey was a younger son and this was a very difficult position for a man to be in. A sixteenth-century man wrote that to be a younger son

> is of all stations for gentlemen most miserable, for if our father possess 1000 to 2000 l. yearly at his death, he cannot give a foot of land to his younger children in inheritance. [Yet it] doth us good someways, for it makes us industrious to apply ourselves to letters or to arms, whereby many times we become our elder brothers' masters, or at least their betters in honour and reputation.[15]

So what was it that made Henry spend approximately four years of his life with Mary Boleyn? Her portrait shows a very appealing woman, with full lips and big brown eyes. She looks attractive even in the popular gable hood, which covered all the woman's hair, and she appears to have been prettier than her sister. She attracted not only Henry, but King Francis I and numerous other courtiers. The impression we gain from the scant sources on her is of a kind, loving woman who followed her heart.

Although Mary is not thought to have been very close to her sister, we have no records of a quarrel between Mary and the fiery Anne. Considering the previous relationship between Anne's sister and Anne's husband, there were grounds for jealousy and resentment on the part of both sisters – but Mary does not seem to have been viewed as a threat. Ridolfo Pio, the papal nuncio in France, wrote that Anne had pretended to be pregnant in 1534 and to fool people she had insisted that only her sister may attend on her.[16] This, although clearly false, indicates that the sisters trusted each other and Mary was often with her sister at court.

Over the course of four years – where we have no proof or even a suggestion of the king having another mistress – Mary and her royal lover are likely to have become very close. Mary would not have been able to break off the relationship even if she had wanted to as few would risk rejecting the king, so she may have tired of him much earlier. This was not the great love of Henry's life, but it was a long-term relationship. And we can only speculate as to how she felt when he fell so publicly in love with her sister.

Throughout the 1520s Thomas Boleyn's career was in the ascendant, undoubtedly because he was an efficient and competent servant, but his daughter's affair with the king can only have helped, at the very least to bring Thomas more firmly to Henry's attention. In 1522 Thomas had recently been made Treasurer of the Household and would soon become a Knight of the Garter. In 1525 Sir Thomas Boleyn was made Viscount Rochford. Known as a Francophile, the French obviously felt Boleyn had influence; they paid him the same size pension as the king's closest friend, the duke of Suffolk. He was an astute politician and an able servant – he deserved the new title for his dedicated service to the king. But there's every chance that this was a reward to mark the end of Henry's relationship with Mary; and perhaps was a sweetener as he began to woo Thomas's other daughter.

Within two years of his relationship with Mary Boleyn ending, Henry had proposed marriage to her sister, and although Henry's surviving love letters to Anne Boleyn are undated, they indicate that he was madly in love with her by 1526. Henry would have been unlikely to continue his affair with Mary while she was pregnant and so, in 1525, his eyes would have wandered – and Mary's sister was nearby. Circumstantial evidence suggests that Mary was cast off in favour of her younger sister.

We can only speculate as to why the affair ended, but 1525 was a watershed year for the king's love life. It was in 1525 or 1526 that Henry discovered that Queen Katherine was going through the menopause, and he began to seriously consider how to rid himself of his wife. He probably already had a young daughter – Catherine Carey is thought to have been born in 1523 or 1524 – and possibly two illegitimate sons, Henry Fitzroy and, in 1526, Henry Carey. But his only legitimate heir was a young girl – the future of England was now uncertain. It was in 1525 that Henry VIII began to pour honours on Bessie Blount's boy, Henry Fitzroy, leading many to assume that Henry was planning to make his son the next king of England.

Another possibility is that Henry, being informed that his wife was beginning to go through the menopause, made a last-ditch attempt for another legitimate child. The king, like most sixteenth-century Christians, saw all events in his life as potential judgements from God. Henry may have felt guilty that around the time his mistress was pregnant, his wife was becoming infertile. Leaving the state of adultery and returning to a pure married life – albeit only for a few months – may have been Henry's attempt to pacify his deity and obtain what he wanted above aught else: a legitimate son.

Chapter 5

Bastards of the King

Mary Boleyn had two children during the 1520s – Catherine and Henry Carey. There has long been dispute as to whether they were the children of Henry VIII. Catherine's year of birth has been estimated at between 1523 and 1529, but a date of around 1524 now seems most probable. She went to court as maid of honour to Anne of Cleves in November 1539, married in April 1540 and had her first child in 1541. Therefore she must have been born around 1524. It was once thought that Henry Carey was born in 1524, from the dates given on his tomb, but it is much more likely that he was born in March 1526.[1] This places both Careys' conceptions within the period of the king's relationship with their mother.

After William Carey's death in 1528, Henry Carey was made his aunt's ward and stayed at court in Anne's household. We are unsure about his sister Catherine, but she presumably stayed in the custody of her mother, and thus spent most of her time at court with the rest of her family. This was a great opportunity for young Henry Carey. He was educated by Nicholas Bourbon, a well-respected French poet, who Anne Boleyn had saved from the French Inquisition. He also studied at a renowned Cistercian monastery.

The two Henrys probably spent time together, as the boy was in the custody of Anne and living at court. Children were usually sent to live with other noble families, or more influential relatives, to cement connections and alliances. Anne may have sought to have young Henry with her as a reminder to the king of what a Boleyn girl could provide him with: a healthy son. This was until his aunt's fall in 1536. Henry Carey was probably then returned to his mother and stepfather and there is no record of further contact with the king until 1545.

As Mary became pregnant with her daughter in 1523 or 1524, and her son around June 1525, there seems to be a good chance that both Catherine and Henry Carey were Henry VIII's children. Surviving documents from Henry's reign and from Elizabeth I's have only a couple of hints that the Careys were royal bastards, which perhaps indicates that they knew better. Nevertheless the dates seem to match. In 1532 Henry wrote to Charles V when trying to arrange a marriage for Henry Fitzroy, duke of Richmond. In the letter, he referred to Richmond as: 'our only bastard son.'[2] This does not prove that he did not have others, as he was trying to persuade the emperor that Richmond would have a great inheritance – possibly a crown – and that this would not be shared. Henry Carey was just a small child at this time.

Carey was, like the sons of many courtiers, named after the reigning king. In this case, it may have been because of a more personal relationship between the baby boy and his sovereign. It was easier to recognise children by an unmarried woman than children conceived by double adultery. With Henry Fitzroy, Henry VIII did nothing publicly for the boy until he was six years old, past the age at which a child was in most danger of succumbing to a childhood disease. By the time Henry Carey turned six, it was 1532 – and Henry VIII was battling to marry young Carey's aunt.

At this time, the king was defying the whole of Christendom by seeking an annulment of his first marriage. To have acknowledged the Carey children as his own would have caused widespread embarrassment and a serious weakening of the moral stand he was trying to take. He was seeking to portray himself as an honourable man, and to depict Anne as from a good family – it would not have helped his chances to admit that her sister had borne his children. In fact, it would have shown that any marriage to Anne Boleyn was legally dubious.

Even after Henry annulled his marriage to Anne – on the grounds of his previous relationship with her sister – to recognise the Careys as his children was to air his dirty laundry before all of Christendom. Henry Fitzroy had already proved that the king could father healthy boys, so he no longer had a point to prove, and Henry was not a man who was entirely comfortable with his adultery. He was often condemning of infidelity in others and would have seen Mary Boleyn, especially after she married William Stafford, as a fallen woman. Although he too had married far beneath himself for love, and damn the consequences, he believed that God had guided him to do so. By 1536 the Careys' mother was in disgrace and their aunt and uncle had been executed for treason. The twelve-year-old girl and ten-year-old boy may have been condemned with the rest of their clan in the king's eyes.

Henry could be ruthless, even with his children. When his daughter Mary refused to publicly state that she was a bastard, the product of an incestuous and illegal union, few were surprised. But Henry made little effort to cajole her out of her defiance, and used harsh measures, such as separation from her mother and her father, threats and banishment, to get his way. Throughout this episode, Henry repeatedly showed that he was willing to disown his daughter; not only was she stubborn and disobedient, she was a constant reminder of her mother. Henry's behaviour towards Mary showed he could switch off his paternal feelings. His merciless streak included discarding both his daughters when their mothers displeased him and after Henry Fitzroy's death in 1536 he did not even organise a decent funeral. Yet Henry loved his children, even if out of sight could be out of mind.

Mary's children had their lineage, but with William Carey dead, their mother disgraced and their mother's family annihilated, it could have been difficult for them to obtain a place at court. Their Boleyn grandparents soon died and there was no one left to put in a good word for them with the king, except their great-uncle, the duke of Norfolk, who had many other relatives to secure positions for. When Henry VIII felt guilty about something he had done it was always someone else's fault, and Henry sending his wife, brother-in-law and friends to their deaths must rank as something he should have felt very guilty about. This should have damaged the Careys' chances of ever obtaining the king's favour, yet Mary's daughter Catherine was chosen to be a maid of honour to Anne of Cleves, and her son Henry obtained a place at court when he was nineteen.

There were rumours about Henry Carey's paternity at the time. In his portrait, Henry Carey seems to have resembled neither Henry VIII nor Sir William Carey. John Hale, vicar of Isleworth, was part of a group opposing Henry's marriage to Anne Boleyn; it would have been a good rumour to start that Anne's nephew, who was in her care, was in fact the king's son. Hale was arrested in 1535 for criticising the king; two priors and a priest were also arrested around this time for similar gossip.[3] Hale blamed his words on 'a fervent ague … Several falls from my horse, from one of which was troubled in my wits, as also by age and lack of memory.'[4] He had said: 'Mr. Skydmore did show to me young Master Carey, saying that he was our sovereign lord the King's son by our sovereign lady the Queen's sister, whom the Queen's grace might not suffer to be in the Court.' Hale also recounted that:

> Master Skydmore … [and] I had several conversations concerning the King's marriage and other behaviours of his bodily lust. Once Cownsell the porter said that our sovereign had a short of maidens over one of his chambers at Farnham while he was with the old lord of Winchester [Wolsey].

There are other suggestions that Henry housed women near to where he stayed, although it is unlikely to have been a harem as this source seems to imply. As with most of Hale's words, there is probably some truth behind the exaggeration.

Neither Carey made a particularly advantageous marriage. Henry married Anne Morgan, the daughter of Sir Thomas Morgan of Herefordshire, in 1545. They had twelve children – including nine legitimate sons – and Carey also acknowledged illegitimate children. One of his bastard sons, Robert Carey, became the 1st earl of Monmouth. It could be said that he was too fertile to be Henry VIII's offspring! Elizabeth's Privy Council considered Henry's son, George Carey, as a potential fourth husband for Mary Queen of Scots; this was opposed by Henry Carey. This suggests that Elizabeth had a very high level of trust in the Carey family. It has also been seen as an attempt to keep Henry's bloodline on the throne of England, as Mary, Queen of Scots was then the likely heir to the kingdom.

Henry Carey was knighted in November 1558, soon after Elizabeth's coronation. He quickly became the 1st Baron Hunsdon; Hunsdon had been one of the manors given to Anne Boleyn by Henry VIII when she was created Marquess of Pembroke in 1532. He was made a Knight of the Garter in 1561, a member of Elizabeth's Privy Council and Captain of the Gentleman Pensioners in 1564; this placed him in charge of her personal security. In 1569 Carey became lieutenant-general of the royal army and he helped suppress the Northern Rising of that year; he also became the Lord Chamberlain and the MP for Buckingham. Carey does not seem to have been a natural courtier, but a soldier, who was honest, trustworthy and popular with his queen and his troops.

The earldom of Ormonde should have passed to Henry Carey on the death of his mother, as often occurred, but instead it was given to Piers

Butler, the cousin of Thomas Boleyn who had previously challenged him for this. His grandfather's other earldom, Wiltshire, had been limited to the male line; as George Boleyn died without issue, it reverted to the crown. However, the earldom of Ormonde had been given to the heirs general, and so should have descended through the female line to Henry Carey. Even during the reign of his cousin Elizabeth, Carey did not secure the title, which had few lands to go with it. On his deathbed, Elizabeth offered him the title but he insisted that if she had not thought him worthy during his life then he could not accept it when he was dying. Elizabeth I signed herself 'your loving kinswoman' in letters to the Careys. This has been taken as 'proof' that she knew them as her half-siblings; however, as her cousins, this was an appropriate form of address.

Catherine Carey married Sir Francis Knollys, a privy councillor and vice-chamberlain of the Royal Household, and they had sixteen children. Catherine became a very close friend of the queen and was appointed her Chief Lady of the Bedchamber. Catherine's daughter, Lettice Knollys, would not be such a good friend to Anne Boleyn's daughter – she secretly married Robert Dudley, earl of Leicester, the love of Elizabeth's life. Lettice's son from another marriage, Robert Devereux, was the surprising replacement in the queen's heart; until he committed treason and she had him executed. This man – Robert Devereux, earl of Essex – was the great-grandson of two of Henry's mistresses, Lady Anne Stafford and Mary Boleyn. Perhaps Elizabeth could have married her much younger love; but one Boleyn reaching the throne of England was astonishing enough.

Catherine and Francis Knollys were two of the Protestant courtiers who felt the need to leave the country during the reign of Queen Mary. When they left, Catherine's cousin Elizabeth sent her a letter signed 'Broken Heart'. This gives a clear indication that the cousins were friends in childhood as well as in later life. The Knollys family initially went to Basel, but by 1557 were in Frankfurt. They returned soon into Elizabeth's reign.

Catherine died in 1568 or 1569 at Hampton Court Palace. Elizabeth paid £640 2s 11d for the funeral, far exceeding what she had paid for other cousins. The queen was said to have been so distraught that she became *'forgetful of her own health'*.[5] In 1596 Henry Carey was buried in Westminster Abbey, where his sister Catherine had been buried. All Henry VIII's legitimate children, Mary, Elizabeth and Edward, as well as Katherine of Aragon's stillborn children and those who died young, were also buried there.

It is likely that Henry's marriage to Katherine of Aragon was celibate from 1524, and it is from around this time that several children were born who were rumoured to have been the king's. Katherine had conceived many times, but all of her children had died, except one girl. Now the pregnancies had stopped too; by this time she was thirty-nine and had not conceived in six years. Henry was not attracted to her and she was no longer his confidante. She was not involved in the social life of the court – she was becoming dispensable. Hall wrote that 'he would not come to her bed'[6] from around 1526, and other accounts agree that it was over by this date, and probably before. Henry continued to be a regular visitor to Katherine of Aragon's rooms, and even visited her thus after he had begun annulment proceedings, but it was only as a part of court ritual.

The six-year age gap between Henry and Katherine was showing more than ever. Francis I said that: 'The King of England is young, but his wife is old and deformed.'[7] She had been constantly pregnant or recovering from childbirth for nine years of her life, and it had taken a toll on her body and her health. Henry's decision to annul his marriage has often been attributed to his love for Anne Boleyn. But there is evidence from the time Katherine went through the menopause that he was considering all options to secure the succession.

The problem was exasperated by the king's lack of a younger brother – Henry desperately needed a male heir. He married Katherine of Aragon when he was eighteen and there had been several pregnancies during the first ten years, including five births. We know of no serious medical problems suffered by Katherine or Henry that could explain this; but Henry came to believe that he knew what the problem was – God disapproved of him and Katherine. He needed to figure out why.

In June 1525 Henry Fitzroy turned six years old. His father considered him ready to receive the honours due to the king's only son. Fitzroy had survived the most dangerous years in a child's life and Henry now wished to organise the boy's education and household. Queen Katherine apparently attended the celebrations for the boy's elevation to the peerage, at the manor house that Henry had commissioned for his mistress.[8] She seems to have dealt with this with dignity; but for a woman who could no longer conceive, to see her husband's healthy young son being fawned over must have been heartbreaking.

Henry VIII heaped titles on his son. Fitzroy was made a Knight of the Garter, keeper of the city and castle of Carlisle and duke of Richmond and Somerset. He was also given the titles of earl of Nottingham, Lord Admiral of England, Ireland, Wales, and the previously English-run territories of Gascony, Aquitaine and Normandy, which were in reality under the control of the King of France. He was also created Lord Lieutenant of Ireland and Warden of the Scottish Marches – these were both titles Henry had held as a child. Fitzroy was made the highest noble in the land, apart from his father, the queen and their legitimate daughter. On the same day, Sir Thomas Boleyn, the father of Henry's mistress, Mary, was created Viscount Rochford.

The titles of Richmond and Somerset were significant ones. Henry VIII's upbringing had been shaped by his grandmother, Margaret Beaufort, countess of Richmond. A fiercely maternal woman, as shown by her tireless campaign to make her only son the king of England, it is likely that she made quite an impression on her young grandson. When Henry gave Fitzroy the title of Richmond, his grandmother is unlikely to have been far from his mind. The title of Somerset had last belonged to Henry VIII's younger brother Prince Edmund, and caused resentment when, after Henry VIII's death, it was taken by Edward Seymour, the Lord Protector. It was felt to be an inappropriate choice because of its quasi-royal connotations. In 1397 John Beaufort, marquess of Somerset, had been a royal bastard – who was then declared legitimate by papal bull and by royal charter. It was through the Beaufort line that the Tudor dynasty claimed the throne.

It had been four hundred years since a king of England had given his illegitimate son a title. Even then, when Henry's ancestor and namesake, Henry II, had honoured his son, it had only been an earldom; a double dukedom for a young boy was unprecedented. When the duke of Richmond was given an income of £4,000 per year, Queen Katherine complained that *his* household had more spent on it than his legitimate half-sister's.[9] Henry was outraged by this criticism and dismissed three of her Spanish ladies. Katherine may have been worried that Richmond's elevation threatened Mary's position as unofficial princess of Wales. This is the first record of his wife making any complaint about his infidelity since the scandal surrounding his affair with Anne Stafford.

Charles V apparently believed that Henry had decided to give the throne to his illegitimate son Fitzroy. He believed that Mary had been quickly engaged to a French prince in order to get her out of the way. The Venetian ambassador even thought that Fitzroy had been legitimised.[10] If there was any truth in this, these ideas may have been put on hold when

Henry realised that he could annul his marriage. And he would conceive a legitimate son, if God was pleased with him. And why would God not be pleased with Henry VIII?

Around this time, Fitzroy's stepfather, Gilbert Tailboys, was knighted and appointed sheriff of Lincolnshire, a large and notoriously troublesome county during Henry VIII's reign. From 1522 to 1525 the Tailboys had been at court, in Wolsey's retinue; Bessie's son may have been with them. On 26 July 1525, the little duke left London for Sheriff Hutton, Yorkshire, a long journey north where he was entertained at the homes of gentry families on the route. He was on his way to establish a semi-royal residence in the north of England, with a train of six hundred servants, as the figurehead of the Council of the North. At the same time, Gilbert and Bessie Tailboys left court for their estate in South Kyme, Lincolnshire.

South Kyme Castle is now only a ruin. It was in an isolated position, which may have been difficult for the couple to adjust to; they who had enjoyed the festivities of court. Bessie had never lived there before and she was now several days' travel away from her eldest child. They would have socialised with the country gentry and entertained the locals at feasts and hunting; both their families had influence in the area dating back many decades. Their deer park would have attracted visitors and money, and the fens would have been a good source of food for the family and all around – there would not have been the fear of starvation and disease that existed elsewhere.

The newly created duke had his court set up royally in Sheriff Hutton Castle. The accounts show that actors and singers were frequently performing for the boy and his attendants. The ruins of Sheriff Hutton can still be seen. He would have spent the winters at Pontefract Castle, also now a ruin. Richmond seems to have been a forceful child, admiring the girls with his best friend, the earl of Surrey, hitting others when he was angry, and skipping lessons to hunt and play sports. He seems to have grown up the spitting image of his father, with his red hair and his boisterous personality. The king described his son as his 'worldly jewel' and ensured that he had a household worthy of a prince.

Many of the men who became leading lights later in the century were at Sheriff Hutton with Richmond: John Dudley and Edward Seymour, who would both lead the country during Edward VI's reign; Queen Katheryn Parr's brother, William; Queen Catherine Howard's nephew, Andrew Baynton; and Henry Grey, Lady Jane's father, who would later seize the throne for her. They would have been hoping for great things when Richmond grew up – they also would have been likely to support him against his half-sister, Mary, if he ever challenged her for the crown.

The young duke's tutors included the renowned scholars Richard Croke and John Palsgrave. Both had links to Bessie Blount, which suggests she had some influence in appointing men to these sought-after positions. Although Croke was distantly related to the Blounts, he was a commoner and felt that Richmond was being encouraged by his guardians to treat the renowned scholar with disdain. Croke was deeply upset by this and perhaps hoped that Cardinal Wolsey, another low-born man who had worked his way up by talent alone, would help him. The king and the cardinal had little interest in helping Croke assert his authority over his charges. Croke felt that the men in charge of the duke's household, Sir William Parr of Horton, Richard and George Cotton, were leading the duke astray by persuading him to not attend his lessons.[11]

Croke's letters to Wolsey remain, and in them he is highly critical of nearly everyone within the duke's household – but not of the duke himself. Perhaps when he was writing that the others' lack of responsible boundaries for Richmond would spoil him, he meant that the child was spoilt – but he could not possibly criticise the king's son. Palsgrave, Fitzroy's chief tutor from 1529, had a different experience. He wrote to his friend, Thomas More:

> And to make the child love learning, I never put [him] in fear of any manner [of] correction, nor never suffer him to continue at any time till he should be wearied, but devise all the ways I can possible to make learning pleasant to him, insomuch that many times his officers know not whether I learn from him or play with him, and yet have I already brought him to have a right good understanding in the principles of the grammars both of Greek and Latin … On my faith I knew never a more singular wit, neither rich nor poor, than he hath already.[12]

Henry Fitzroy appears to have grown into a lively young man. Nicholas Throckmorton, one of the boys lucky enough to be educated alongside him, wrote that

> By parents' heast, I served as a page To Richmond's Duke, and waited, still at hand, for fear of blowes, which happen'd in his rage …[13]

Many young boys, being constantly feted and rarely contradicted by their contemporaries, would have had tantrums and struck out; it is little reflection on the man he may have become.

Yet this is not the only complaint recorded about the young duke. In 1534 Richmond and his friends were riding over fields and destroying farmland during their sports. He was clearly enthusiastic about one of his father's favourite pastimes – hunting. 'Here in this country where I lie I have no park or game to show sport nor pleasure to my friends when they shall resort unto me,' he complained to his father.[14]

Some of the Blounts were given an education fit for royalty alongside the duke of Richmond. This was one of the few benefits Bessie's family received. His cast-off clothes were passed on to his younger half-brothers and they received a small increase in their status. The Blounts never moved up from the gentry to the aristocracy, but remained a family on the fringe of the court. If Richmond had lived, he would have become increasingly powerful and his family would probably then have fulfilled their ambitions.

There was increasing speculation about the duke's future. There was the possibility of 'legitimising' him, especially as the Catholic Church was eager to keep Henry onside. In 1714 the Church 'legitimised' all of Louis XIV's known bastards. Louis issued a decree placing them in the line of succession, after his legitimate descendants, but before his legitimate nephew. There could be no argument that they were legitimate in the usual tense – their parents had never been married to each other. This policy was meant to be for the offspring of couples who later married but the Church was prepared to make an exception for the King of France. There is little doubt that, if Charles V had not objected, the Pope would have done the same for Henry VIII of England in the 1520s.

The English representatives in Spain told the emperor, in 1525, that Henry was looking for a foreign princess to marry young Richmond. Their instructions read that they were to say that the duke 'is near of the King's blood and of excellent qualities, and is already furnished to keep the state of a great prince and yet may be easily, by the King's means, exalted to higher things'.[15] It was rumoured that he would marry Princess Eleanor of Portugal, Charles V's niece. The English envoys said that she might find 'another dauphin' (heir to the throne) if she broke off her engagement to Francis I's son. If Charles V's niece was Fitzroy's queen consort, this might be good enough compensation for the offence to his aunt and cousin that Richmond's elevation would cause. These negotiations were being conducted two years before Henry announced his intention to annul his marriage to Katherine.

It was only in the thirteenth century that marriage had been clearly defined by the Catholic Church, and public opinion had slowly followed. The distinction between wife and mistress, legitimate child and bastard developed little by little, but was reasonably clear by Henry's reign. It had been thought that when a man decided to marry, this was simply to satisfy his lust, and so the Church had frowned upon marriage altogether, advocating a life of celibacy. It had been a long time since the reign of the illegitimate William the Conqueror, but it was possible that England would accept Henry VIII's bastard as their next king.

There were other royal possibilities debated for Henry's only son. Chapuys said there was a rumour that Henry Fitzroy would be made King of Ireland.[16]

One wild suggestion was to marry Henry to his half-sister Mary.[17] This was supported by the Pope; although it was against church law, there were precedents in the Bible itself, including Abraham marrying his half-sister, Sarah.[18] It had also been common practice amongst the Egyptian pharaohs to keep the royal bloodline pure. Incest was not illegal in England until the twentieth century, and although it was condemned, this condemnation was not nearly as strong as it would be today.

By 1536 Richmond was seventeen, a man ready to fill his father's shoes. Henry's second marriage had not produced any boys. The earl of Sussex, a close friend of Richmond's father-in-law, suggested to Henry that as 'the Princess [both Mary and Elizabeth] was a bastard, as well as the Duke of Richmond, it was advisable to prefer the male to the female, for the succession to the Crown. This opinion [was not] ... contradicted by the King.'[19] It was the law that bastards could not inherit from their fathers, but an exception to this was made for the bastards of princes. Henry may well have wanted people to believe he had options, as he would not have wanted to appear vulnerable – and an ageing king with no son and heir was vulnerable indeed.

Yet illegitimate sons could be dangerous, especially when the king had no legitimate boys. James, duke of Monmouth, was the bastard son of Charles II. When his father died in 1685, he claimed that his parents had been secretly married and then tried to claim the throne. His uncle, James VII of Scotland and II of England, succeeded in hanging on to the throne and

Monmouth was executed. However, the venture showed how dangerous illegitimate children, raised almost as if they were princes, could be. And Richmond was raised in a similar style to his legitimate sisters.

Henry turned down a proposed marriage between Richmond and the daughter of the King of Denmark, who was also the niece of Charles V, although he had initially been seeking out such a match. It would have been a fantastic endorsement of Henry's position in Europe. Perhaps Henry was paranoid that his son might challenge him for the throne with foreign support. His own father had kept him away from politics as a child, probably for this very reason.

Henry VIII had four problems with his own claim to the throne. His father was a descendant of Edward III, but through an illegitimate line. The fact that John of Gaunt married his mistress *after* she had borne him several children did not make those children legitimate in many people's eyes. Henry actually had a greater claim to the throne through his mother, Elizabeth of York; her father had been the great Edward IV. However, when Edward died, evidence was found that he had secretly married in his youth and then left his wife for Elizabeth Woodville. Therefore Edward IV's children by Elizabeth − including Henry's mother, Elizabeth of York − were illegitimate. This may have been fabricated, but it was a damaging assertion. Edward IV's mother had claimed that Edward himself was illegitimate; if either of these allegations were true, then Henry VIII could not use descent from Edward IV as one of his claims to the crown of England.

Henry's great-great-grandmother was Katherine, the widow of Henry V of England and a French princess. However, Henry VIII was not descended from her royal husband, but from her liaison with a commoner, her Welsh clerk of the wardrobe. It has often been assumed that, as they had several children, they must have had a marriage ceremony. But there is no evidence of this; the couple were forced to separate when King Henry VI and his councillors discovered his mother's clandestine relationship. Therefore the Tudors, through four relationships, could be considered an illegitimate branch of the royal family tree − and so they were open to coups at any time. If Henry married Bessie and made Richmond his heir, he would have solved the succession problem for the moment, but there would always have been a risk of a return to the Wars of the Roses.

There was no definite need for a son. The England of the 1520s was probably ready for a queen regnant. As Mary was near childbearing age when the Great Matter began, Henry could have had an adult grandson before he died, if he had arranged an early marriage for his daughter. The English would certainly have accepted a female ruler if she was married to one of her English royal cousins. Yet the last female heir to the throne had been Matilda, four hundred years before, and that had been a disaster. Yet there was no reason to assume that Mary's accession would lead to another civil war. There were many contemporary examples of powerful female rulers, such as the Regent Margaret of the Netherlands, Margaret of Navarre and Mary, Queen of Hungary, who proved that women could reign successfully.

In the summer of 1536 Henry passed an act, which meant that his proclamations were as legally valid as acts passed by Parliament. He then passed an act giving him the power to name his own successor. Most people at the time believed that this was so he could make Richmond his heir. There is much evidence that it was at least a back-up plan. What is certain is that the time around 1524 to 1526 marked a watershed in Henry's love life, and in his political direction. He would make significant changes to the country based on this.

Henry was a private man and many of his affairs would have gone unrecorded. Of the many rumours of his dalliances a large proportion are no doubt false; however, even these, by their very number, are suggestive of a womaniser. Henry was not interested in prostitutes, and there are no stories of him with low-born women, but many of the ladies at court would have succumbed to the king's charms. In 1546 Henry instructed all brothels to be closed. He had always been strict with the brothels that were popular in Southwark and towards the courtesans who followed his armies into battle. In contrast, King Francis kept his own official prostitutes at court, the *'filles de joie'*, literally the girls of joy. Henry's arrangements, though similar, were far less crude.

It is alleged that several courtiers were involved in recommending obliging women to Henry. There is evidence that William Compton made his Thames Street house available for the king's discreet liaisons. There are even suggestions that Cardinal Wolsey, archbishop of York, was *'the King's bawd, showing him what women were most wholesome and best of complexions'*.[20] Greenwich Castle, near his main residence of Greenwich Palace, was allegedly used for housing his mistresses and this was refurbished in 1526.[21]

Henry was supposed, wrongly, to have taken lovers at a very young age. As well as the rumours accusing him of being Anne Boleyn's father, Edward Neville, a close companion of Henry's from his early years, and his distant cousin, was also said to be his son. This was due only to his resemblance to the king, and despite only a small age difference between the two. Charles Brandon, duke of Suffolk, and Henry apparently looked so similar that Brandon was assumed by some to be Henry's bastard brother. This was given credence when Brandon was elevated from the son of a knight to a duke within the first five years of Henry's reign. Yet Brandon's marriage to Henry's sister, Mary, makes these rumours especially unlikely. Gossip started about anyone who looked like the king.

Henry was apparently 'living in sin, sometimes with two, sometimes with three of the queen's maids of honour'.[22] Although we cannot take Sander's account seriously, Henry was certainly more forward and less prudish than he has often been described. One story explains how

> A man called William Webbe was out on his horse near Eltham Palace one day, with his pretty sweetheart riding pillion, when he chanced to encounter his sovereign on the road. The King pulled the girl from the horse and kissed her in front of the aghast Webbe, then took her straight back to the palace with him

where he is said to have kept her for a while.[23] Webbe was a courtier, but there was nothing he could do about this, except complain to others.

It was written that: 'All it took to please him was an apple and a fair wench to dally withal.'[24] Yet he did have some morals; George Wyatt refers to the king's pursuit of a certain woman, who Henry then forsook once he realised that Sir Francis Bryan was seriously interested in the lady. His relationships seem to have caused little offence at court. But Henry certainly 'kept' mistresses, away from the court where he could visit them discreetly. As well as smaller castles and rented houses, hunting lodges would have been a convenient place to house a mistress.

There is a story that Henry 'had a fair lady whom he loved and lodged in the park', though unfortunately the year of this is unknown. He was said to have been spontaneously composing poetry for her and encouraged Sir Andrew Flamock to join in. Henry is said to have started with: 'Within this tower/There lieth a flower/That hath my heart.' Flamock added a humorous second verse, which apparently so angered his monarch that Flamock was told to leave. People have made up their own endings, as unfortunately the original was lost. One version reads: 'Within this hour/She pissed full sour/And let out a fart.'[25]

In the Lansdowne MSS, there is a story that a former mistress of the king had been banished from court for taking another lover, and the woman is

named as the sister of Sir Anthony Browne. She is said to have been confronted about her immoral behaviour and replied that she was no worse than
the queen, Anne Boleyn. Another version names the brother one of Henry's
'most strait-laced councillors' – this would describe Sir Anthony Browne well
– and says that his sister had accused the queen of sexual intercourse with
Mark Smeaton and George Boleyn.[26] This, he said, is what led to Anne's adultery being reported to the king.

It is more likely that this is referring to Browne's daughter rather than
his sister – Elizabeth, countess of Worcester. John Hussey described her
as 'beareth the name to be the principal' lady against Anne.[27] Certainly
Elizabeth Browne, along with her brothers, was prominent in the downfall of Anne Boleyn. She was a lady-in-waiting to Anne Boleyn and Jane
Seymour, but there is no record that she was the king's mistress.

Another alleged lover of Henry VIII's was Mary Berkeley. We know
very little about her, except that she was the daughter of James Berkeley, a
courtier. Estimates of her date of birth range from 1495 to 1500, making her
a little younger than Henry. She married for the second time after her husband's death in 1531, to Sir Thomas Jones. Her third child, Sir John Perrot,
was born around 1527. She is alleged to have borne two bastards to Henry:
Perrot and Sir Thomas Stucley.

This shows how confused these stories are – Thomas Stucley's mother
wasn't Mary Berkeley, it was Jane Pollard, the daughter of Sir Lewis Pollard,
and his father was Sir Hugh Stucley of Affeton. There is certainly nothing to prove a connection to King Henry VIII. Stucley lived from around
1525 – towards the end of Henry's affair with Mary Boleyn – until 1578. His
portrait shows a tall man posing in a Henrician style, but there is no obvious
resemblance to the monarch, and it is this alleged resemblance that is the
basis for the claim.

Stucley did not manage to impress Henry's legitimate children. He was
imprisoned in the Tower of London by Edward VI. Stucley claimed to the
Council that the French were planning to invade Calais; they did not believe
him. He was released by Queen Mary but began counterfeiting coins, ran
up huge debts and became involved in piracy. He married Anne Curtis,
although they had no children. In 1569 Stucley was committed to prison
for insulting Queen Elizabeth to others. Lord Burghley described him as
having 'the highest degree of vainglory, prodigality, falsehood'.[28]

Stucley was in the service of Edward Seymour, the Lord Protector of
England at the beginning of Edward VI's reign. When Seymour became the

victim of a coup in 1549, Stucley fled to France to avoid the wrath of the new rulers. He worked for Henri II of France, probably as a spy against the English. In 1552, the Council imprisoned Stucley in the Tower until Edward VI's death a year later. He then worked as a mercenary for the duke of Savoy, and became involved in piracy.

Elizabeth I, pretending to be outraged by Stucley's piracy, which was being criticised by the European powers he was robbing, arrested him in 1565 but soon gave him a full pardon. Stucley then went to Ireland, but seems to have lost Elizabeth's favour and in 1569 was accused of treason. He fled to Spain in 1570, where he was made duke of Ireland; it was a good rumour for the Spanish to start, that Stucley may have had a claim to the thrones of England and Ireland. He again plotted treason, planning to lead a Spanish invasion of Ireland, which was being ruled by the English. In 1577 Pope Gregory XIII gave him money to invade Ireland, a Catholic country being dominated by its Protestant neighbour. Instead he decided to fight for Portugal against Morocco and was killed in battle.

It was the bishop of Aquila, the Spanish ambassador, who first started the rumours about Stucley. King Philip II may have been taken in, but he had never seen Henry VIII. The Spanish were also keen to believe that John Perrot had a claim to the throne, and they supported an impostor claiming to be the illegitimate child of Elizabeth I and Robert Dudley. If there was the slightest reason to believe that the unpredictable Stucley was a son of the late king, Elizabeth I would have kept him tightly under her control.

Perrot had a similarly adventurous career to Stucley's and was around the same age. Sir Robert Naunton started the myth that he was Henry's son. Naunton was married to Penelope Perrot, John's granddaughter, and no doubt wanted to spread the rumour that his wife and children were descended from a king. He wrote that: 'If we compare his picture, his qualities, his gesture and voice with that of the King ... they will plead strongly that he was a surreptitious child of the blood royal.'[29] This was hardly solid evidence. The Berkeleys did not receive regular grants around 1527, which would have indicated a relationship between Mary and the king. She did not achieve a glittering second marriage either.

John Perrot was born in Wales around 1527; this would place his conception at the time that Henry was beginning seriously to pursue Anne Boleyn. Henry's letters indicate that he was still involved with other women in 1526, when Perrot was probably conceived. There were apparently rumours at the time that Perrot was illegitimate and later there were comments about his resemblance to King Henry. It sounds likely that Perrot was happy to allow people to think that this may have been the case, but there is no evidence. He died in September 1592 after marrying Ann Cheyney and later Jane Prust; both marriages, like Stucley's, were childless.

Perrot was around twenty when Henry died, but received nothing from him. He did not meet Henry VIII until he was involved in a fight with the king's servants. Apparently Perrot inspired Shakespeare's character Falconbridge in *King John*.[30] He was made a Knight of the Bath at Edward VI's coronation, imprisoned by Queen Mary for harbouring Protestants, but found favour with Queen Elizabeth and was appointed lord deputy of Ireland. If Elizabeth had suspected that he was her half-brother, she would not have given him this opportunity, which he could have used to build a power base against her. He was convicted of high treason in 1591 and died of natural causes in the Tower of London a year later.

There are also rumours that Henry had an illegitimate daughter, Ethelreda, sometimes called Esther or Audrey. It is perhaps less likely that Henry would have acknowledged an illegitimate daughter than an illegitimate son, as she would have been of less worth. Nevertheless, she could have been a useful marriage pawn. Ethelreda was the child of Joan Dingley, who was said to have been a royal laundress. Joan subsequently married a man named Dobson. John Malte, the king's tailor, acknowledged the young girl as his own child. The lands Henry granted to Ethelreda may have been only a thank you to her parents – his servants – so that the girl could make a good marriage.

During Queen Mary's reign, Ethelreda and her husband served Elizabeth Tudor while she was in the Tower. They also benefited from a grant after the dissolution of the monasteries. John Malte left part of his estate to Ethelreda in his will, which indicates she probably was his child. Like John Perrot and Thomas Stucley, Ethelreda was most likely born between 1525 and 1527 – in the three years after Katherine of Aragon went through the menopause, and when he ended his relationship with his mistress, Mary Boleyn, to around the time Henry first made promises of marriage to Mary's younger sister, Anne. Ethelreda Malte married John Harrington in 1547, the year that Henry VIII died. She died around 1558, without having had any children. If Henry's bloodline continued, it was not through these three alleged offspring.

There are also suggestions that Richard Edwardes was Henry's son. The evidence rests on him receiving an Oxford education that his family could not have afforded. There are many possible explanations for this: he could have had a benefactor, a scholarship, or perhaps his mother was the mistress of a rich man. Richard or his family may have impressed someone influential. Perhaps it was his father who paid – but there were many men who could have afforded to pay for this and there is no reason to assume that it was Henry VIII. Richard Edwardes has many descendants who believe he was Henry's son. This rumour seems to have originated from the Edwardes family themselves and not from any contemporary source. Much of our (more dubious) information comes from family histories.

Edwardes' mother, Agnes Blewitt, was not a courtier. She was from Somerset and is unlikely to have met Henry; he may have had affairs with low-born women, but they were unlikely to have lasted long. Mistresses needed to be able to dazzle at courtly accomplishments, and this usually meant having had an aristocratic upbringing. It could cause offence to target the wives and daughters of the highest in the land, but the king was also not expected to keep the company of women who were too far his social inferiors. A commoner may have held Henry's attention long enough for a casual fling and perhaps to conceive a child. Yet Henry may have considered his social inferiors for long-term mistresses, as he happily picked low-born ministers.

Edwardes was a poet, musician and composer who spent some time at Elizabeth's court. He married Helene Griffith, which does not seem to have been an advantageous marriage. They had only one son, William, who continued the Edwardes line by having sixteen children. Richard Edwardes died in 1566, three years after his marriage, and there is no evidence that links him to Henry VIII during their lifetimes. Nevertheless, these rumours persist.

Henry did mix with the 'common people' far more than his father did. At the christening of the first son of Henry and Katherine of Aragon, who lived for only a few weeks, the king allowed peasants at the celebrations to rip his clothes off him, while he just laughed. He always made an effort to appear merry and generous to his subjects and they, on the whole, loved him. It is likely that while travelling around London, hunting in the countryside or on a royal progress around the houses of his prominent subjects, a woman or two caught the eye of the monarch. It is perfectly possible that Henry did have a bastard by a low-born woman, as he might not have publicly acknowledged this or might never even have known.

If Henry had other bastards, they would probably have received great honours, unless there were complicated circumstances, as there were in the case of the Carey children. As there was no mention of Henry Fitzroy until he was six, his mistresses may have suffered miscarriages and stillbirths or had children who died in their infancy. If Henry had other illegitimate children – and it is likely that he did – it was probably the children of Mary Boleyn. It is at least possible that Henry's bloodline did continue, whether through the Careys' many children or through another illegitimate child that we, and perhaps Henry, have no knowledge of.

These rumours were easily started and almost impossible to categorically disprove. Perhaps a DNA test on their remains is all that could possibly be done to put these theories to rest, one way or the other. Many people would like to believe that Henry VIII's bloodline did continue, but if it did, it was almost certainly through the Careys. It is possible that it was Mary, the runt of the high-flying Boleyn litter, whose children helped continue Henry VIII's lineage. Henry's four acknowledged children all died without having children themselves.

Chapter 6

'The Woman in the World that I Value the Most'

'Grudge who will, but none deny ...'

Henry spent the summer of 1526 travelling around the country with his court, and enjoyed spending time at his new palace at Grafton. Sixty-two years earlier, a momentous event had happened nearby. A beautiful woman, Elizabeth Woodville, had refused to become the mistress of Edward IV – so at Grafton, Edward had made her his wife. Henry may have thought of his grandparents as he spent time there, especially as he much resembled Edward IV both in looks and in personality; we can but wonder if their example inspired him to propose to Anne Boleyn. If it did, it should not have. Despite their happy marriage and many children, after Edward IV's death, doubts about the legitimacy of this union led to civil war.

Henry seems to have been attracted to Anne Boleyn from 1525 or 1526; in one of his letters he says that he was *'struck with the dart of love'* for Anne for over a year and yet he still did not know if she was interested but by 1527 she had agreed to marry him. Henry showed everyone that he had a new courtly love in February 1526, when he jousted with the motto 'Declare I dare not' and an emblem which showed a heart in a press, and on fire.[1] Why would Henry be worried about declaring his feelings? This may have been because he had just finished his relationship with her sister.

In 1526 Henry wrote letters to his sister Margaret extolling his hatred of divorce and declaring that her soul was in danger of damnation. His hypocrisy is obvious, as he was soon petitioning the Pope for an annulment himself.

Margaret Tudor was allowed to annul her marriage to the earl of Angus on the grounds that he had a previous precontract. She soon married her lover, Henry Stewart, Lord Methven. Henry had a much better case for annulment than his sister but this did not guarantee success. When his other sister, Mary, secretly married the duke of Suffolk, Henry accepted them back into the country on condition that they paid him cripplingly large fines for the rest of their lives. As far as he was concerned, they were just using marriage to satisfy their lust.

Henry told Parliament during the Blackfriars trial that he was not annulling his marriage to satisfy his desire for another woman, 'for I am forty-one years old, at which age the lust of man is not so quick as in lusty youth'.[2] He had enjoyed his youth, spent time with many lovers, but he was now ready to settle down with the love of his life. He was still an impressive and attractive man at this stage, although 'bald like Caesar', according to the Venetian ambassador. The English were hopeful that he could have sons but they were not prepared for the popular Queen Katherine to be discarded against her will in order to make this happen. In his own mind, Henry was obeying his conscience and correcting the mistake he had made in living with Katherine all these years – the succession was only a small part of the bigger picture for him, once he had convinced himself of the righteousness of his position.

Hall reported that: 'The common people, being ignorant of the truth and in especial women and others that favoured the Queen, talked largely and said that the King would for his own pleasure have another wife.' For them, this could set a dangerous precedent, putting ideas in the head of every man who would prefer to discard his middle-aged wife for a younger woman. There is even a report of women daring to shout 'Back to your wife!' at the king as he passed them.[3] The men were more pragmatic; it was women who hated 'the concubine' and everything she represented.

Anne Boleyn was the determined younger woman who had got her claws into good Queen Katherine's husband – she was every married woman's worst nightmare and to some devout adherents of the Roman Catholic Church, she was the Devil incarnate who had led Bluff King Hal astray. Eustace Chapuys wrote to Charles V that the public's feelings about Henry's treatment of Queen Katherine were so strong they would be happy to join an uprising against him. Henry agreed, reportedly saying that

> The Lady Katherine is a proud, stubborn woman of very high courage. Had she taken it into her head to act, she could easily have mustered an army and waged war against me as fiercely as ever her mother did in Spain.[4]

Henry still felt the desperate need for a legitimate son. The Tudor line was not secure – it is only with the benefit of hindsight that we see the Wars of the Roses as ending in 1485. Henry nearly died in two accidents, while hunting and jousting, in 1524 and 1536, and some of his Yorkist cousins still posed a threat. Had he died then, with only one or two young daughters to succeed him, it is likely that one of their male cousins would have sought the throne, perhaps marrying the young Princess Mary or Elizabeth, or perhaps his daughters would have shared the fate of the Princes in the Tower. It would also have left England open to invasion from Scotland for centuries to come, because the Scottish king's claim was best after Princess Mary's – and she was only a young girl. The annulment has been put down to a midlife crisis, but it was a complex issue. Henry's health was declining from this time onwards and he must have been aware of his own mortality. In 1527 the problem with his sore leg – probably a varicose ulcer – began, which was to plague him for the rest of his life.[5] By 1531 he was suffering from insomnia.[6]

Lust for his mistress was only one motivation, but it was a strong one. The most pragmatic decision would have been to marry a French or Spanish princess, forming an alliance and receiving a big dowry. He could then have married someone who was younger; Anne Boleyn was approximately twenty-six when he first proposed and thirty-three when they married. This was considered old to bear a first child. Out of his love for her, he risked his kingdom; not just by the annulment, or by the dissolution of the monasteries, but by not arranging an alliance with another power, based on a second marriage, which could have helped support him against the Pope and the emperor.

But he had chosen Anne and her position at court was developing in a way that her sister's and Bessie Blount's had not. Mistresses were often used as intermediaries to the king. Cavendish wrote that it was

> judged, by and by, through all the court, of every man, that she [Anne], being in such favour with the king, might work mysteries with the king and obtain any suit of him for her friend.[7]

Anne would have been petitioned by courtiers, offered gifts, flattered, in the hope that a request for something coming from her would have more success than if they were to ask themselves. She could use this to win influential aristocrats to her cause; those who allied themselves with her now would gain the gratitude of the king and the future queen. There was little to be gained by siding with the ageing Katherine, who was now an inconvenient embarrassment in the eyes of any ambitious person.

There were accusations that Anne Boleyn was quite low-born, the product of an upstart family of merchants. In fact, her pedigree was similar to most of the upper class – a mixture of ancestors who were already nobles and those who became aristocrats by exceptional ability or cunning. Her great-grandfather, Geoffrey Boleyn, is the basis for these slurs. He was a merchant and an alderman who become lord mayor of London. He then married the daughter and co-heiress of Lord Hoo and their son married the co-heiress of an Irish earl, Margaret Butler. Their son was Thomas Boleyn, Anne's father, who married into the well-established Howard family. As Ives points out so well:

> Anne's great-grandparents were (apart from Geoffrey) a duke, an earl, the granddaughter of an earl, the daughter of one baron, the daughter of another, and an esquire and his wife. Anne Boleyn came, in fact, from the same sort of background as the majority of the Tudor upper class. Indeed, she was better born than Henry VIII's three other English wives; marrying her did not, as has been unkindly said of Jane Seymour, give the king 'one brother-in-law who bore the name of Smith, and another whose grandfather was a black-smith at Putney'.[8]

Anne Boleyn was a woman who attracted slander, but the wildest rumour about her was that she was Henry's daughter. As conspiracy theories go, this is a particularly fanciful one. Not only would Henry have been ten when Anne was born but there is nothing to prove that Henry ever had an affair with Lady Boleyn. This rumour was being spread around the time of the annulment, when Henry's subjects, in particular the women, were prepared to repeat any malicious slur about the other woman in the royal marriage.

Sander alleged that this was not only true but also that it was well known at court. His story was that when Henry was 'visiting' Elizabeth Boleyn, he had fallen in love with her daughters, first Mary and then Anne. He insisted that Mary Boleyn took Katherine of Aragon's side during the 'Great Matter' and she planned to 'assert it publicly' that Henry was Anne's father.[9] Sander, as with his other yarns, has nothing to corroborate this. We should accept Henry's words, when he was asked about the rumours that he had been the lover of both Boleyn sisters and their mother – 'Never with the mother'.[10]

For a long time it was believed that Anne had been born around 1507, when Henry was sixteen. This would at least have made the accusation of incest more likely, but at this age Henry was being kept away from the bad influences of court by his father; he did not have the freedom to chase an attractive, older lady-in-waiting, especially one who had been busy for eight years having a child a year, and so is unlikely to have seemed an attractive prospect to a young prince. There could have been an affair later on, but it is highly unlikely. This rumour probably arose from the convention of so many different spellings and pronunciations for one person's name. Elizabeth's surname was written as Bullen, Boullant and Boleyn; it would have been easy for someone to confuse Elizabeth Blount with Elizabeth Boullant, and spread the rumour that it was Anne's mother who had been the king's mistress. Compounding this, it may have been known that Henry had previously conducted an affair with a Mistress Boleyn, and the mother could easily have been confused with her daughter Mary – gossip that he had relationships with two sisters could easily be expanded to include the mother.

In 1513 Anne Boleyn was appointed as a maid of honour to the most powerful woman in Europe, Margaret, regent of the Netherlands. Margaret was also archduchess of Austria, a Hapsburg princess and the daughter of the Holy Roman Emperor Maximilian and Mary of Burgundy. She was the aunt and guardian of Charles V, who was only a year older than Anne. Within three years, he would become the king of Spain and in 1519, while still a teenager, Charles was elected the Holy Roman Emperor and controlled vast swaths of Europe. Margaret's court would have been a very exciting place to be.

This formidable woman reigned over a court that was the model of chivalry and sophistication; she was clever, religious and capable. This year cannot have failed to have a profound effect on the way young Anne saw the position of women in society. The Burgundian court was that which all other European courts aped, with the best dances and entertainments; the country had a tradition of patronising the arts. Henry VIII was much more interested in adopting these practices than his father had been.

Anne was then twelve, the minimum age to be a maid of honour. From 1512 to August 1514, Thomas Boleyn was a diplomat in Brussels. He must have had good relations with Margaret of Austria to be able to secure such a sought-after post for his young daughter. Margaret was known to be strict with her maids of honour and they were not allowed to spend their time gossiping and flirting with the men of the court. Studying, reading, religion and the maintenance of personal and family honour were requirements of Margaret's ladies, and so Anne, at a time where she was beginning puberty, was carefully observed at all times. Courtly love was widespread in Burgundy, but it had clearly to be courtly love, with no hint of physical contact.

Anne was probably chosen to go to Burgundy ahead of Mary because she was a bright child and considered more likely to cope well abroad, or Mary may have been ill or had an offer elsewhere. But it was unusual for the younger daughter to be offered such an opportunity. In a letter from Anne at the Burgundian court to her father in 1513, she wrote: 'I understand from your letter that you wish for me to be a woman of honest reputation when I come to court.'[11] From the information we have on the Boleyn sisters as adults, it seems that Anne kept to this, and it is likely that she was the more promising of the two from a very early age.

Anne impressed Margaret. The regent wrote to Thomas Boleyn: 'I find her so bright and pleasant for her young age, that I am more beholden to you for sending her to me than you are to me.'[12] But when Princess Mary left England to marry Louis XII, Henry VIII requested that Thomas Boleyn's French-speaking daughter became Mary Tudor's maid of honour. A surviving letter from Thomas asks Margaret to release Anne. This permission may not have been readily granted; Anne seems to have taken longer to get there than the party who travelled directly from England.

The only definite proof we have that Anne did go to France in 1514 and not at a later date is from the French ambassador, de Carles, who knew Anne well. He wrote in 1536 that: 'I am well aware that Anne Boullant first came from this country when Mary [Tudor] left to go to join the king in France to bring about the alliance of the two sovereigns.'[13] Margaret may have dragged her heels over sending Anne to France – her family's enemy – to attend on the marriage of the English princess who had been promised to her nephew; therefore only one Boleyn girl, 'Marie Boleyn', is shown on the original records.

Mary Boleyn's reputation and experiences at the French court have already been documented here. Anne seems to have behaved herself well and managed to remain at the French court long after the death of Louis XII. At first she was kept, along with her sister, as a maid of honour to the new queen, Francis's wife Claude. Her father, as ambassador, had influence at the French court and managed to arrange these positions. Claude was a shy and devout fifteen-year-old, who had little influence on the tone of the court. Serving as her maid of honour would have been a more sedate existence than serving Mary, the French queen, had been.

Louise of Savoy, Francis's mother, ran the government while her son was busy enjoying himself. The Boleyn sisters would have seen clearly that strong women *could* control a country, as long as they could control the king. At some point before 1521, Anne was transferred into the service of the Duchesse d'Alençon, King Francis's sister.[14] Throughout her time there, she was learning the skills and grace that would wow the English court on her return.

In France, she developed an impression of what it meant to be a royal mistress. There were those, like her sister Mary, who were discarded quickly and laughed at by the courtiers. And then there was Françoise de Foix. Françoise maintained the upper hand with Francis I, insisting on taking other lovers and arguing with him publicly. By playing harder to get than the other women at court, Françoise held him in thrall for ten years. This was from 1518 to 1528 – including some of the time Anne Boleyn was at court and throughout the beginning of her relationship with Henry. Although there were aspects of Françoise's position she had no desire to emulate, Anne may have admired how this woman kept the interest of the lecherous Francis for so long.

During the time of Mary Tudor's marriage to King Louis, the French court had been a constant round of festivities. Men and women would have mixed at these celebrations, and love affairs would have developed. But when Louis died, the way the court was organised changed. The constantly pregnant Queen Claude kept her household very separate from her husbands, although the men and women of the two establishments socialised frequently. Here Anne would have spent most of the time with the other ladies.

In June 1520 Anne was probably at the Field of the Cloth of Gold as Queen Claude's attendant. On the English side, her parents were definitely there with several attendants, and George and Mary would almost certainly have been among their number. Thomas Boleyn ended his term as ambassador to France shortly beforehand. Anne returned to England, at her father's request, in 1521. Relations were then bad between France and England, and most English people in Paris left around the same time. But this was not why Anne was recalled; she was then of an age to marry. Her father had just married off one daughter, and he and the king had a suitable man in mind for Anne – James Butler.

Butler was at court as a member of Wolsey's household. But it was another of the cardinal's noblemen that Anne was interested in marrying: Henry Percy, heir to the earl of Northumberland. Cavendish wrote that:

> When it chanced the Lord Cardinal at any time to repair to the Court, the Lord Percy would then resort for his pastime unto the Queen's chamber, and there would fall in dalliance among the Queen's maidens, being at the last more conversant with Mistress Anne Boleyn than with any other; so that there grew secret love between them that at length they were ensured together, intending to marry.

The romance with Percy was brought to an abrupt end. Wolsey berated Percy saying: 'I marvel not a little at your peevish folly, that thou wouldst entangle thyself with a foolish girl.'[15]

We do not know if Anne truly loved Henry Percy, but we know that she wished to marry him. For this sophisticated lady-in-waiting, being countess of Northumberland would have been preferable to being countess of Ormonde in tribal Ireland. But it was also expected that children, even when they reached adulthood, would obey their parents. This was a very important part of English culture and the Christian faith. Percy and Anne did not know better than their elders and would have to do as they were told.

According to Cavendish, who was writing thirty years after these events, this marriage was prevented because from 1522, when Henry was probably involved with Mary Boleyn, he was secretly in love with Anne. Kings of England rarely had affairs with the wives of people with titles and lineages as grand as the Percys, so Henry may have been attempting to end this match to save a scandal later on. Yet this is unlikely; the earl would have been extremely angry if his eldest son had married beneath him. Henry Percy was already betrothed to Mary Talbot and the king, the earl and the cardinal were united against this love match.

Anne's marriage to James Butler was important, as the Boleyns and Butlers were arguing over the earldom of Ormonde. The Boleyns had the better claim, but the Butlers were based in Ireland. The Butlers had allegedly decided that it would have to be defended by force and they had been speaking to other Anglo-Irish nobles, requesting assistance. The marriage would solve a problem that could spiral out of control in a territory in which no English king ever fully felt secure. There is nothing else to suggest that Henry was interested in Anne before 1526.

Anne had arrived in England a polished product after living at the two most sophisticated courts in Europe and she could easily arrange another match. At the English court there was a galaxy of stars, but only one sun, and all revolved around him. It would have appeared glamorous, even to Anne. However, people still threw the contents of their chamberpots out of their windows, or even on the floor in palace corridors. Churches and castles suffered from this as well as more humble dwellings, and apprentice and aristocrat alike were guilty of it. People were simply used to the dirt and the smell.

There were around 100,000 Londoners during Henry's reign. Theirs was a growing, bustling city without room for its entire people and the constant incoming chancers looking to make their fortune. It was dirty, messy and crowded in the slums, yet was, in many ways, similar to the palaces of the royal family. Courtiers' clothes would often be grubby but great effort and time had been put into making them opulent and ornate. They rarely washed, seldom cleaned their clothes and hardly ever washed their hair or cleaned their teeth, if at all. The palaces, much like their inhabitants, were brightly coloured and ostentatiously decorated, but filthy.

After time at the Burgundian court and seven years in France, Anne appeared to the court as an exotic French mademoiselle. Anne's reputation may have been damaged by her sister's, but around the time she arrived at court, her sister was the king's mistress, which could open doors for the family. Anne was first mentioned at court on 1 March 1522, in a masque, although she had probably become a maid of honour a year before. She was described as skilled at singing and dancing;[16] her position in the entertainments was assured. In the masque, *The Assault on the Castle of Virtue*, Anne was dressed in white satin and a gold headdress to play 'Perseverance'. The eight women defended the castle while the men tried to bombard them into surrender by pelting them with fruit. The women eventually acquiesced and they danced with the men, who were, of course, the king and his closest friends. This seems to have been almost prophetic; the masque was about a man desiring a woman who was determined to hold out, but eventually gave in.

Descriptions of Anne's appearance and personality varied from one extreme to the other. The Venetian ambassador, who had little reason to be biased, described her thus:

Madam Anne is not one of the handsomest women in the world; she is of middling stature, swarthy complexion, long neck, wide mouth, bosom not much raised, and in fact nothing but the English king's great appetite, and her eyes, which are black and beautiful.[17]

This is probably a fair description. She knew how 'to use [her eyes] with effect'.[18] Anne Boleyn was a woman not classically beautiful, but very alluring —the king was not the only man to notice her. Sander showed his bias by describing her as

> rather tall of stature, with black hair and an oval face of sallow complexion, as if troubled with jaundice. She had a projecting tooth under the upper lip, and on her right hand, six fingers. There was a large wen under her chin, and therefore, to hide its ugliness, she wore a high dress covering her throat … She was handsome to look at.[19]

This bizarre description was written by a man who was only nine when she died; there is no evidence that Anne 'wore a high dress', which was not fashionable at this time. Her portraits show that she did not usually cover her neck. Often the accusations of witchcraft marred people's descriptions of her – how else could she have made good King Henry forsake his devoted wife and the Pope?

George Wyatt described Anne's 'beauty [as] not so whitely as clear and fresh'. This was at a time when paleness was an important attribute; women would begin to paint their faces white and pencil in blue veins during the reign of Anne Boleyn's daughter. Sallow skin was meant to be a sign that the woman would not be as pleasant or as obedient as a fair-skinned woman.[20] It could simply be that Anne had an olive complexion, which would now be considered attractive. She is said to have had long black hair, and been graceful at the courtly pastimes of dancing and playing musical instruments; 'albeit in beauty she is to many inferior, but for behaviour, manners, attire and tongue she excelled them all, for she had been brought up in France.'[21] 'No one would have taken her to be English by her manners, but a native-born Frenchwoman.' She was also reportedly clever, witty and ambitious. Anne was a woman who belonged at the court. She loved the celebrations, the power and politics, the flirting. Anne was not considered as beautiful as Bessie Blount or her own sister Mary, but her confidence and wittiness were seductive to many.

By 1527 it was common knowledge that Anne was Henry's latest love interest, but so far there was little to show that she would be any different from his former mistresses. Yet Anne was refusing to become his lover and Henry was a king who was not used to being denied anything. He therefore wanted her even more and could not bear it that Anne denied him. We cannot know if her rejection was calculated or sincere. That it inflamed Henry's interest is unsurprising; what is astonishing is how far he went to attain her.

There are some Catholic sources that suggest that Anne was not eager to be Henry's mistress – and they would be the most likely to accuse her of targeting the king. These sources, and George Wyatt, assert that Katherine tried to protect her pretty maid of honour from the monarch's amorous advances. Wyatt wrote that Katherine went about this by constantly playing cards with Anne in order to expose the malformation on one of Anne's nails; this is hardly likely. However, Henry had not been especially generous to his former lovers and Anne may have been bold enough to reject him simply because she was not tempted by the offer. He worked hard to win her round, giving her diamonds and rubies, bracelets and brooches and gems arranged into lovers' knots and hearts. There is a long list of the presents that Henry showered on Anne in 1527, which were far more than a mere mistress might expect. In this year, her father was given the earldom of Ormonde which he had been disputing for several years. Plain Mistress Anne was now Lady Anne.

Henry went to mass three times a day and often five times on holy days. He was a man of conscience – and he believed that his conscience was God speaking directly to him. He was a man who liked all things in his life to be legal and above board, including sex. His conscience just conveniently reflected what he already wanted to do. He repressed and executed others for following their consciences, but he was God's representative in England – he would always believe himself in the right. And his conscience was telling him that Anne Boleyn should be more than his paramour.

Henry now believed that Katherine of Aragon, like Bessie Blount and Mary Boleyn, had been his mistress, and that he had really been a bachelor his whole life. That the king had lived in sin with his brother's widow was the cause of the outbreaks of plague and other catastrophes in England during the mid-1520s. Everything that happened in the kingdom was a judgement from God, and as God's favourite Englishman, Henry felt that they were mainly judgements on himself and those around him.

He still respected Katherine and basked in her admiration. He saw her as an adviser, companion and friend, and perhaps something of a mother figure. Certainly he did not see her as a lover, and the couple had grown apart since he had worn her colours in the jousts. More importantly, she could not give him what he wanted. He therefore chose to thrust aside the woman who had been so good to him, just as he would later discard Wolsey, More, Boleyn, Norris, Cromwell, Carew and many others to whom he had once been close.

He finally told his wife of eighteen years his feelings. Henry seems to have believed that Katherine would accept his decision and live a religious life, as it was little different to the routine she then followed. Katherine had become increasingly pious, and her life was a constant round of masses and prayers. As far as he was concerned, she was no longer sexually desirable and could not have more children; she was fit only for a convent. Her marriage to his brother meant their marriage had been unlawful from the start. By this, Henry showed he did not understand the woman who had been his consort for so long.

The king gave his ministers the impression that he had no real wish to remarry, but that he might wed a French princess for the sake of the realm. His true intentions are made obvious by his correspondence; from the beginning of the process, it was Anne Boleyn he wished to marry. In September 1527 Henry applied for a dispensation to overcome all impediments caused by 'affinity arising from ex illicito coitu [illicit sex] in any degree, even in the first'.[22] 'In the first degree' could only refer to Anne's mother or her sister. The Pope granted this within three months. This further confirms that Henry did have an affair with Mary Boleyn, and proves his hypocrisy in discarding Katherine on the same grounds; by this request, he was acknowledging that, under Church law, Anne Boleyn was his sister.

The Tudors still needed to bolster what could be seen as an upstart dynasty with careful marriages – not by marrying the daughter of a viscount. If the annulment was so Henry could produce a legitimate son and heir, then one conceived by a foreign princess would have had higher status. If the annulment was not accepted by the Stuarts – and it was not – then James V and his descendants would always be seen as alternative monarchs. For a king to choose to marry one of his subjects for love, and Henry did this four times, was extremely unusual, even if they were noblewomen.

Some historians have come to the conclusion that in 1528 Henry had ten mistresses. However, the likelihood at this time is that he was living chastely, faithful to the beguiling Anne Boleyn. This rumour comes only from a misreading of the list of his New Year's presents. It was expected that Henry would give gifts to all the court. He gave to 'thirty-three noble ladies' and 'ten mistresses'. By the term 'mistress' he was showing they were gentlewomen, rather than noblewomen. The word did not then have an exclusively sexualised meaning.

Anne Boleyn was firmly in possession of Henry's heart at this point. In July 1528 the abbess of Wilton died. An abbess held an important and potentially lucrative position, and at Wilton Abbey there were many women who belonged to the gentry. The nuns were meant to elect a successor from amongst themselves, but in reality it was decided by a patron of the convent, such as the king or an important noble. Wolsey told them to elect their prioress, Lady Isabel Jordan. However, the sister of William Carey, Dame Eleanor Carey, was also a nun at the abbey and Anne was asked to intercede with Henry for the position. This was normal procedure, but it was also a test of the political influence of Henry's sweetheart versus his chief minister.

It emerged that Dame Eleanor had two children by two different priests and had recently been the mistress of Lord Broke's servant. It is unlikely that she had chosen the religious life herself – her family probably lacked a dowry for her. The Carey family then tried to obtain the post for Eleanor's elder sister, but there seem to have been skeletons in her closet too. Henry wrote to Anne Boleyn that:

> Though there is not any evident case proved against [the elder Carey sister] … I have done that neither of them shall have it, whereby the house shall be better reformed (whereof I ensure you it had much need).[23]

It cannot have done the Carey family's reputation much good to have the king and cardinal investigating their relatives' scandals. Neither Anne nor Wolsey got their way; Henry had shown that it was he who was in control.

Anne was spending every moment in Henry's company from 1528 onwards, while she was at court, but she would not consummate the relationship. She was often at Hever between 1527 and 1531, and this seems to have helped keep Henry's interest. But Katherine was still the queen, despite Henry's wishes. Katherine apparently

> showed (to Mistress Anne, nor to the King) [not] any spark or kind of grudge or displeasure … [The Queen] dissembled the same, having Mistress Anne in more estimation for the King's sake.[24]

She dealt with the situation with incredible dignity, and showed that she saw Anne in the same category as Anne Stafford and Bessie Blount – women who entertained the king and to whom she would be civil, but not as a threat to an anointed queen.

On 12 May 1528 Henry's close friend, the duke of Suffolk, received a belated papal dispensation for the annulment of his marriage to Margaret Mortimer. He had married twice since he had left Margaret in 1507, once to Anne Browne, who had died, and then to Henry's sister, Mary, the French queen. Suffolk's dispensation had been granted on very similar grounds to the king's. Henry probably saw this as a sign that his annulment would be equally easy to obtain and so he was prepared to bide his time. He continued to treat Katherine with respect. Then an event occurred which led many to think that Henry's actions had displeased God – sweating sickness spread through the country.

Sweating sickness had been introduced to England in 1485, the year the Tudors took power. It intensified during the summer months and the court was dismissed, with Henry taking a small number of servants and moving around various locations in the countryside, far from London where many were perishing. He had good reason to panic. The French ambassador wrote of the sweat:

> One has a little pain in the head and heart. Suddenly a sweat breaks out and a physician is useless, for whether you wrap yourself up much or little, in four hours, sometimes in two or three, you are despatched without languishing.[25]

This is an exaggeration; most people survived it. It was known as 'the English plague' to foreigners as it recurred so regularly in England. Henry, always terrified of illness, fled from place to place until the outbreak had died down, leaving both Katherine and Anne behind him.

Several of the king's courtiers died during this outbreak, including Sir William Compton, his close friend and the lover of his ex-mistress, Anne Stafford, and Sir William Carey, Mary Boleyn's husband. Mary and her two children were left destitute, and she was pregnant with her third child. It seems that Mary had not returned to her husband at the end of her affair with Henry as a faithful wife. The king thought that when William Carey died, Mary was pregnant by another man.[26] Anne Boleyn, her brother, her father and her uncle, the duke of Norfolk, were also afflicted, although they recovered – was this God's judgement on the Boleyns and Henry himself? When William Carey died, there were many debts to be sorted. Henry wrote to Anne:

> As to your sister's matter, I have caused Walter Weltze to write to my Lord [Thomas Boleyn] mine own mind therein … for surely whatsoever is said it

cannot so stand with his honour but that he must needs take her his natural daughter now in her extreme necessity.[27]

Anne had evidently asked for Henry's help, but Henry offered no assistance. Thomas Boleyn is not thought to have been being miserly with his daughter; he was extremely ill and in danger of dying of the sweat himself. Anne stepped in and arranged for Mary to receive a pension of £100 to pay these debts off – Mary had been reduced to pawning her jewellery. Anne was the best advocate anyone at court could have had if they wished to wring concessions from the king.

Chapter 7

The Lady is All-Powerful

From 1528 Anne was no longer a maid of honour to Queen Katherine, but was still often at court in the awkward and ambivalent position of queen-in-waiting. Previously, courtiers had petitioned Wolsey rather than the king directly; now the cardinal's power had waned and the king and his fiancée were taking the reins. For the last twenty years, Henry had been so occupied with his friends and lovers, hunting, jousting and entertaining, that he had left the day-to-day running of the country in his chief minister's hands. Now that Wolsey was failing to secure an annulment – the Pope was continually dragging his feet – Henry's respect for his chief adviser was diminishing. Anne Boleyn was apparently convinced that Wolsey was secretly hindering the process; his fall in 1529 was a sign of the great influence Anne now enjoyed.

Chapuys reported that 'The Lady is all powerful here' and Anne was given her own court, which rivalled the queen's. Henry was determined to show that he was deeply committed to marrying her. Wolsey wrote to the Pope, describing

> the approved, excellent virtues of the said gentlewoman [Anne], the purity
> of her life, her constant virginity, her maidenly and womanly pudicity, her
> soberness, chasteness, meekness, humility, wisdom.[1]

Henry was giving Anne every honour he could, every mark of respect – she was being openly treated as if she were already queen. Yet many saw her simply as a mistress who had risen above her position.

In 1529 Cardinal Campeggio wrote that Henry 'sees nothing, he thinks of nothing but Anne; he cannot do without her even for an hour. He is constantly kissing her.'[2] She appeared to be equally enamoured with him, writing to her suitor of 'the joy that I feel in being loved by a king whom I adore, and to whom I would with pleasure make a sacrifice of my heart, if fortune had rendered it worthy'.[3] We cannot know if Anne was ever genuinely attracted to, or in love with Henry, although there is every reason she would have been: he was still a handsome, charismatic man.

The imperial ambassador was still doggedly determined to persuade Henry that a second marriage was no guarantee of a son. The king angrily responded: 'Am I not like other men? Am I not? Am I not?' Chapuys was brave to broach this subject, as not fathering a boy could be considered both a slur on masculinity and a judgement from God. Yet the prevalent belief was that infertility was never the man's fault. Bessie Blount had proved that Henry was capable of fathering a male heir, and he was determined to have another – but this one would be legitimate. Yet Henry also insisted that, 'if I were to marry again, I would choose her [Katherine] above all women' for her 'gentleness, humility and buxomness'.[4] He insisted that it was the illegality of their marriage that was the reason for the annulment; if he was proved wrong, he would happily return to Katherine.

In December 1529 Thomas Boleyn was made earl of Wiltshire, a title his family had a small claim to. The earldom of Wiltshire had been in Thomas Boleyn's mother's family, the Butlers, before their lack of a direct male heir had led to it being given to the Staffords. The title of Ormonde, which he had been given two years previously, could travel down the female line as well as the male, and so should have been Boleyn's years before. The king ended the dispute over the title by giving Boleyn's cousin, Piers Butler, another earldom so he would drop his claim.

At the same time, Anne's brother George was knighted and created Viscount Rochford, and Anne became known as Lady Anne Rochford. Henry and Anne were acting as a married couple, and Anne was given precedence at a banquet over every woman present (Katherine was not invited). On 1 September 1532 Henry showed that Anne, dressed in crimson velvet, was no mere scarlet woman; he created her marquess of Pembroke. This title could be passed onto her children – and the decree omitted the usual phrase 'legitimately born'. This was completely unprecedented. Henry also promised her an income of £1,000 per year and her investiture ceremony was attended by courtiers and foreign diplomats.

Anne Boleyn was the first mistress of an English king to achieve such a level of official recognition. She was now guaranteed financial security if the king's attentions moved elsewhere, which would override any damage to her marriage prospects that their relationship may have caused. Yet it was not a sign that they had given up on obtaining an annulment, it was merely a safeguard and a stepping stone to the throne. They had been constantly together, sometimes in adjoining bedrooms, for five years, but they probably had not consummated their relationship – until now. A month after she received her title, Anne became pregnant.

Had Henry really been physically faithful to Anne Boleyn for six years? His medical records show he had problems with his bladder around this time, which may have caused impotence. This could have helped him remain loyal to Anne throughout the long build-up to their marriage. And from 1527 onwards he expected the situation to be resolved soon. No one realised that it would be dragged out for six long years. The Spanish ambassador, Diego Hurtado de Mendoza, wrote that: 'Nothing … annoys this king so much as the idea of not accomplishing his purpose.'[5] Once he had made the commitment to Anne publicly, he could not back down.

Yet Katherine could not admit defeat either. Her two symbols were an arrow sheaf and the pomegranate, representing her parents' military triumph in Granada. She had been raised on the road, as her parents led their troops into battle. A daughter of Ferdinand and Isabella was never going to accept being sidelined. For the Tudor upstarts to marry into such an august dynasty was a considerable achievement. There was a clear social hierarchy and royals married royals. That she would be discarded for Mistress Anne Boleyn went against the whole accepted structure of sixteenth-century society.

Henry's love letters to Anne reveal much about their long, drawn-out courtship. We have the original notes he sent her because they were stolen, and ended up in – of all places – the Vatican, where they remain today. They depict a man whose mistress has the upper hand, and who is desperately unsure if she reciprocates his feelings. Unfortunately, we do not have her replies, but it is clear that she was, at this point, rejecting the king.

The love letters began at some point between 1523 and 1528, probably in 1526. Henry drew love hearts around Anne's initials in his letters. All correspondence he addressed 'to my mistress', but initially in a courtly sense. He signed his letters to Anne: 'H. Autre AB ne cherche R' (Henry loves AB and no other). The annulment proceedings had begun by March 1527 and he seems by then to have proposed to Anne Boleyn. His early letters imply he wanted her as a mistress; his intentions do not seem to have been honourable from the start.

Henry wrote that he was anxious to discover if she had any feelings for him. He had been 'above one year struck with the dart of love' and still had no idea if she was interested in him. He even offered to make her his sole mistress, the coveted position of *maîtresse-en-titre* that women were prepared to kill for in other European courts. No woman in England had ever officially had such a status. Anne rejected this, and still chose to stay away from court, even though she could have accepted the option of being constantly chaperoned by relatives. He assured her that if he 'knew for certain that you wished it of your own will' he would cease importuning her and 'put from me little by little my mad infatuation'.[6]

Although her hold on him increased, even Anne's extensive influence and power depended entirely on the king. Mistresses could never have any real independent power in an absolute monarchy, because they were nothing without the king's say-so. Henry was pursuing her in the tradition of courtly love, declaring himself to be her servant, yet Anne insisted that as she was unworthy to be served by a noble king, she could only serve him. 'Although it does not appertain to a gentleman to take his lady in place of a servant, nevertheless in compliance with your desires, I willingly grant it to you …' Anne was defying the customs, which encouraged Henry to do the same.

The letters show a confused suitor, a man who is used to having his every whim satisfied, trying to work out if this young woman is genuinely refusing him or if he needs to offer her more. It is likely that in the beginning Anne was not as calculating as she has been portrayed; she probably did not know that there was a possibility of marriage. She may well have been genuinely reluctant to embark on a relationship with a capricious womaniser. The affair with her sister, which the king had only ended very recently, would also have discouraged her.

In September 1529 Henry sent Anne a hart he had killed himself.[7] 'I can no less do than to send her some flesh representing my name, which is hart's flesh for Henry, prognosticating that hereafter, God willing, you must enjoy some of mine.'[8] The tone in some of the letters is clearly sexual: 'Wishing myself (especially of an evening) in my sweetheart's arms, whose pretty duckies [breasts] I trust shortly to kiss'[9] and 'Henceforth my heart will be dedicated to you alone, and wishing greatly that my body was so too, for God can do it if He pleases; to whom I pray once a day for that end.'

As well as praying that Anne would have sex with him, he also wrote to her of his all-consuming passion for her:

> Bringing to my mind a point of astronomy, which is, that the further the days are from us, the farther too is the sun, and yet his heat is the more scorching; so it is with our love, we are at a distance from one another, and yet it keeps its fervency, at least on our side. I hope the like on your part, assuring you that the uneasiness of absence is already too severe for me; and when I think of the continuance of that which I must of necessity suffer ...[10]

He was completely besotted with this aloof woman, describing her in 1527 as

> The woman in the world that I value the most.

Around 1527, he wrote to Anne:

> I must of necessity obtain this answer from you, having been for more than a year, struck with the dart of love, and not yet sure whether I shall fail, or find a place in your heart ... I will take you for my only mistress, casting all others, that are in competition with you, out of my thoughts and affections.[11]

Here he acknowledges that others have been 'in competition' with Anne; she was not the only woman he had been pursuing.

We have one example of Anne's response to Henry's poetic declarations of love. They both wrote in an illuminated book of hours, which they passed between them during mass in the royal chapel:

> If you remember my love in your prayers as strongly as I adore you, I shall hardly be forgotten, for I am yours.
> Henry R. forever

Anne replied: 'By daily proof you shall me find/To be to you both loving and kind.'[12] The ice maiden was thawing as the months turned into years; but they were still little nearer their goal. And it was Katherine of Aragon who stood in their way.

The royal couple continued to lead lives which were mostly separate, but some old habits remained. Katherine still embroidered all her husband's shirts, much to Anne Boleyn's disgust. But Katherine had always sewn his shirts and Henry saw little reason for this to change. For the neglected Queen, it was important that she continued to act as his wife in any capacity she could. She could not consider agreeing with an annulment and there could be no compromise. It was written of her that:

> She was a character tempered by steel ... Under extreme pressure, Katherine of Aragon had not broken; but she had also not learnt how to bend.[13]

The duke of Suffolk described Katherine of Aragon as 'the most obstinate woman that may be'.[14]

Katherine continued to present herself well, dressing in expensive garments. All through 'the King's Great Matter', as the annulment proceedings came to be called, she continued her duties as queen exactly as before; she could do nothing else. Part of this was to spend most of her time with her ladies-in-waiting – including Mistress Boleyn. She seems to have remained civil to Anne, in marked contrast to Anne's wild jealousy towards Jane Seymour. There is only one story of Katherine, ever regal, acknowledging to Anne that she was a rival. She is said to have been playing cards with Anne and coolly said to her: 'You have good hap to stop at a king, my lady Anne, but you are not like others, you will have all or none.' Even this story is of doubtful authenticity.

Katherine insisted that she treated Anne well because: 'I have been a true and obedient wife, ever comfortable to your will and pleasure ... being always well pleased and contented with all things wherein you had any delight or dalliance ... I loved all those whom ye loved, only for your sake.'[16] On the face of it, Anne Boleyn was very different to Katherine of Aragon, yet both were stubborn, intelligent and determined. Henry was unsure which way to turn, caught between two women of steel and with little idea of how to resolve the issue. The result was six years of limbo for the court and the country.

Throughout this time, Henry kept his illegitimate son close by. The duke of Richmond returned to court in August 1529, aged ten, to take his place in Parliament. Richmond remained with the king from then on and saw him daily. This must have worried both Katherine and Anne. Anne complained to Henry that she saw her time and youth had been wasted in vain, as she would now never make an honourable marriage and did not know what would become of her.[17] This was a good speech but Henry felt he could do little without the Pope's approval, which he remained convinced would arrive any day.

Katherine was then told by Henry that she was to join her daughter in Richmond or at the very least remain in her apartments. She chose to stay at court, insisting that her place was near her husband. Then at Christmas 1529, it was Queen Katherine leading the celebrations, playing the role of consort; Anne was nowhere to be seen. Henry simply did not dare to go any further at this stage, for fear of his subjects' reactions and the international response. The king and his queen were at an uncomfortable stalemate.

During 1530, Katherine did not see Henry from New Year to April, but she joined him as his queen for the summer progress. This gave some people hope that Henry was tiring of Anne, but it was simply a show of unity for his subjects. Katherine still appeared convinced that his relationship with Anne Boleyn would peter out and he would return to her. She believed that if the Pope sent Henry an order to separate from Anne, then their marriage could return to normal. It was believed throughout Europe that Anne would give in to Henry's advances eventually and then his desire for an annulment would cool. Katherine must have expected that, in the end, Anne would follow the example of her cast-off sister. She underestimated not only her rival but her husband, who would do anything to have his way.

The papal representatives were aware that Anne probably was still not Henry's lover and this was her trump card. Cardinal Campeggio found it amusing that Anne had all the status of a *maîtresse-en-titre*, but without becoming his *maîtresse* at all, in a physical sense. Ortiz reported from Rome that Anne had suffered a miscarriage in 1531, but there is no evidence to support this. There were also rumours that Anne had already borne Henry children. As Anne proved her fertility regularly during the three years that she and Henry were married, it seems unlikely that they were cohabiting long before Anne became pregnant with their daughter, Elizabeth. Any children she had borne would have spurred Henry to legitimise the union, and he would have married her immediately. All the evidence goes against their relationship becoming sexual before the autumn of 1532.

It had been four years since Henry had announced his intention to annul his marriage and he was little nearer to his goal. Wolsey's endeavours had yielded nothing from the papacy and after discarding the cardinal, there was no Englishman who had much influence with the Pope. Henry and Anne were not getting any younger. In July 1531 Henry finally cut his links to his first wife and had her sent away from the court, without saying goodbye; he never saw her again. This ended the ridiculous situation that had endured for so long, of a court with two rival queens; but it did not solve the situation – there was still no annulment, and no marriage to Anne.

Anne continued to be detested by the women of England, including Henry's ex-lover, Elizabeth Amadas. In 1533 there were reports that 'Some part of such ungracious rehearsals as Mistress Amadas at sundry times hath spoken before divers persons', saying that she had 'looked this twenty year upon prophecies' and that the king was 'cursed with God's own mouth' and the Scots would have conquered England by the end of the year. She also said:

> My lady Anne should be burned, for she is a harlot; [that] Master Norris was bawd between the King and her; that the King had kept both the mother and the daughter, and that my lord of Wiltshire was bawd both to his wife and his two daughters.

Elizabeth also told of her own former relationship with Henry:

> The King had often sent her offerings and gifts, and that Mr. Daunsy had come the bawd between the King and her to have had her to Mr. Compton's house in Thames Street.

William Compton and Henry Norris had both been Henry's Gentleman of the Stool and as such were probably involved in procuring women for him.

Elizabeth's anger seems to have been inflamed because her own husband had left her. 'Because the King has forsaken his wife, he suffers her husband to do the same, but the good Emperor will deliver all good wives when he comes, which shall be shortly.' She also declared, 'I care not for the king a rush under my foot; it is the king of heaven who rules all.'[18] Henry's previous affection for Elizabeth Amadas did not save her from being arrested for her comments.

Elizabeth's account gives us a clear idea of how Henry arranged his liaisons in the early part of his reign. It has been inferred that Elizabeth's account was of a recent affair, and thus he had been unfaithful to Anne. However, Compton had died in 1528, and so it was at some point before this that Henry had allegedly pursued Elizabeth Amadas, and it may have been very early in his reign. Elizabeth was older than Henry and is unlikely to have attracted him later in his reign; but as a teenager, he seemed to prefer older women.

Elizabeth was the wife of Robert Amadas, the court goldsmith who became the richest of his profession in the country. Although Elizabeth was the sister of Hugh Bryce the younger and a gentlewoman, her position would have been somewhat ambiguous as her husband, although very wealthy, worked for his living. He had inherited the position from Elizabeth's father; her brother had died without issue, and so Elizabeth had inherited his wealth and entitlements. Through this, Robert Amadas became the master of the Mint and the keeper of Henry VIII's jewels. By her marriage with Amadas, Elizabeth had two daughters, Elizabeth and Thomasine.

Around the time of Elizabeth's outbursts, Robert Amadas owed the king 1,771 *livres*, 19s 10d for missing plate.[19] This seems to have been dealt with and Robert died soon afterwards. Elizabeth quickly married again, to Sir Thomas Neville on 28 August 1532. Neville was the fifth son of Baron Abergavenny. Elizabeth was, at this time, the sister-in-law to Katheryn Parr, who would become Henry's sixth wife. Elizabeth died within the next four months, in 1532, before Henry married his '*harlot*'.

Even by 1532, many of Henry's subjects were not aware that he wished to marry a maid of honour. Some were convinced that he had come up with a more sensible plan to secure the succession – by marrying the mother of his son. Helwighen

> mentioned a report that the King wished to marry this lady to legitimate by subsequent marriage a son whom he had by her; but the Dean said that this son was by another lady, who was already married. Said he had never heard of this, and he thought that the King's love for another than his wife must be for the mother of his son … Asked him if he knew these two ladies and whether they were beautiful, worth leaving his wife for. He said he knew them both, and the mother of his son was eloquent, gracious and beautiful but the other lady was more beautiful still.[20]

Bessie had been widowed on 15 April 1530. There is nothing to suggest that Henry ever considered marrying her; he had already gone too far in his commitment to marry Anne. He was happy at this time to give his blessing to his cousin's wish to marry Bessie and so clearly had no intentions of marrying her himself. Bessie was now a wealthy widow, the mother of a duke, and so was sought-after. Throughout 1532, Bessie repeatedly refused marriage to Lord Leonard Grey, a younger son of the marquess of Dorset and the king's cousin through Henry's maternal grandmother, Elizabeth

Woodville. Bessie would have made a good queen in many ways; she was the same age as Anne Boleyn and had already proved her fertility. She also had an eleven-year-old son by the king, almost old enough to reign.

Bessie had gone on to have three children by Gilbert Tailboys: George, Robert and Elizabeth, all of whom died childless. Her daughter Elizabeth became Baroness Tailboys when her brothers died without issue. Because she claimed the title in her own right, her husband could not represent her in Parliament and as she was a woman she could not attend herself. She was not prepared to accept this and petitioned against it, in vain. Bessie's daughter, Catherine Clinton, from her second marriage, later married William, Lord Burgh. She was the only one of Bessie's children to continue the family line.

As Gilbert had become Baron Tailboys, when he died Bessie was left a wealthy widow. From July 1531 she was based mainly in South Kyme. Her unmarried sisters were sent to her, where she endeavoured to marry them off. Around 1534, Bessie chose to marry Edward Fiennes, Lord Clinton, twelve years her junior and a man who would go on to become the first earl of Lincoln after her death. When the king gave grants to the family, they tended to be given solely to Bessie or to Bessie and her children, not to Lord Clinton. It may have been significant that Bessie remained a widow for four years, from 1530 until after Henry had finally married Anne Boleyn. Perhaps Bessie was hoping that the king would tire of Anne over the years and see the sense in marrying her. However, she appears not to have been often at court during this time, although her New Year's present in 1532 was one of the most expensive that year, a gold goblet.

Edward Fiennes, Baron Clinton, was born around 1512 in Lincolnshire; his lands bordered Bessie's. At the time of their wedding, Bessie was around thirty-four years old and so was still young enough to produce more children. This was an equal match; he was a very talented young man with a title and she was the mother of the duke of Richmond and Somerset. Bessie bore him three daughters, Bridget, Catherine and Margaret, before she died in 1539 or 1540 aged around thirty-nine. Clinton outlived his wife by forty-five years, becoming an earl, an ambassador and an admiral.

Anne Boleyn was determined to show the whole world that she would be a better wife for Henry than either Bessie or a French princess. She would not have been a complete stranger to the rulers of Europe who she wished to impress. She knew Francis I from her nine years at the French court. Charles V had been brought up in Burgundy, and would have been there during Anne's two years as maid of honour to his aunt. They were of a similar age, although there is no evidence that they knew each other personally. Now she wished to build on these links.

On 11 October 1532 – about a month before Anne became pregnant with Elizabeth, and around the time she consummated her relationship with Henry – Anne and Henry set off to Calais to meet Francis I. This showed the world that the King of France supported the annulment. It was very important for Henry to have some international support. Among the thirty ladies accompanying Anne to Calais and Boulogne was her sister, Mary Boleyn. We can only imagine what Mary thought of this voyage – to try to persuade her ex-lover, the King of France, to support her sister's marriage to another of her ex-lovers, the King of England.

The group sailed on *The Swallow* from Dover and stayed in Calais for ten days. It would have been very different from when Mary Boleyn travelled there as a maid of honour to the new queen of France. Now Mary Boleyn was the prospective sister-in-law of the King of England and could look forward to a glittering second marriage. However, as the discarded mistress of her sister's fiancé, she must have been a slight embarrassment to the proceedings. Anne and Mary, who had not been brought up together and who were chalk and cheese in terms of looks and personality, do not appear to have been particularly close; neither does Henry appear to have retained any affection or respect for her.

Here Mary will have seen Francis and perhaps other men she had been involved with during her time in Paris, although Anne was the lady who first led Francis onto the floor and spent most of the night talking privately to him, perhaps reminiscing about her and her sister's time at the French court. She is likely to have been as much a politician at this meeting as she was with the French ambassador, who she showed great favour to. Mary Boleyn is barely mentioned in the accounts. She could easily have been a thorn in Henry's side, especially as he was insensitive enough to pursue her sister so soon after the end of their affair. There is no evidence that she did anything to anger her sister and new brother-in-law until she later married without their approval.

The accommodation for this meeting was beautifully and ostentatiously decorated. No restraint was shown in displaying to the French how rich and successful the English king was. One hundred and seventy dishes were served to the nobles. Six women were involved in the masque, where no one was expected to know who the ladies were, but of course it was Anne who led the women and approached the King of France to dance. All the ladies were dressed in expensive matching garments, 'loose, gold-laced over-dresses of cloth of gold, with sashes of crimson satin and tabards of cypress lawn'.[21] It was not as competitive as the bankrupting extravaganza of the Field of the Cloth of Gold, but nonetheless a statement was being made before all of Christendom – Henry's fiancée was accepted by the French.

The king wanted the whole of England to know that Francis had received Anne and he ensured this by commissioning a pamphlet, *The Manner of the Triumph at Calais and Boulogne*, to be distributed throughout London within the week and then spread across the rest of the country. It seems to have been very carefully worded. In the pamphlet, all the key attendants were named, including the new marquess of Pembroke. Precedence was very important in sixteenth-century society and Anne, as the highest-ranking English lady there, was correctly written first.

Next on the list should have been Anne's aunt, Dorothy, countess of Derby. However, the second name was 'my lady Mary'. Nobody would have thought immediately of Mary Boleyn, the widow of a knight, as 'my lady Mary' – this was the term used to describe Henry's daughter. It was probably written thus to persuade people that Mary supported her parents' annulment and had attended this gathering. Nobody at court would have been fooled, but the citizens of London may have believed that Katherine of Aragon's daughter was now on her father's side.

Two of the party were left behind with the French nobles: the thirteen-year-old duke of Richmond and his close friend, the earl of Surrey. Henry probably consummated his relationship with Anne at this time; he was now looking forward to conceiving a new – and legitimate – son. He was unlikely to need the duke of Richmond as his spare heir anymore. The boys joined the French princes, who led a wild life riding horses in a noisy gang through the streets in the middle of the night, firing pistols and throwing stones at people. Richmond became very close to the French princes, which could have been very useful to him in the future. Anne Boleyn may have been pleased that this rival for her lover's affections was now so far away.

Chapter 8

'Grudge Who Will, But None Deny'

The fact that Anne Boleyn kept Henry's attention, and kept him faithful for six years is astonishing. But finally, on 25 January 1533, the whole charade came to an end, and Henry secretly married his pregnant mistress. It was not a grand, triumphant wedding but a quick, secret ceremony in a room at Whitehall. Once it became known, it would not be popular with the common people, especially not with the women. Anne was the first lady in English history to go from king's lover to Queen of England. (Although Edward IV married Elizabeth Woodville for love in 1464, it is unlikely that she physically became his mistress before the wedding. Anne was already pregnant at her wedding, so there can be no doubt. I have discounted earlier examples in history, from when marriage was not clearly defined.) Henry had cared deeply for Katherine of Aragon at the beginning of their marriage and his affairs with Bessie Blount and Mary Boleyn had been of some duration – yet it was surely Anne who was the great love of his life.

That he made this commitment shows Henry's attitude to love and marriage. He was, by this stage, essentially a one-woman man who wanted to legitimise his relationship. Yet this was not his primary incentive; fathering a boy was incredibly important to him, and it was vital that the child be born in wedlock. Henry had still not obtained an annulment from his marriage to Katherine, but this was just an inconvenience that would be dealt with by his ministers. His second marriage was not valid in the eyes of the Catholic Church or English law, but as he was the new head of the Church in England, as well as the man who made the laws, this could be flouted.

The mistress was now the wife, and the wife was just a discarded mistress who had mistakenly believed for years that she was married to the king.

By February 1533 Anne had been secretly married to the king for a month. However, the court was still unaware that it had a new queen. Now that Anne's pregnancy would soon be obvious, she decided to announce her condition in a dramatic fashion. She shouted to a man, thought to have been Thomas Wyatt, that she had

> a furious hankering to eat apples, such as she had never had in her life before … the King had told her that it was a sign that she was pregnant but she had said it was nothing of the sort.

This was apparently in front of dozens of courtiers.[1] After six years, Anne had finally consummated their relationship. As queen, Anne chose 'the most happy' as her motto. All were awaiting the birth, convinced that this child would be a boy.

Soon, the fifteen-year-old duke of Richmond returned to England and married fourteen-year-old Mary Howard, daughter of the duke of Norfolk and first cousin to Queen Anne. They were considered approximately the right age for marriage; it was thought dangerous to consummate a marriage any younger. Legally girls could be married from the age of twelve and boys from fourteen, although the couple often did not live together until they were eighteen, and this seems to have been the plan for the young duke and duchess. Henry VIII's grandmother, Margaret Beaufort, had been thirteen when she gave birth, shortly after her fourteen-year-old husband's death. She bore no children during her three subsequent marriages; this was probably due to the physical damage caused by giving birth before going through puberty.

Mary Howard was a compromise choice as the king's daughter-in-law. The Howards were now the premier family in England, after the Tudors, so she was a good match for the realm's highest-ranking noble. Yet she was not from a foreign royal house that could potentially damage the position of Henry's children with Anne Boleyn. Supporters of Henry's daughter, the Lady Mary, were happy to see her half-brother marrying an English aristocrat rather than a niece of Charles V, who could have dented international support for Mary's right to the throne. Henry had never shown any enthusiasm for the Pope's suggestion of marrying the duke of Richmond to his half-sister.[2]

Mary Howard was also Anne's first cousin, so if Mary and her young husband ever challenged the rights of Queen Anne's children, Richmond could not automatically rely on the support of his wife's family. Mary did not even bring a dowry; this match seems to show Queen Anne's influence; she had secured a magnificent marriage for her cousin and friend to a man who could have wed a European princess. However, Mary was not only a Howard but also the granddaughter of the late duke of Buckingham, so had some claim to the throne herself. It was still a potentially dangerous combination.

In May 1533 Anne was crowned and became the anointed Queen of England. The archbishop of Canterbury had declared Henry's first marriage invalid and his marriage to Anne legitimate. After a coronation, a queen was considered divinely appointed to her position. The monarchy were put there by God, and those who did not fully agree with this were aware of the treason laws; they could not even criticise the king's choices, or, after her coronation, Queen Anne. The awe-inspiring pomp and display, plus the free wine, also ensured compliance.

Some contemporary accounts say that Anne was booed by the crowds.[3] Even Henry was well aware that his subjects were unhappy with his decisions. Londoners were said to have seen the entwined initials 'H' and 'A' and shouted 'Ha! Ha!'. Some reported comments from the crowds that included 'The Queen's Grace was a goggle-eyed whore'[4] and the abbot of Whitby denounced her as a 'stewed [professional] whore', and shouted 'God save Queen Katherine, our own righteous queen' and that he would never take 'that whore Nan Bullen to be Queen'.[5] There were allegedly 'too many caps on heads'[6] but the Venetian ambassador praised 'the utmost order and tranquillity of the day'[7] and he had little reason to be partisan.

There is evidence to dispute mass hostility to the king's mistress becoming the queen – no doubt her swollen belly reiterated the importance of this marriage. The coronation would have been an impressive sight by any standard and many of the king's subjects had never seen anything like it; it had been twenty-four years since Henry and Katherine had been crowned. Few people would have dared to jeer an anointed queen, even if they had doubts as to the legitimacy of her title. The truth was probably that some people grumbled, but there was no open defiance of the king's wishes. The people came out to enjoy the show and to see the woman for whom the country had been turned upside down.

During the coronation there were numerous references to virginity – which was ironic as the queen was heavily pregnant. Anne Boleyn was regularly linked with St Anne in the writings of the time. Now, as she was about to bear the heir to the throne, the association was with St Anne's daughter – Mary, mother of Jesus. Many parts of the pageant tied in with this theme. There were also references to the virgin Aestrea with a long scroll: 'Queen Anne, when thou shalt bear a new son of the King's blood, there shall be a golden world unto thy people.'[8]

Boats filled the route along the Thames from Greenwich to the Tower of London four miles away. The cannons fired so much that every single pane of glass was shattered in the Tower and in nearby St Katherine's Church. Anne wore her hair loose and flowing at the coronation, as only queens and unmarried women were permitted to do. All the monks of Westminster were to follow the new queen in her coronation procession, despite what had been done to the monks so the king could marry her.

Now that Anne Boleyn was finally in the position to which she had aspired, she was concerned that one of her maids of honour might become Henry's mistress. As the ladies were from the highest families in the land, they were often clad in gorgeous clothes and had been raised to exhibit many of the accomplishments and skills which the king admired. They were often young and unmarried as many women semi-retired from the court when they had children. Anne was by now about thirty-two. These younger, nubile women had no baggage, and had not had to fight for years to be where they were. They would be a welcome diversion for a king who was widely perceived to be henpecked; a strong woman, especially an argumentative one, might be considered an interesting mistress, but a curse on a husband. Henry expected Anne to transform into a queen and fulfil that role – which did not involve criticising his infidelity.

There was no suggestion that Henry was unfaithful during Anne's pregnancy. Their daughter, Elizabeth, was born on 7 September 1533. The common Christian belief of the time was that if the parents had been adulterous or promiscuous, then the children would not be healthy. This was because sexual intercourse had been designed solely for creating children, and if it was used wrongly then it would cause defects. This was especially the case if the couple had sex other than in the 'missionary' position. To have a healthy boy would prove their union was approved of by God. A healthy girl was better than nothing, but was hardly the sign they had been looking for.

After the announcement that England had a new queen, Henry had happily devoted himself to Anne – but this changed when the baby was born a girl. During Anne's next pregnancy, Henry began to work his way through her maids of honour – many of whom lacked all honour and were certainly no longer maids. Having to spend all day playing cards, sewing and attending mass with women who were sneaking off to her husband at night would have been humiliating for the proud woman who had dominated the king's thoughts for seven years. Katherine had accepted it stoically, but Anne was not known for her calm and composed nature.

In 1533 Chapuys was told that the king had always been inclined to amours.[9] Henry was married to Anne, but he was not likely to change now that he had achieved his goal. In November 1534 Henry invited many women to court for the festivities and Chapuys reported that: 'He is more given to matters of dancing and ladies than he ever was.'[10] As Anne was now his wife, Henry expected her to act as such, which left a vacancy for a new mistress.

On 27 September 1534, Chapuys reported that the king

has renewed and increased the love he formerly bore to another very handsome young lady of the Court; and whereas the royal mistress,[Anne Boleyn] hearing of it, attempted to dismiss the damsel from her service, the King has been very sad, and has sent her a message to this effect: that she ought to be satisfied with what he had done for her, for, were he to commence again, he would certainly not do as much; she ought to consider where she came from and many other things of the same kind. Yet no great stress is to be laid on such words ... [Anne] knows perfectly well how to deal with him.[11]

This woman sounds like a genuine danger to Anne's position; she was said to be close to the Lady Mary, and Chapuys wrote that during this affair many courtiers made an extra effort to pay court to the king's elder daughter. According to Chapuys, the handsome young lady had written Mary a letter, describing herself as 'her true friend and devoted servant'.[12] He believed that this unnamed lady was a positive influence on Henry, and that Mary's conditions improved at this time. The relationship seems to have ended soon after. She is referred to as a previous mistress of Henry's, but we have no further clue as to her identity. This relationship was significant enough that it was well known abroad. Charles V wrote:

It is said that the English nobles are ill-disposed towards Anne on account of her pride and the insolence and bad conduct of her brother and relations. For the same reason the King's affection for her is less than it was. He now shows himself in love with another lady, and many nobles are assisting him in the affair.[13]

Chapuys did not fully agree. He replied to the emperor:

With regard to the Lady it is quite true that occasionally this king seems to be angry with her, but, as I have already observed in some of my previous dispatches, such outbreaks are merely lovers' quarrels, of which no great notice need be taken, unless, indeed, the King's passion for the young lady, about whom I once wrote to Your Majesty, should continue and wax stronger than it is at present ... I hear from the Grand Esquire (Guildford) that upon the Lady [Anne] addressing certain remonstrances to the King, and complaining that the young lady in question did not treat her with due respect in words and deeds, the King went away in a great passion, complaining loudly [about Anne] ... Rochford's wife was dismissed from court owing to the above.[14]

The 'very handsome' young lady's name is unfortunately not recorded in any surviving documents. Chapuys' portrayal of the lady, both in looks and personality, is very different to his description of Jane Seymour or Bessie Blount. She was certainly one of Anne's attendants, and to contact the Lady Mary and insult Queen Anne shows confidence; Chapuys also wrote that she had the support of many courtiers. But this level of hostility to Anne's reign is what Chapuys wished to hear, and what he paid his informants to tell him. Therefore we can be unsure as to whether this mistress's influence was as great as he reported it to be.

Despite Henry's commitment to Anne, she could not accept sharing her husband's affections. Cromwell praised 'the great modesty and patience she [Katherine] had shown ... the King being continually inclined to amours'.[15] Anne did not have his first wife's ability to turn a blind eye. In October 1534 Viscountess Rochford, Anne's sister-in-law, was dismissed from court for conspiring against Henry's lover. Although we do not know the details of this plot, Henry was clearly showing Anne who was in charge. At the same time, Anne lost another ally from her household when her sister, Mary, was banished for secretly marrying a commoner. Within only a year of achieving their goal, the Boleyns did not seem to be in a much better position than before.

We hear little about Mary Boleyn during the reign of her sister. We can see from the records that in November 1530 Henry gave his wife twenty pounds to retrieve a jewel from Mary. This may have been gambled during cards or could have been a family gem that Anne particularly wanted. By 1534 Mary had been a widow for six years. Perhaps her family felt that once Anne was established as queen, they would be in a stronger position to arrange a glittering match for Mary. Perhaps she refused to marry or she was simply forgotten about in the excitement over her sister's elevation. If so, this would have been unusually short-sighted for a shrewd man like Thomas Boleyn.

In 1534 Mary secretly married William Stafford, a commoner. Her new husband was distantly related to the late duke of Buckingham and Henry's ex-mistress, Anne Stafford, but he was not a gentleman. He had been born around 1500 in Blatherwycke, Northamptonshire, and was the second son of Sir Humphrey Stafford and Margaret Fogge, the daughter of Sir John Fogge of Ashford – minor gentry. Stafford is listed as an attendant at Queen Anne's coronation. He may have first met Mary there, or in Kent, where his mother's family were based, as were the Boleyns. It is most likely that they met when he was part of the group who went to Calais in 1532 to meet Francis I. She only informed her family when her pregnancy could no longer be concealed. The Boleyns would never have accepted Mary marrying so far beneath her. Anne had, on several occasions before this, used her influence with Henry to help Mary, but this was not acceptable behaviour for the sister of the Queen of England; it reflected badly on Anne and confirmed people's opinions that Mary was a wanton who could not control herself.

Without her family's support, Mary had to beg for help from Henry's chief minister, Thomas Cromwell. Her letter survives and is worth quoting in full.

Master secretary,

After my poor recommendations, which is smally to be regarded of me, that [I] am a poor banished creature, this shall be to desire you to be good to my poor husband and to me. I am sure that it is not unknown to you the high displeasure that both he and I have, both of the king's highness and the queen's grace, by reason of our marriage without their knowledge, wherein we both do yield ourselves faulty, and acknowledge that we did not well to be so hasty nor so bold, without their knowledge. But one thing, good master Secretary, consider; that he was young, and love overcame reason. And for my part I saw so much honesty in him, that I loved him as well as he did me; and was in bondage, and glad I was to be at liberty; so that, for my part, I saw that all the world did set so little by me, and he so much, that I thought I could take no better way but to take him and forsake all other ways, and to live a poor honest life with him; and so I do put no doubts but we should, if we might once be so happy to recover the King's gracious favour and the Queen's. For well I might a had a greater man of birth and a higher, but I ensure you I could never a had one that should a loved me so well nor a more honest man; and besides that, he is both come of an ancient stock, and again as meet (if it was his grace's pleasure) to do the King service, as any young gentleman in his court.

Therefore good master secretary, this shall be my suit to you, that, for the love that well I know you do bear to all my blood, though, for my part, I have not deserved it but smally, by reason of my vile conditions, as to put my husband to the king's grace that he may do his duty as all other gentlemen do. And, good master secretary, sue for us to the king's highness, and beseech his highness, which ever was wont to take pity, to have pity on us; and that it will please his grace of his goodness to speak to the queen's grace for us; for, so far as I can perceive, her grace is so highly displeased with us both that, without the king be so good lord to us as to withdraw his rigour and sue for us, we are never likely to recover her grace's favour: which is too heavy to bear. And seeing there is no remedy, for God's sake, help us, for we have been now a quarter of a year married, I thank God, and too late now to call that again; wherefore of is the most alms to help. But if I were at my liberty and might choose, I ensure you, master Secretary, for my little time, I have tried so much honesty to be in him, that I had rather beg my bread with him than to be the greatest Queen in Christendom. And I believe verily he is in the same case with me; for I believe verily he would no forsake me to be a king.

Therefore, good master secretary, seeing we are so well together and does intend to live so honest a life, though it be but poor, show part of your goodness to us as well as you do to all the world besides; for I promise you, you have the name to help all them that hath need, and amongst all your suitors I dare be bold to say that you have no matter more to be pitied than ours; and therefore, for God's sake, be good to us, for in you is all our trust.

And I beseech you, good master secretary, pray my lord my father, and my lady to be good to us, and to let me have their blessings and my husband their good will; and I will never desire more of them. Also, I pray you, desire my lord of Norfolk and my lord my brother to be good to us. I dare not write to them, they are so cruel against us. But if with any pain I could take with my life I might win their good wills, I promise you there is no child living would venture more than I. And so I pray you to report by me, and you shall find my writing true, and in all points which I may please them in I shall be ready to obey them nearest my husband, whom I am bound to; to whom I most heartily beseech you to be good unto, which, for my sake, is a poor banished man for an honest and godly cause. And seeing that I have read in old books that some, for as just causes, have by kings and queens been pardoned by the suit of good folks, I trust it shall be our chance, through your good help, to come to the same; as knoweth the (Lord) God, who send you health and heart's ease. Scribbled with her ill hand, who is your poor, humble suitor, always to command,

Mary Stafford[16]

If Mary ever expressed these sentiments to her sister, it is no wonder she was banished. Mary had disobeyed the queen's wishes and was declaring that she was happier than Anne, despite Anne's crown and, technically at least, Anne having all that she had set out to achieve. This letter depicts an articulate and passionate woman, not the 'runt of the litter' as she has sometimes been portrayed. Anne did not take Mary back as her lady-in-waiting and so was without this potentially useful ally at the time that she needed friends most.

Mary appears only to have argued with her family when it came to her choice of men. A woman who chose to marry for love in an age where this was considered sheer madness was either very brave or very stupid. One married to ensure that one's children would have enough income not only to keep them in the style to which the nobility were accustomed, but also to ensure that they never had to work. Marrying below one's station could cause problems for one's descendants for generations. This determination to be with the one she loved (or inability to control her lust), and her friendly and easy-going manner may have seemed endearing and refreshing to Henry, who lived in a court of vultures. If so, this was only during their affair; later, he had even less sympathy than Anne for Mary when she got herself into trouble.

The timing was upsetting for the Boleyns. Now Anne was finally crowned and the mother of the king's child, Mary could have made a magnificent match. The Boleyns had climbed to the top through good marriages – she had just taken the whole family down a peg. They had all been benefiting from Anne's marriage, but the new Mrs Stafford was now in financial trouble. Her long, eloquent appeal to Cromwell was to no avail. Cromwell insisted that Thomas Boleyn should help, but he refused. Eventually, Anne was the first to relent. She sent Mary a golden cup and some money. However, there is nothing to suggest that the sisters ever saw each other again.

After her dismissal, Mary seems to have settled down to country life and very little more is mentioned of her. She probably lived at the family residence in Rochford, Essex for the rest of her life. There is no mention of her visiting her doomed brother and sister; no mention of her writing to them or to her parents about them. At a distance from the court, Mary was safe from accusations of intrigue and being arrested along with her siblings – like Bessie Blount, she was living away from the seat of power – and thus had ceased to be of any consequence. Only recently have people thought to research this woman, so attractive she enticed two kings; so close to the centre of power, yet seemingly indifferent to it.

Mary and William Stafford are said to have had a boy in 1535, who died as a child.[17] There are also rumours of a daughter named Anne, perhaps named defiantly after her aunt. Banished to the countryside, the couple lived a happy and simple life away from the chaos of court. Her pursuit of love rather than riches made her the most successful of the Boleyns – she managed to survive Henry's wrath against the rest of her kin.

The contrast between the Boleyn sisters was never clearer than when Henry allowed Anne to be executed on phoney allegations of adultery. Mary and her husband, banished from court, avoided all the schemes that Mary's two siblings were fatally the victims of. Mary, like her mother and father, is not known to have made any contact with Anne or George after their arrests; it would have been foolhardy to have done so. Both Boleyn girls had gone against the social norms when arranging their marriages – Anne by aiming too high, Mary by aiming too low – but it was very clear who had received the happier ending.

In April 1538 Elizabeth Boleyn died and her husband followed her in 1539. The Staffords benefited somewhat from the deaths of Mary's parents and siblings. Although Mary no longer had what was left of the family's influence to rely on, she was heir to many of their possessions. She inherited these, including those that had been in jointure to her sister-in-law, Jane, Lady Rochford, and the lands of Mary's paternal grandmother, Margaret Butler. Mary died on 19 July 1543. Her husband benefited little from her inheritance as the majority went to her son, Henry Carey. Nevertheless, Mary was able to leave her husband several manors around Rochford, Essex, where they had settled.

This marriage gave Stafford great opportunities for advancement, even after his sister-in-law's fall. He was knighted on 23 September 1545 towards the end of Henry VIII's reign. He had earlier been given minor positions at court; in 1540 he was made a gentleman pensioner; in 1541 he became an esquire of the body, and during Edward VI's reign he was a standard bearer. He continued his military career, fighting in France in 1544 and in Scotland the following year, where he served under Edward Seymour, earl of Hertford and the uncle of the young Prince of Wales. This connection helped him progress at court when Seymour took control of the Council during the early years of Edward VI's reign. Stafford was also acquainted with Lord Clinton, the husband of the late Bessie Blount, who he accompanied to France in 1551 to attend the christening of a French prince. His Protestant beliefs would have brought him closer to both these men.

Stafford became a Member of Parliament, along with his stepson, Baron Hunsdon, and managed to keep his position after the fall of Edward Seymour, ingratiating himself with the new duke of Northumberland. He later became lord of Chebsey. He married his kinswoman Dorothy Stafford, the daughter of Henry Stafford, 1st Baron Stafford, within a year of Mary's death, and had five children by her. In March 1554, early into Queen Mary's reign, he took his wife and several relatives to Geneva, Switzerland, where John Calvin was based, and other English religious refugees followed. His son's godfather was Calvin himself. Stafford died on 5 May 1556 in Geneva. His wife returned to England after his death, with her children, despite John Calvin's insistence that the children remained with him. Dorothy Stafford served Queen Elizabeth for forty years.

Anne Boleyn's line died out with her virgin daughter, but Mary's descendants prospered. She is an ancestor of Winston Churchill, Charles Darwin, Vita Sackville-West and Thomas West, Baron de la Warre, who Delaware State in the U.S.A. is named after. Diana, Princess of Wales, and Elizabeth Bowes-Lyon, the wife of George VI are also descended from her. Anne Boleyn may be famous as the mother of Elizabeth I, but Mary's descendants include Elizabeth II.

Most of the king's mistresses had been the queen's ladies. Anne Boleyn, Jane Seymour and Catherine Howard had all been serving their predecessors when they had caught Henry's eye. Anne Stafford, Jane Popincourt, Bessie Blount, Mary Boleyn and Elizabeth Carew all served the first Queen Katherine, and Mary Shelton and the 'handsome young lady' served the first Queen Anne; Anne Bassett and Katherine Willoughby served more than one of his queens. Anne Boleyn does not seem to have expected the king to be unfaithful. This situation could, understandably, be very awkward for both wife and mistress. Different queens reacted to these challenging circumstances in different ways. Henry was no longer so attractive − by 1535, we know he had a fifty-four-inch waist. But there were still many benefits to being close to the king.

In this year, a French admiral was the guest of honour at a court celebration. Apparently, Admiral De Brion was talking to the queen and realised that he did not have her full attention as she was looking about the hall. She then burst out laughing, though apparently with tears in her eyes. The admiral was shocked, and asked: 'How now, Madam! Are you amusing yourself at my expense or what?' Anne explained, 'He went to fetch your secretary, but he met a lady, who made him forget the matter!'[18] Anne clearly felt humiliated by her husband's attentions to other women and did not hide her emotions. This was the normal situation for the wife of a prince. Katherine of Aragon had been raised as a princess and had felt sure that she would remain the first lady in the kingdom, however many lovers Henry had. But Anne was now in a very different position and her ego was used to Henry's absolute devotion. For the new queen, it was a bitter blow.

The 'handsome young lady' seems to have been forgotten by Henry within months, but it was clear that sooner or later he would begin an affair with another woman and it was important that, unlike the last mistress, this woman would not be pushing for improved relations with Katherine and Mary. Anne must now have been very concerned about the influence Henry's lovers could have over him. Detested by many at court, with most of Christendom insisting that she was merely Henry's mistress and many ladies hoping to oust her from her position, it is unsurprising that she was described at this time as bad-tempered and unpredictable. Henry had proved once that he was willing to discard his wife for another woman − and Anne, daughter of an Englishman, would be far easier to discard than Katherine, daughter of Spain had been. A dangerous precedent had been set. In February 1535 Anne was once again pregnant and sexually unavailable, and Henry was attracted to the perfect candidate to overthrow the queen.[19]

On 25 February 1535 Chapuys wrote: 'The young lady who was lately in the King's favour is so no longer. There has succeeded to her place a cousin german [first cousin] of the concubine, daughter of the present governess of the Princess.'[20] (This could possibly refer to Elizabeth Carew, who was both a first cousin of Anne Boleyn's and the daughter of Mary's governess, Margaret Bryan. Elizabeth has been linked to Henry in other documents. However, Chapuys later makes it clear that it is 'Mistress Shelton', daughter of Anne Shelton and the woman in charge of running Mary's household, who he was referring to.) This was Mary Shelton, daughter of Anne, Thomas Boleyn's sister, and Sir John Shelton, commander of Princess Elizabeth's guard. The family had a respectable lineage. The Shelton line could be traced back centuries; Nicholas de Shelton had been involved in the signing of the Magna Carta and conspiring against King John. For many years it was thought that Chapuys, in his writings, was referring to Margaret, or Madge, Shelton. Mary did have both a sister and a sister-in-law called Margaret; the confusion was probably caused by how the 'y' was written, making 'Mary' look like 'Marg' for Margaret. However, it is clear from two contemporary sources which name is correct, and that it was Mary who was Henry's lover.*

Mary Shelton's dates of birth and death are disputed. She was probably born around 1520 and died around 1570, though she could have been born as early as 1512 and Remley suggests she died in 1560. When she married in 1557/8 she was still fertile, indicating a date of birth no earlier than 1520. Although she may have been fertile in her forties, marriages were not usually contracted for women of this age unless they were particularly wealthy. This would make her at most fifteen when she had her affair with the king. Her second husband is thought to have been born around 1528,[21] so an earlier birth date is unlikely.

Mary had nine siblings: three brothers and six sisters. Along with John, Anne, Ralph, Gabriella, Elizabeth, Margaret, Thomas and Emma, she was brought up at Shelton Hall, Shelton, Norfolk, which is now in ruins. Mary's

---

* Her sister-in-law was Margaret Shelton, *née* Parker. Her sister Margaret married Thomas Wodehouse of Kimberley, Norfolk.

parents married in 1512, but we do not know when she was born. She did not marry until around 1545 so was probably very young in 1533 when she became a maid of honour, possibly the minimum age of twelve or thirteen. Her close friends at court, Mary, duchess of Richmond and Lady Margaret Douglas, were born around 1520 and so we can assume that Mary Shelton was of a similar age.

The Sheltons were some of the many enjoying the benefits of being closely related to the queen. Mary and her family were therefore indebted to Queen Anne and would hopefully support her rather than put forward a rival. This is why some historians think it highly convenient that Henry's new mistress was a member of the Boleyn family and that perhaps Anne herself arranged for her cousin to try to attract the king, to lure him away from someone who was more of a threat. This is a possibility – the reformers were probably concerned, and rightly so, about the influence the conservative 'handsome young lady' could have on Henry and so may have tried to counter this.

If this was true, it was a dangerous game to play. Mary was an individual, not merely a member of her family, and could have been dazzled by the possibilities on offer. Anne's extended family were also disappointed that they were not receiving greater financial benefit from the royal marriage, and may have felt that Henry would be more generous to the family if he was infatuated with a more compliant member of it. If this was arranged, Anne was unlikely to have been involved. It does not seem to have been in the queen's character to hope her husband would become attracted to another woman, especially one who was very like her, but twenty years younger. Her passionate and furious responses to Henry's infidelity with the unnamed lady and Jane Seymour show us that she wished to be the only woman in Henry's heart. Anne declared to Henry that 'whenever she hears of his loving another woman but her, she is broken-hearted'.[22]

Although they were cousins, this did not mean that their families were allies – not all Boleyns supported the queen and so she could not rely on Mary Shelton's loyalty. When Anne was arrested, five women were chosen to be her attendants in the hope they would report her words, so they could be twisted into evidence against her. Among these five were Mary's mother, Lady Shelton, and Anne's aunt by marriage, Lady Boleyn. Anne complained to Kingston, the lieutenant of the Tower, that it was 'a great unkindness in the King to set about me as I never loved'. Kingston replied that they had been chosen by the king because he thought them 'honest and good women' and not out of malevolence.[23] We should not, however, tar Mary with the same brush as her mother – she was not among the women selected.

It has also been alleged that the duke of Norfolk – always ready to offer up one of his relatives to the king – was concerned that the Howards were losing their influence and so tutored Mary Shelton to attract the king. This is almost as unlikely; Mary was Anne's first cousin through the Boleyn side, not the Howard, and so he would have had less to gain. Yet the duke was a religious conservative and came to dislike his niece. He was not gaining as much as he would have liked from Anne's position; he once called her a 'grande putaine' (great whore).[24] Therefore, he may have been part of a group hoping to keep the king happy with another woman, who was the close friend of his daughter, Mary, duchess of Richmond and was a part of the Howards' network. It is likely that Henry noticed the attractive newcomer on his own.

Lady Shelton was in a difficult position, running the household which included the Princess Elizabeth, heir to the throne, and her half-sister, the Lady Mary, who had been stripped of her title and inheritance but could still be reinstated. John and Anne Shelton tried not to offend anyone, while still reaping the benefits of being the aunt and uncle of the queen. Anne Shelton was criticised by the duke of Norfolk and by Queen Anne for treating the Lady Mary with too much respect. In 1535 there were rumours of a plot to poison Mary, and Chapuys told Lady Shelton that if anything were to happen, she would be implicated. Had Mary Shelton kept Henry's attention, she could have been a serious threat, as she had access to both the king's daughters. It is likely that Anne found it difficult to keep her temper around Mary once she knew the truth about the girl's relationship with her husband – and Anne could make her ladies' lives very difficult if she chose to.

Mary seems to have been a beautiful girl; she was probably only a teenager when she was Henry's lover. Christina, duchess of Milan, was famed for her beauty and the king considered marrying her in 1538. In the reports, Christina was described as 'very high of stature … a goodly personage of body, and competent of beauty, of favour excellent, soft of speech, and very gentle in countenance … she resembleth much one Mistress Shelton, that sometime waited on Queen Anne'.[25] According to Chapuys, this affair lasted from February 1535 for six months.

Mary seems to have happily accepted the role of mistress and not pressed for more. Yet Henry viewed his relationships as private, and was not always the best target for a gold-digger. He did give presents, titles and grants of land to his lovers' relatives – but never enough to sustain them. It is even possible, with the exception of the women he married, that the gifts given to his lovers' families were earned by their hard work for the king – not solely because their relative had attracted him. It was only the unattainable Anne Boleyn who came close to achieving the level of influence and financial standing that was normal on the Continent for a king's paramour, and her refusal to accept just these gifts and to hold out for marriage led indirectly to her death. Yet Henry was, at times, exceptionally generous to his lovers – in 1532 he became the first king of England to give his mistress, Anne Boleyn, a title, and he was the first to give a dukedom to his illegitimate son. But if a woman was hoping to snare Henry now, she would go for a crown. Other women would be more ambitious than Mary Shelton, as Anne would soon discover.

Chapuys also hinted at other sexual relationships that the king was conducting. In the summer of 1535 the king stayed three nights at Wulf Hall, the home of the Seymour family – although it is unlikely that he began his pursuit of Jane Seymour at this point. Throughout this period, the most influential woman in the king's life was still his wife. He no longer wanted her to play the part of political adviser, as he had allowed during their courtship, but she was still a force to be reckoned with. We know of one argument between his spouse and his sweetheart. Apparently

a book of prayers which belonged to one of her maids of honour called Mistress Mary Shelton [was] presented unto her highness wherein were written certain idle poems ... the queen her majesty, calling her before her presence, wonderfully rebuked her that would permit such wanton toys in her book of prayers ... and upon this occasion commanded the mother of the maidens to have a more vigilant eye to her charge.[26]

It may not have been just notes in her prayer book that Anne wanted the mother of the maids to watch her for. Yet Anne and Henry had sat passing love notes to each other in mass before they married. Perhaps this was Anne's real concern – that Mary's poetry was for the king.

This flirtatious behaviour, the type that one can imagine the young Anne Boleyn having indulged in, was no longer appreciated by the queen – at least not in others. She had not only become embittered from eight years of constantly trying to hang on to her power, she was now only thirty-four in an era where ninety per cent of English people died before they reached forty – and life expectancy was thirty. She was aware of the danger that alluring young maids of honour could pose for their ageing queen. Anne, like her predecessor, tried to ensure that her ladies were respectable and devoutly religious.

The ladies-in-waiting to Katherine of Aragon had been expected to pray with her for hours every day; Anne Boleyn's attendants did this, but were also kept busy sewing for the poor. Secular poetry, in particular tales of romance, was frowned upon as an improper use of a woman's time and a possible tool for corruption. Thomas Wyatt had already broken down some of these taboos, but tales of past kings and queens and religious writings remained the only fully accepted writing at court. We must judge Mary and her group by the standards of their time and it was highly controversial, and potentially dangerous, to be writing such verses.

The group of courtiers Mary associated with were well-educated in the humanist tradition, reformers who debated theology and wrote secular poetry. If Mary was the flighty young woman she has sometimes been portrayed as, she would never have been accepted into the social circle of scholars and poets. Her two closest friends at court were Lady Mary Howard and Lady Margaret Douglas. These women were socially superior to Mary – Margaret Douglas was the king's niece, the daughter of his sister Margaret, and Mary Howard was the duchess of Richmond and Somerset, the daughter of the duke of Norfolk, the king's daughter-in-law, and another first cousin of Queen Anne. These three friends were very popular at court, but their friendship did put each other at risk – all three women liked romance. Margaret Douglas was brought up at the English court, and as she was now at a good age to marry, she could be a useful diplomatic pawn for her royal uncle. Mary Howard, who may have caught the king's eye later in his reign, was a very similar character to Queen Anne. These women were heavily involved in the writing of what is now called 'the Devonshire MS', which was once wrongly believed to have belonged to Anne Boleyn.

In this book, the earl of Surrey, his sister Mary Howard, Margaret Douglas, the poet Thomas Wyatt and several others wrote verses, as it was passed around the court, and in particular between the Howard kin. You were to read and enjoy the poems, and then add a composition of your own or a poem you liked that was not already there. Mary Shelton was by far the most industrious writer in the book and seems also to have played the role of editor. Her writing shows an articulate and forthright woman, defending her gender.

Mary copied into the manuscript poems by Chaucer, but not verbatim. She adjusted them, often putting a female slant on them, several of them critical of men who boast of their affairs with women, and of the double standard which meant that the woman was shamed by the liaison and the man was not. She may well have been related to John Skelton, poet laureate to Henry VII and tutor to Henry VIII. His origins are unclear, but on Skelton's retirement he settled in Diss, Norfolk, near the Sheltons' lands. If she was, then there was a family tradition of poetry.

This shows that Mary Shelton, unlike other of Henry's lovers such as Jane Seymour and Catherine Howard, was both literate and literary. This love of poetry seems to have also been a love of poets; it is thought that Mary's paramours included at least two of the prominent bards of the age, Thomas Clere and Henry Howard, earl of Surrey.[27] The group's writing seems to have been more than an enjoyable educational pursuit – it was also used to convey messages of lust and love from one member of the group to another. Mary Shelton appears to have copied into the manuscript a series of poems written between Margaret Douglas and Thomas Howard while they were both being held in the Tower of London, charged with illegally contracting marriage.

Mary Shelton was around sixteen years old when she attracted the king. Another man admired her, who had also fallen for the allure of her elder cousin – Thomas Wyatt. Wyatt has gone down in history not only for his innovative secular poetry but also for his pursuit of Anne Boleyn, which he had to swiftly end when the king showed his desire for her. He wrote many poems about 'Brunet', who is widely believed to have been Anne. In 1536 Wyatt was arrested along with Anne and was lucky to escape being executed as one of her alleged lovers.

In the Devonshire manuscript, there is a record of another woman Wyatt pursued: Mary Shelton. He wrote a poem, the first letter from each stanza spelling out SHELTUN, as he once had done for ANNA. In this he writes that he is 'suffering in sorrow' and wishes for the woman to 'ease his pain', but although he is being rejected, he ends each stanza with 'to serve and suffer still I must'. A reply was written directly under the poem, rejecting him and signed 'Mary Mary Shelton'.[28]

Mary appears to have loved the pageantry and display of the court. And although she was young, she was clearly interested in the men of the court and had a powerful effect on them. At the time of her relationship with the king she was betrothed to Henry Norris, a trusted courtier. But neither Mary nor Norris seemed in a rush to marry and she enjoyed spending time with her friends, writing romantic poetry and indulging in courtly love. Mary's flirtatious nature was partly responsible for sending both her fiancé, Henry Norris, and a man who was courting her, Francis Weston, to the scaffold – accused with the queen of treason and adultery.

Norris was around forty-five, much older than his teenage fiancée, and already had a son and heir. He would often have slept in Henry's room or a side room, and would have delivered vital and personal messages for the king. As Henry's Groom of the Stool he would have known most of the king's secrets and would have been well aware of his fiancée's relationship with the monarch. There are suggestions that Norris had helped the king arrange clandestine liaisons with other ladies.[29]

Like his predecessor in the post, Sir William Compton, Norris was a go-between for the king and his lovers. This may have made him less inclined to marry Mary – either through concern about her promiscuity or through fear of offending the king. If the affair continued, even sporadically, Norris would have been well aware of this and Chapuys would probably not have known. This engagement should have been a way to cement the Sheltons' ties with the monarch and gain further favour; it ended as a mess Mary had to distance herself from. Henry's relationship with Mary ran its course within a few months, and her family did not greatly benefit from it. Anne was soon pregnant again and Henry was looking for a new mistress. This time his affection grew for a far more dangerous rival among Anne's ladies-in-waiting – Jane Seymour.

Mary was intelligent, but could be reckless. Her friendships with Margaret Douglas and the Howard family got her into trouble repeatedly, first after helping to arrange the illicit marriage of Margaret, the king's niece, to Thomas Howard. Mary was lucky that Henry remembered her with fondness – she could have gone to the Tower, as Margaret and Thomas Howard did just a month after the execution of Anne Boleyn. But Mary was careful in May 1536; she would doubtless have been alarmed at the arrests of her fiancé, her cousins and her friends and realised that there was a chance that she, or her immediate family, could be implicated.

Mary later attended Catherine Howard up until her arrest, and then spent time at Kenninghall, Norfolk, on the estate of her friend Mary Howard.

There Mary Howard, Mary Shelton and Margaret Douglas, spent much of the next year, until there was again a queen to serve. Sir John Shelton, Mary's father, died on 21 December 1539, aged sixty-two. The family then suffered financial problems which seem to have put any marriage for Mary on hold. Mary went instead to a convent at St Helen's, Bishopsgate, which was popular with gentlewomen. By 1545 their situation had improved and Mary was engaged to Thomas Clere, in what seems to have been a love match. Unfortunately, Clere died on 14 April 1545, although he left 'lands in Hockham Magna ... [to] ... Mary [Shelton]' in his will.[30] Surrey immortalised their love in his elegy to Clere: 'Shelton for love, Surrey for Lord thou chase.'[31] Mary was now around twenty-six years old and soon married her cousin, Sir Anthony Heveningham, a gentleman from Suffolk. Their children included Arthur and Abigail Heveningham, and through Arthur, Mary is thought to be an ancestor of Diana, Princess of Wales.

This was not the end of scandals involving Mary. Shortly before Henry's death, her long-term friend Henry Howard, earl of Surrey, was arrested. It was recommended that: 'It may please your good lordships to examine Mrs Heveningham, late Mary Shelton, of the effect of the earl of Surrey his letter sent unto her, for it is thought that many secrets have passed between them before her marriage and since.'[32] Some have suggested this source is hinting at a love affair between the two. This may have been the case, but although the two had maintained a friendship for at least twelve years, there is no evidence that this had developed into a romance. She managed to survive Surrey's arrest and execution unscathed. Her husband died around 1557 and Mary married Philip Appleyard; she was then aged around thirty-eight. Mary died three years later, in 1560, during Elizabeth I's reign. The Shelton family had remained close to Elizabeth through the reigns of her two siblings and were rewarded for their support when she inherited the throne.

Throughout 1535 and 1536, Katherine of Aragon was exiled to remote castles, without any contact from her beloved daughter or husband. Even after Henry's marriage to Anne Boleyn, Katherine of Aragon had her staff's clothes embroidered with entwined H's and K's. Henry and Anne's relationship had undergone a transition but it still seemed strong. He had been madly, slavishly in love with the tempestuous and uncontrollable Anne Boleyn from 1526 to 1535. The royal couple seem to have enjoyed drama – the theatrical conflicts, the passionate reconciliations – 'as usual in such cases, their mutual love will be greater than before'.[33] But now Henry was no longer so besot-

1. Henry VIII by Hans Holbein. Despite his modern reputation for morbid obesity and rapacious cruelty, the young Henry was a romantic, athletic figure, who sought a male heir above all else. Desperate to secure the bloodline of the upstart dynasty that had brought to an end decades of bloody turmoil, he should perhaps not be judged so harshly. (*THP Archive*)

2. Crest of Henry and his first wife, Catherine of Aragon. As the widow of Arthur, Prince of Wales, Catherine's marriage to his brother Henry required papal dispensation. (*THP Archive*)

3. Henry Fitzroy, duke of Richmond. Fitzroy was the product of Henry's affair with Elizabeth Blount and the only one of Henry's illegitimate offspring to be acknowledged. *(The Royal Collection © 2005 Her Majesty Queen Elizabeth II)*

The Lady of Richmond.

4. Mary Howard, duchess of Richmond. A compromise choice for Henry's daughter-in-law, Mary's family posed no threat to the succession of his children. After her husband's death, the King reposessed much of his property, claiming the marriage was invalid on the grounds of non-consumation. Mary's brother, Henry, earl of Surrey, encouraged her to seduce King Henry, but she refused. *(The Royal Collection © 2005 Her Majesty Queen Elizabeth II)*

5. Mary Boleyn. Although the details of the Boleyn girls' early lives have often been confused, it is now widely believed that Mary was the eldest of the three children to survive infancy. *(The Royal Collection © 2005 Her Majesty Queen Elizabeth II)*

6. Blickling Hall, Norfolk. Birthplace of Mary Boleyn, and Anne if she was born before 1505. Some historians contend that Anne was born in 1507, by which time the Boleyn family had moved to Hever Castle, in Kent. *(Courtesy of The National Trust)*

7 and 8. Hever Castle and grounds. Anne Boleyn grew up here with her siblings until 1513, when she was sent to the French court to be educated. After the executions of George and Anne Boleyn and the death of their father, Thomas, the castle came into the hands of King Henry, who in 1540 bestowed it upon his fourth wife Anne of Cleeves following the annulment of their marriage. *(Author's Collection)*

9. Catherine Carey. Born c.1524, Catherine was the daughter of William Carey and Mary Boleyn, although there is evidence to suggest that she was in fact the issue of Mary's affair with Henry. *(The Royal Collection © 2005 Her Majesty Queen Elizabeth II)*

10. Mary Shelton by Hans Holbein. First cousin of the Boleyn children and maid-of-honour to Mary Boleyn, she was reported by Imperial ambassador Eustace Chapuys to have had a six-month affair with King Henry in 1535. *(The Royal Collection © 2005 Her Majesty Queen Elizabeth II)*

11. Jane Seymour by Hans Holbein. Betrothed to Henry on the day of Anne Boleyn's execution, Jane was his second wife's polar opposite in appearance, education and demeanor. She died of puerperal sepsis soon after giving birth to the male heir Henry craved. *(THP Archive)*

12. Henry VIII with his parents and Jane Seymour. Her reputation rendered forever irreproachable by the birth of Prince Edward and her subsequent early death, Jane's spectre haunted Henry's subsequent marriages; she remained his 'true wife', and it was beside her that he was buried in 1547.

(The Royal Collection © 2005 Her Majesty Queen Elizabeth II)

ted, and was finding it difficult to accept Anne's behaviour. He would have compared this to Katherine's dignified manner and his second wife would have been seen as lacking; the qualities that had attracted him to her were unsuitable in a queen and she had not yet given him a male heir. But in November 1535, Anne was pregnant for the third time and his relationship with Mary Shelton appeared to have come to an end. There was nothing to suggest that Anne was in a particularly precarious position. But Henry could not have two ex-queens still alive, and so rejecting Anne at this point could only have meant reconciliation with Katherine.

Chapter 9

The Year of Three Queens

'All goodly sport
To my comfort
Who shall me let?'

On 8 January 1536, Katherine of Aragon died. A growth was found on her heart that was 'completely black and hideous' leading some to pronounce that she had died of a broken heart. Henry declared himself relieved that there was now no danger of invasion and the royal couple wore yellow, paraded Princess Elizabeth and danced all night. From Katherine's deathbed, she wrote one last letter to the man she still considered her husband, who she had devoted herself to for twenty-seven years. She signed off: 'Lastly, I make this vow, that mine eyes desire you above all things. Farewell.'[1] Anne miscarried on the day of the funeral. This would have been seen as more than a coincidence by the people of the sixteenth century – Henry may have felt that this was proof his second marriage had offended God.

Katherine was buried in Peterborough as the dowager Princess of Wales, merely the widow of Prince Arthur and sister-in-law of Henry VIII. Her legacies were the controversial reign of her daughter, who went down in history as Bloody Mary and led a very unhappy life, and the end of the Catholic Church's authority in England and Wales. It was not what she would have wished for – but she has also been remembered as a woman of great courage, who followed her conscience no matter what the consequences.

On 17 January 1536, nine days after Katherine's death, Henry had an accident that ended his jousting career. He fell from his horse and remained unconscious for two hours; onlookers feared he was dead. Many of his later medical problems – his headaches and dramatic mood swings – may have been caused by this, and a strong argument has been made that he suffered brain damage. Falls like this can cause a major change in someone's personality, and from this point on we see an increasingly grumpy and irritable middle-aged man replacing the jovial and energetic young king. The loss of his great love, jousting, would have been a terrible blow to him and may, coupled with the effects of his injuries, have caused serious depression. Within four months of the fall, he had discarded the woman he had loved so passionately for ten years and married her attendant.

On 31 March 1536, Thomas Cromwell told Chapuys that although Henry was 'still inclined to amours', he believed the king's marriage to Anne was solid and that the king would 'henceforth live honourably and chastely'.[2] This appears to have been a case of saying one thing with words and another with body language; Chapuys came away with the impression that the king might repudiate Anne soon. It was already known that Henry was enamoured with Jane Seymour, and had 'latterly made very valuable presents' to her.[3] Chapuys had reported on Henry's pursuit of Jane, but did not think this would topple Queen Anne from her position. The ambassador reported that Henry could not bear to be parted from Jane for even an hour,[4] but this still appeared to be just another infatuation – his latest mistress. The world had seen what Henry was prepared to do for a woman who would not consent to be his lover, yet few considered the plain and passive maid of honour any match for Anne Boleyn. It was probably these very qualities that attracted Henry to Jane.

Polydore Vergil described Jane as 'a woman of the utmost charm both in appearance and character'[5] and Sir John Russell said she was 'the fairest of all his wives'.[6] John Skelton, the poet laureate, had written a poem describing the beauty of Jane's mother, but few could honestly say as much for Jane. Chapuys was less complimentary than Vergil and undoubtedly more accurate:

> She is of middle stature, and no great beauty, so fair that one would call her pale than otherwise. She is over 25 years old. I leave you to judge, whether being English she would not hold it to be a sin to be still a maid … Seymour is not a woman of great wit, but she may have good understanding. It is said she inclines to be proud and haughty.[7]

The physical description confirms what we see in her portrait.

Thanks to the tutoring of her family and their allies, Jane succeeded in entrancing the king. Playing on her virginity and virtuous manner, Jane delighted the king by being everything his feisty wife was not. Plain in both looks and personality, Jane was happy to play her part until the king agreed to discard his wife. Jane may have lacked Anne's abrasiveness, but she did not lack her ambition. As Anne was being tried for treason, Jane was choosing her wedding dress.

Jane's character is something of an enigma. Cardinal Pole described her as 'full of goodness'.[8] She does not seem to have ever had the strong influence on her husband that Katherine of Aragon and Anne Boleyn had enjoyed, but he was now older and more aware of his own power. This does not prove that she was placid, but perhaps that she had learnt to be obedient. Any woman who Henry fell in love with would now be very aware of the women the king had loved before and the potential danger they were in.

It was not until Jane Seymour that any woman came close in Henry's eyes to Anne, the woman he had loved obsessively for ten years. He was not discreet although he did not flaunt her as he had Anne in front of Queen Katherine. On 18 March 1536 Chapuys wrote that: 'The new amours of this king with the young lady of whom I have written still go on, to the intense rage of the concubine.' Jane was only about seven years the queen's junior – so around twenty-seven or twenty-eight in 1536 – and seems to have had none of her sex appeal, intelligence, wit and charisma.

Jane was allegedly encouraged to criticise Anne to Henry, in the company of those who would agree with her. She had known and served Anne for years. Jane had the support of the whole conservative faction, plus her very able brother Edward Seymour, who under the reign of Jane's young son would rule the country. Various court factions joined together, united temporarily in their dislike of Anne Boleyn and in pursuit of the benefits of backing the right horse. The whole court was watching to see which way the wind would blow.

In many ways, Henry's pursuit of Jane echoed his courtship of Anne Boleyn: the handwritten notes, the declarations of love, the offer of anything she wanted if she would only consent to be his mistress. He showered Jane with presents and on one occasion sent her a purse filled with coins and a letter. Jane was well aware (or had been made well aware) that to accept money from the king would leave her open to accusations of impropriety. Jane handed back the letter to the messenger, then dropped to her knees and told him to

> ask the King on her behalf to consider carefully that she was a gentlewoman, born of good and honourable parents and with an unsullied reputation. She

had no greater treasure in the world than her honour which she would rather die a thousand times than tarnish.

She added that if the king wished to give her money, he could do so when she made a good marriage. Henry responded that she had behaved 'very modestly'; exactly how a woman should behave.[9]

This was a very shrewd response, and is likely to have been the work of shrewd advisers. Jane had as many allies as Anne had enemies, who now included the Machiavellian Thomas Cromwell. Henry was utterly charmed by this shy young woman who needed his help and protection. His sweetheart's brother, Edward Seymour, was made a gentleman of the Privy Chamber, which gave him constant access to the king. Seymour and his wife were also placed in the room next to Henry's, with a private passageway between the rooms. This was so that Henry could sneak along to meet Jane regularly, but always chaperoned, so no doubt was cast on her virtue.

Everywhere Henry and Jane went, her brother accompanied them. Chapuys wrote that Jane had been ordered by her brother 'not in any wise to give in to the King's fancy unless he makes her his queen'.[10] Anne now seems to have realised that her marriage was in danger, although she was probably only thinking of annulment. She began making overtures towards Chapuys, the Imperial ambassador, who had still not acknowledged her, and even to Henry's daughter, Mary; neither could be persuaded to recognise her as Queen of England.

Now that Cromwell was sure the king wanted rid of his wife, he began to look for evidence to justify an annulment, and Henry's former mistress, Mary Shelton, had her name mentioned in some of the reports. We have the details of two conversations Anne had about her cousin in the lead-up to the arrests: one of these condemned Mary's fiancé and the other condemned the man paying court to her. Henry Norris had been engaged to Mary for a long time, and the queen is said to have asked him why they were not yet married. He replied that he 'would tarry a time'; Anne was upset at this and accused Norris of wanting to marry the queen herself. 'You look for dead man's shoes', Anne is said to have shouted, 'for if aught came to the King but good you would look to have me.' Norris was shocked at this suggestion and the two argued loudly – loudly enough for others to hear.[11]

Anne was often reported as unable to keep her temper, but this time it was very costly for both of them. She realised how her words would sound when the quarrel was gossiped about – for Norris and Anne to talk about the king dying, and for Norris to allegedly be wishing for it, was high treason, and thus punishable by death. Anne asked Norris to seek out the witnesses and promise them that she was a 'good woman'. He agreed.[12] Although they probably did not know it, the plot was already forming and the faction round the Seymours were trawling for the names of those they could 'prove' were Anne's lovers. Norris had just nominated himself.

Perhaps the queen's response was an ill-judged attempt to remind herself that she was attractive, and she was hoping for compliments. Anne may have encouraged Norris to name the day because she wanted someone to rein in Mary's behaviour; Norris may have prevaricated because he was unsure if he wished to marry someone who had acquired a reputation – or perhaps he was standing aside because of the king's interest in his fiancée. It may also be an indication of Mary's young age. If Mary Shelton married and became pregnant, she would probably be sent to his country estate and therefore not be a temptation to the king; a situation Anne would probably have been pleased with. Now all the queen's conversations and flirtations were being reported to Cromwell, including those of a man who was probably closer to Mary Shelton than Norris was.

Another courtier, Francis Weston, also had a conversation with the queen about Mary. She playfully scolded him for flirting with Mistress Shelton and not paying enough attention to his wife.[13] Weston replied that there was someone there who he loved more than Mary or his wife. When Anne played the innocent and asked who this was, he replied that it was her. This was normal court banter, but now it was enough to convict him of adultery. Both men were executed alongside the queen and the other men accused with her. It is a possibility, though there is nothing to corroborate the theory, that Weston's pursuit of a woman so recently the king's mistress may have counted against him when the witch-hunt to find 'lovers' of Queen Anne began in earnest. We cannot be sure exactly when or why Henry's relationship with Mary Shelton ended, or whether Weston's friendship with Mary was courtly love or a sexual affair.

These reports show that Mary was part of the same social circle as Queen Anne. As three of the five accused men were closely linked to Mary – her first cousin, George Boleyn, as well as a man who was courting her and her fiancé – it was important that the Sheltons showed their loyalty to the king. There was nothing she or any of her family could do to help them. Norris had significant influence at court and throughout London; Weston's family offered the king everything they had. It made no difference.

On 1 May 1536 Henry left Greenwich without saying goodbye to his second wife; he never saw her again. (With the four wives who he annulled his marriages to, he did not say goodbye, but left without their knowledge and sent a messenger. The only one he ever saw again was Anne of Cleves.) Sir Henry Norris was soon arrested; over the next few days other courtiers were questioned and several men were sent to the Tower, where the queen was now also contemplating the change in her fortunes. Chapuys described Anne around this time as 'that thin old woman'; she was no longer the striking young girl who had attracted Henry ten years previously; she had become a thirty-five-year-old virago. Henry VIII did not appear devastated to find out that the love of his life had committed adultery with dozens of men and had been plotting to have him killed.

It was reported that: 'You never saw a prince nor husband show or wear his horns more patiently and lightly than this one does. I leave you to guess the cause of it.'[14] He was showing 'the joy and pleasure a man feels in getting rod of a thin, old and vicious hack in the hope of getting soon a fine horse to ride'.[15] Henry visited Jane regularly during May, while putting out the rumour that he had no desire to marry again and would only do so if his Council insisted it was his duty to do so. No one was fooled.

Henry then announced he had been 'seduced and forced into this marriage by means of sortileges and charms'[16] – he probably now believed this. She was no longer 'our most dear and most entirely beloved wife, the Queen'; she was a woman who had bewitched him into marrying her. Henry's grandmother, Elizabeth Woodville, had been accused of using witchcraft to persuade Edward IV to marry her. Witches were thought to routinely indulge in incest and sodomy (sodomy was a word used to describe various sexual practices, including male homosexuality, bestiality and anal intercourse between men and women. Laws against sodomy had only recently been enacted in England), which may be the reason for the charge of sodomy against Anne and all the accused men except Norris.

Cromwell initially planned for the accused men to walk through the streets of London, so that the people of the capital could see the traitors; he hoped it would win sympathy for the cuckolded king. This was cancelled, however, apparently because Norris was so popular with the common people they feared it would cause a riot. Despite Anne's deep unpopularity, opinion again swayed to the underdog and few seem to have believed that she was guilty, even at the time. The common people were now singing songs in the streets of London criticising the king's new love, Jane Seymour; it was widely known she was in the background.

Thomas Boleyn was excused from sitting in on the trials of his children – although he delivered a 'guilty' verdict on the four men accused with them, just as all the other jurors did. Despite Thomas's fiery temperament, which he had passed on to both Anne and George, all three Boleyns involved in the trials appear to have kept calm and the siblings attracted admiration for their dignified conduct. The same could not be said for Henry Percy, the new earl of Northumberland and Anne's old paramour. He claimed he was ill and left before the end of her trial.

Over two thousand people attended the trials of George and Anne Boleyn. Both were well known for their intellect and wit; both impressed the audience with their courage in the face of the inevitable. The charges of incest and adultery were patently absurd; Cromwell had not even bothered to make the dates sexual intercourse was meant to have occurred plausible. For some of the times he specified, Anne was still under constant supervision, recovering from the birth of her daughter. But some of the charges relating to George Boleyn appear to have been true.

Anne 'was likewise charged, as was her brother, with having ridiculed the King, and laughed at his manner of dressing, showing in many ways that she did not love him, and was tired of married life with him'.[19] Anne and her friends also seem to have insulted the king in other ways. 'There were certain ballads, which the King himself is known to have composed once, and of which the concubine and her brother had made fun, as of productions entirely worthless, which circumstance was one of the principal charges brought against them at the trial.'[20] Henry was the absolute ruler of England; it seems that the Boleyns may have begun to take for granted his support for them.

At George Boleyn's trial, it was revealed that Anne 'had said to his [George Boleyn's] wife that the King was impotent. This, however, was not read in public; it was given to him in writing, under protest that he was only to say yes or no, without reading aloud the accusation; but to the great annoyance of Cromwell and others, he read it aloud and said that he was unwilling to engender or create suspicion in a matter likely to prejudice the issue the King might have from another marriage. He was likewise charged with having spread the rumour or expressed a doubt as to Anne's daughter [Elizabeth] being the King's, to which charge, however, he made no answer.'[21] Jokes within their risqué circle of friends were now treasonous, but George's response suggests that Anne had indeed made some of these comments.

The two siblings, who were often with each other, may have criticised the king's sexual performance, which George might have heard about from both his sisters, at least one cousin and others at the court. It was claimed that: 'The King was incapable of making love to his wife and he had neither skill nor virility.'[22] Perhaps the pressure of trying to conceive with Anne caused sporadic impotence, although he was still able to perform with other women; yet all the letters from this time show that Henry was still powerfully attracted to his wife. One possible explanation is that Henry suffered from a condition causing sexual dysfunction. The theory that Henry had syphilis was widely believed up until the twentieth century, but this rumour started long after his death. Henry did not have any of the conventional treatments for syphilis, such as sweating or mercury.

There is only one mention of Henry and syphilis in contemporary documents: that Cardinal Wolsey tried to infect the king with it. This bizarre accusation was included in the bill of attainder against Wolsey, which was rejected by the House of Commons. The attainder stated that

> The same Lord Cardinal knowing himself to have the foul and contagious disease of the great pox, broken out upon him in divers places of his body, came daily to your grace, rowning in your ear, and blowing upon your most noble grace with his perilous and infective breath, to the marvellous danger of your highness, if God of his infinite goodness had not better provided for your highness. And when he was once healed of them, he made your grace believe that his disease was an impostume in his head, and of none other thing.[23]

It is possible that the cardinal suffered from syphilis, but there is no evidence for this and no reason is given as to why he would try to infect his benefactor. This could have been an attempt to explain away Henry's syphilis, but the attainder specifically states that Wolsey was unsuccessful in his attempts to infect the king.

Francis I of France was a famous victim of the disease, and his syphilis-ridden body apparently burst in its coffin. There has been a suggestion that Mary Boleyn caught syphilis from the King of France and gave it to the King of England, although the evidence clearly refutes this. Neither she, nor any other of Henry's wives or known mistresses, showed any symptoms of the illness as far as we know, and nor did any of his children. An ulcer on the thigh, like Henry's, would more likely be caused by syphilis than be a varicose ulcer, but that is not proof that Henry had this sexually transmitted disease. It is, however, impossible to diagnose any medical conditions from a distance of nearly five centuries.

Neither is Henry's unfortunate lack of heir proof of any disease. Anne Boleyn conceived three times in three and a half years (Katherine of Aragon had four children who were stillborn or died shortly after birth, at least two miscarriages, two Prince Henrys (who lived only a few weeks) and Princess Mary. Three of those stillborn children were boys. Anne Boleyn gave birth to the Princess Elizabeth and suffered at least two stillbirths. This used to be considered a sign that Henry had given his wives syphilis, but there is nothing to support this. This record does not suggest any serious fertility problems. Katherine's religious devotions were thought to have made her periods irregular and Anne Boleyn and Jane Seymour produced healthy children. It is only after 1540, when he was forty-nine, that he shows signs of infertility.

After Anne was condemned, she was kindly allowed to have her usual ladies attending her – this did not include Mistress Seymour, who was apparently busy preparing for her wedding. Anne's attendants may have now included Mary Shelton, who had not given evidence against the queen. Surprisingly, none of Anne's ladies were accused of aiding and abetting her adultery, despite Henry's claims 'that upwards of one hundred gentlemen have had criminal connexion with her'.[24] This was in contrast to the arrest of Catherine Howard. As Anne's ladies would have been with her twenty-four hours a day, unless she was with the king, a number of them must surely have helped her arrange these rendezvouses. Mary, as one of Anne's ladies and closely associated with the others accused, was an obvious target if someone wanted to blame one of Anne's attendants. The king's former affection for her and her parents' influence may have helped protect her, but the fact that no women were implicated shows, as if further proof was needed, that the entire case was a farce.

Anne was to die, not with the status of queen, but as the king's former-mistress. Before the executions, Chapuys wrote that

> I have also been informed that the said Archbishop of Canterbury had pro-nounced the marriage of the King and of his mistress [Anne] to have been unlawful and null in consequence of the King himself having had connex-ion with Anne's sister, and that both he and she being well aware and well acquainted with such an impediment, the good faith of the parents could not possibly legitimise the daughter [Elizabeth].[25]

Shortly after Anne Boleyn's death, the Succession Act was passed. One of its clauses made marriage between two people, who had been made siblings through permitted or illicit sexual conduct, illegal. We know that at this time, Henry Percy wrote to the Council insisting that he had never had a precontract with Anne – there had been rumours the royal marriage would be annulled on these grounds – and so it would have been very difficult to use this to dispute the validity of the marriage; yet Henry's ego could not allow his first marriage to be declared valid after all. Henry claimed he had never been legally married and had no legitimate children. It was the final insult to Anne, who was now to be executed for adultery despite the proclamation that she had never been legally married.

Anne and the five men accused with her were convicted. It was thought that if George Boleyn had denied all the charges, he would have been spared; bets were being made that he would be found 'not guilty'. William Brereton, a man Anne had not known well, Francis Weston, Henry Norris, Mark Smeaton and George Boleyn were beheaded on 17 May 1536, fifteen years to the day since the execution of the duke of Buckingham. The lieutenant of the Tower said Anne was the first condemned prisoner he had seen who was anxious for death. Two days after the executions of the accused men, she was beheaded by a French swordsman, and no one had even thought to arrange a coffin for her, putting her in an empty arrow chest with her head tucked under her arm. Her initial hysteria had given way to impressive self-control by the time of her trial. At her execution it was reported that: 'In her dignity and composure she had never looked more beautiful.'[26] Anne's last words were the same as Katherine of Aragon's: 'To Jesus Christ, I commend my soul.' Katherine spoke them in Latin, the language of antiquity, tradition and Catholicism; Anne was said to have spoken them in English. Both women were now in Henry's past.

From the moment Henry decided to marry his mistress, Anne Boleyn, every woman he glanced at was a potential queen of England. Therefore, women who would have been more accommodating in the past were encouraged by their families to aim for a crown. It was this possibility, that there were richer pickings to be had than just some small grants for the family and a besmirched reputation, that was one of the reasons Henry married six times. Yet the king was always the one who held the power.

None of Henry's mistresses had enjoyed real political authority, until Anne Boleyn. She was astute enough to build a faction around her that was prepared to fight for the royal annulment. She recruited key players in the Reformation such as Thomas Cranmer, who was promoted from her family chaplain to archbishop of Canterbury. She built excellent links with the French ambassador and developed alliances throughout the court; effectively Anne was one of Henry's ministers from 1527, but like many of Henry's other advisers, she became a victim of political infighting. It was often safer not to rise too high at Henry's court; to be a mistress, rather than a wife.

Chapter 10

His 'True Wife'

*'Company me thinketh best
All thoughts and fancies to digest ...'*

Henry went from risking everything for Anne Boleyn, to kindly consenting to her being beheaded by a sharp sword instead of a clumsy axe. The public were said to be appalled.[1] We can only surmise as to the reasons for his rejection of her – her sharp tongue and alleged criticism, his disappointment that she had not borne him a son, or perhaps he had genuinely been convinced that she was a witch. But finally, her enemies had succeeded in overthrowing her, and Henry quickly married Jane Seymour.

Henry was an excommunicate, and any Catholic allied to him risked eternal damnation. Because of the religious changes in England, Henry would have found it very difficult to negotiate a match with a foreign princess who could bring him a decent dowry and an international alliance. It had to be an English woman, and he had chosen Mistress Jane Seymour, of an undistinguished gentry family. Within twenty-four hours of Anne's execution, Henry and Jane were officially engaged. They married on 30 May, eleven days after his last wife had been beheaded. As Jane had been one of Anne's attendants, spending much of their time together, it is extremely unlikely that she could have believed her former mistress was guilty of all the charges.

It was very unusual for a king to marry one of his subjects except when he desperately needed an alliance with her family. Now Henry was marrying a commoner for the second time – and the Seymours were a level below the Boleyns in the social hierarchy. Jane claimed descent from Edward III, but this was through an illegitimate line and was of dubious authenticity. She had little to recommend her to the outside observer, with no title, no beauty and no charisma. But she seemed to be what a woman was supposed to be: submissive. She was the perfect antidote to ten years with Anne Boleyn. Jane had been at court since 1529, but there had been no sign that the king had noticed her before.

Jane was, at around twenty-eight, old to have been unmarried. She was said to have been in love with William Dormer,[2] but his family had not been prepared for him to marry a mere Seymour. Jane's mother was Margery Wentworth, a noted beauty, a quality Jane does not seem to have inherited. Her father was Sir John Seymour, who had been born around 1474 and knighted by Henry VII in 1497 for his assistance at the battle of Blackheath. He was described as a 'gentle, courteous man'[3] with ten children; in fact, the whole Seymour family was remarkably fertile. Sir John was even rumoured to have fathered the children of his daughter-in-law, who was then abandoned by her husband, Jane's brother, Edward. Such a family history of fecundity had helped convince Henry to marry Anne Boleyn, a member of the Howard family; it probably also helped sway him towards her successor.

Henry, as he had for his first two marriages, needed a dispensation to marry his third wife. The dispensation was dated 19 May 1536 – the day of Anne's execution. The wording is revealing; it was a dispensation for those in the 'third degrees of affinity' – second cousins.[4] Henry and Jane were, at closest, fifth cousins but it was Jane's close relationship to his last wife that was the issue – it has rarely been noted, but Jane was Anne Boleyn's second cousin. Jane and the Boleyn sisters shared Elizabeth Cheyney as their great-grandmother. The Boleyns were descended from Elizabeth Cheyney's first marriage to Sir Frederick Tilney, and they became the parents of Elizabeth, Anne Boleyn's maternal grandmother. Jane Seymour was descended from Elizabeth Cheyney's second marriage to John Saye, and they were the parents of Anne Saye, Jane Seymour's maternal grandmother. Elizabeth Carew, who Henry was also linked with, was another second cousin of Jane's. There was now no need to beg for the Pope's approval – Thomas Cranmer, archbishop of Canterbury signed the paperwork immediately.

Henry was looking forward, again, to conceiving a male heir but he was also planning for the future if this did not happen, and these plans seem to have included making the duke of Richmond a potential heir. Shortly after his marriage, the king was pushing through the Act of Succession, which would allow him to name his own successor. The first recorded sign of the duke of Richmond's illness was five days before his death, when he failed to attend Parliament to support this very act. Prior to this he went every day, and was also a guest at weddings and a participant in all the court's activities. The king had spent a lot of time with his son throughout his childhood and was inconsolable on his death.

Henry VIII had always been terrified of death and insisted that Richmond's father-in-law, the duke of Norfolk, organise a quick and private funeral. Henry may have wanted his dead son's corpse taken far away from him. Richmond was originally buried in Thetford, but is now interred at St Michael's Church in Framlingham, near his close friend, the earl of Surrey. It is thought that he died of consumption, although it could have been another lung condition. McNalty concludes that there was a history of pulmonary tuberculosis in the Tudors. It allegedly killed both of Henry's sons, Richmond and Edward VI, contributed to the deaths of Henry's father and brother, Henry VII and Prince Arthur, and his daughter Elizabeth may have suffered from tuberculous laryngitis.[5] The duke was only seventeen, and died on 23 July 1536 in St James's Palace. It was only two months since the execution of his stepmother, who the king had branded a 'poisoning whore', accusing her of targeting both Princess Mary and the duke of Richmond.[6]

Henry refused to provide for Mary Howard, the teenage widow who was now the dowager duchess of Richmond and Somerset. Perhaps this was because it was Anne Boleyn who had arranged the marriage, and Mary, Anne's cousin and one of her most favoured ladies-in-waiting, reminded him of his disgraced wife. Mary had brought no dowry and their marriage had been unconsummated and therefore childless, so £1,000 a year for life was a sum that Henry had no wish to pay. The duchess did not believe that it was the king who was denying her this money, blaming the situation wholly on her father. The duke of Norfolk was doing his best to persuade Henry to settle the matter fairly but the king was insistent that their unconsummated marriage did not count as a legitimate union.

Henry appeared happy in his marriage to Jane, but she never gained a fraction of the power her predecessors had wielded. Perhaps this is why she seems to have made no serious enemies. Henry does not seem to have felt the same passion for her as for his previous lovers and it is likely that he was quickly unfaithful.

> Within eight days after publication of his marriage, having twice met two beautiful young ladies, he said and showed himself somewhat sorry that he had not seen them before he was married.[7]

Henry also asked that all Jane's attendants be *'fair'*; it was important to him that the new ladies-in-waiting were attractive.

Jane was clearly determined, as her predecessors had been, that her ladies would behave virtuously. Anne Boleyn had introduced French fashions and customs, but Jane was a conservative Englishwoman and was determined to return to a more traditional court. It is unsurprising that when Anne Bassett secured a place at court, she was warned that she must not arrive in the 'French apparel' she had worn to meet the queen previously. John Hussey wrote to Anne Bassett's mother that he had seen Anne in the altered head-dress and 'I thought it became her nothing so well as the French hood, but the Queen's pleasure must be done'; the French hood sat further back on the head and showed the hair. Anne Bassett was also warned that she needed to add extra material to her neckline.[8] Queen Jane may have felt threatened by the arrival of this new, and apparently very pretty, young woman; there were later rumours that Henry was attracted to her, and even considering marrying Anne.

Henry told Chapuys that he was now feeling old, and doubted that the queen would conceive, after only three months of marriage. This is unlikely to have been proof of his impotence – she did become pregnant soon after, and on 12 October 1537, Jane gave birth to a healthy boy. She died twelve days after the birth, probably of puerperal sepsis, the infection Henry's mother had died of. Jane had paid the ultimate price for her success, only seventeen months after the wedding. Nevertheless, she had died in a noble cause; she had given her husband the one thing he had craved all his life, that he would shake the foundations of his country for – a legitimate son, the future Edward VI.

Jane may have died, but the Seymours continued to benefit from her refusal to be merely Henry's mistress. During the reign of her son, Edward VI, Jane's eldest brother Edward was made duke of Somerset (which had been a royal title) and was Lord Protector during the first half of his nephew's minority. Her brother Thomas married the queen dowager, Katheryn Parr. Both were executed in the ensuing power struggles and the son she had given her life to bear died before he reached full adulthood. Both her brothers were buried in the Tower of London's chapel, St Peter ad Vincula, near Anne Boleyn and some of her 'lovers'.* Nevertheless, as a family, the Seymours continued to prosper.

Henry had three marriages behind him, and had gone through a turbulent ten years, but finally he had his Prince of Wales. The disappointment of losing the woman he loved was weighed against the joy of the long-awaited arrival of a healthy son and heir. The king was now old by sixteenth-century standards, and was perhaps beyond his days as a man 'inclined to amours'. But he was still insistent that his next wife must be someone he could be attracted to.

In the letters to other monarchs announcing the death of Queen Jane, there were already hints at negotiating for her successor. Henry wore black for over three months after her death (Jane Seymour died on 24 October 1537 and he wore black until 3 February 1538), but England was threatened by the Catholic coalition of France, Spain, the Holy Roman Empire and the Papal States. An alliance with a European power, sealed by a marriage, could bolster England's position on the Continent and prevent a possible invasion. As a man, he could mourn, but as a king, he could not afford the luxury. The future of the Tudor dynasty, and of the country, rested on the health of the king and one baby boy. He knew from painful experience that this was not enough.

Henry's council may have begun enquiries into a fourth wife immediately, but Henry himself was cautious. He wanted to marry, but after the two queens he had discarded, he was determined to choose very carefully this time. Henry now sought all the advantages of a wife and a mistress to be wrapped up in one woman: for her to enjoy the constant celebrations and feasts, and to ornament them; for her to be intelligent and a good

---

* Henry Norris, Francis Weston and George Boleyn were buried in St Peter ad Vincula along with Anne Boleyn. Jane, Lady Rochford joined her husband and sister-in-law there six years later, along with Catherine Howard. Jane Seymour's brothers, Edward, duke of Somerset and Thomas, Baron Seymour of Sudeley joined them in the 1550s. Charles II's illegitimate son, the first bastard to try to claim the throne of England since William the Conqueror, joined them in the seventeenth century.

companion; for them to be in love. He insisted: 'I will trust no one but myself; marriage touches a man too closely.'[9]

Henry said his advisers should choose his fourth wife for him, as they 'would have good sport to make him amorous at his age'.[10] After the death of Jane, there are far fewer reports of Henry chasing ladies. Maybe it was because Henry was less able to womanise, with his ulcerated leg and his obese frame, his headaches, constipation, indigestion and irritability. As he aged, he preferred to marry the women he loved, rather than retain them as mistresses. Yet the reports of Henry between 1540 and 1541, barely able to keep his hands off Catherine Howard in public, show that he was still interested in attractive girls.

By 1538, a year after Jane's death, Henry was enthusiastic about finding a new wife. He enjoyed the negotiations, playing rival off against rival, hoping to obtain the best possible match. Unfortunately, the royal families of Europe were not as eager as they would previously have been – Katherine of Aragon, Anne Boleyn and Jane Seymour had all died in the last two years. Rumours that Katherine had been poisoned, Anne falsely accused and that Jane had died of neglect spread throughout Europe.

At first, Henry was particularly interested in marrying a French noble-woman. He told Francis I that he would like some possible contenders to travel to Calais, so that he could 'see them and enjoy their society before settling on one'. Francis replied that Henry

> would perhaps like to try them all, one after the other, and keep for yourself the one who seemed the sweetest. It was not thus, Sir, that the Knights of the Round Table treated their ladies.[11]

Henry was said to have been deeply embarrassed, and did not pursue this idea. He then wished to marry Mary of Guise, Francis's cousin, but she rejected him in favour of his nephew, James V of Scotland, a man with a smaller kingdom but who was younger and more attractive.

Henry had wished to meet the women before making any commitments as 'marriage is a bargain of such nature as must endure for the whole life of man, and a thing whereof the pleasure and quiet, or the displeasure and torment of the man's mind doth much depend'.[12] Even the sixteen-year-old Christina of Milan's reputation for beauty was not enough for Henry, or that she was said to resemble his former mistress, Mary Shelton; or that she was also the niece of the most powerful man in Europe. He still wanted to check this for himself. He was very pleased that her portrait showed she was tall, as this had been listed as one of his requirements (although the next woman he fell in love with was the diminutive Catherine Howard). He was specific about her appearance – not only must she be beautiful, but as he was now a big man he was in need of 'a big wife'.[13]

While negotiations continued with several French princesses, and their portraits were painted for Henry's approval, the king seemed wholly taken by Christina of Milan. To marry Christina, Henry demanded that his prospective bride be made the heir to Denmark; she was at the time second in line to her elder sister. However, her family were not so eager. Wriothesley went to meet Christina and asked if she wished to marry Henry; he had heard rumours that she did not. She replied, 'What should I say? You know that I am at the Emperor's commandment.' Wriothesley then tried to persuade the evasive princess that this would be an excellent match for her, explaining that Henry was 'the most gentle gentleman that liveth; his nature so benign and pleasant, that I think till this day no man hath heard many angry words pass his mouth'. This was deviating so far from the truth that Christina seems to have struggled to keep a straight face; Wriothesley described her as 'like one that was tickled'.[14]

From the start of the detailed negotiations for Christina's hand, the Hapsburgs seemed lukewarm. As she was the great-niece of Katherine of Aragon, they needed a dispensation for her to marry Henry – and they would only accept this from the Pope, who was unlikely to be helpful. The negotiations continued for over a year, but eventually petered out. No doubt her family had concerns about sending such a young woman to a husband known for disposing of unwanted wives. Neither Francis nor Charles made any serious effort to build a marital alliance with the King of England – it was not just his past record and his age which counted against him, it seems his kingdom was not considered quite attractive enough either.

Archbishop Cranmer had another suggestion for Henry. He thought that the king should marry 'where that he had his fantasy and love, for that would be most comfort for his grace'.[15] Cranmer knew him well; this was a progressive idea, and one that was ignored. Henry wanted a foreign princess, as was expected of him – and no Englishwoman had captured his heart this time. In 1516 Erasmus had published *The Education of a Prince*, in which he criticised the use of princesses as marriage pawns – pointing out that these alliances rarely worked. He advised kings to marry women from their own country; this may have inspired Henry.

In 1538 rumours abounded at court as to whether an Englishwoman would again sit on the throne of England. But with an absence of ladies at court, as there was no queen for them to serve, Henry had few opportunities to fall in love with a young aristocrat. One courtier, John Hussey, wrote:

> The election lieth between Mrs. Mary Shelton and Mrs. Mary Skipwith. I pray Jesu send such one as may be for his Highness' comfort and the wealth of the realm. Herein I doubt not but your lordship will keep silence till the matter be surely known.[16]

Mary Shelton had been Henry's mistress three years before, during his marriage to Anne Boleyn. (If he was considering marrying Mary Shelton in 1538, then she was almost definitely his earlier mistress, not her sister Margaret: he would have been unlikely to marry his ex-mistress's sister after his annulments to Katherine of Aragon and Anne Boleyn. If he had, this would have been the third time in four marriages that he had married a woman who under Church law was his sister.) A woman who had fornicated before marriage was clearly an unsuitable choice as Queen of England – and Henry may not have been her only lover.

Mistress Skipwith is more likely to be Margaret than Mary Skipwith. The sisters were the daughters of Sir William Skipwith of South Ormsby, part of the Lincolnshire gentry. Mary Skipwith married George Fitzwilliam of Mablethorpe around 1550. We are unsure of her date of birth, but her date of marriage suggests she may have been too young to marry at the time of the rumours, twelve years beforehand. It is likely that, as with the Sheltons, Mary and Marg, the abbreviated version of Margaret, were confused here, and it was Margaret Skipwith who Henry was rumoured to be interested in. Margaret Skipwith married three months after this rumour, when the king helped arrange a marriage for her to Bessie Blount's son.[17]

The court had been desperate for a new queen. Without one, its social life came to a standstill, with no ladies-in-waiting. The women who had served Queen Jane, or who hoped to serve a new queen, were eager to gain positions at court. Anne Bassett, who had served Queen Jane so briefly, wrote to her mother that: 'I trust in God that we shall have a mistress shortly … which I hope to God will not be long.'[18] This letter suggests that Anne Bassett, who was later thought a possible candidate for wife number five or six, did not consider herself to be in the running for the position of wife number four. After two years without a queen, negotiations seemed to have come to an end for a French or Habsburg princess. But the shrewd Thomas Cromwell had a match in mind.

She was not a princess from a dominant European family, but she was royal, single and available. Her brother was the duke of Cleves, a small but strategically placed German duchy between the lands of the mighty Habsburgs and France. An alliance between Cleves, Denmark, Guelders and England could cause problems for the emperor, especially in the Netherlands. Cleves had a similar brand of Christianity to England's, in between Catholicism and Protestantism, so they were not perturbed by the idea of their Lady Anne marrying an excommunicate. While the Catholic countries were temporarily allied, England could easily be subjected to a holy invasion. Despite Henry's dislike of Lutheran doctrines, the German principalities could be useful allies.

Chapter 11

'I Like Her Not'

After two years of fruitless negotiations with rival royal families, forty-nine-year-old Henry was finally awaiting his new bride's arrival. Nicholas Wotton, the ambassador who had written the report on Anne of Cleves, was honest and it was clear that she would not make Henry's heart pound. The duke was in debt and so Henry did not even receive a dowry. As Henry had not received dowries for any of his other wives, he seemed unconcerned. If Henry wanted to marry a princess, then Anne of Cleves was the best available.

Henry VIII was fluent in several languages and most European princesses could have communicated with him in at least Latin; but Anne only spoke her native German. She also had none of the social skills so prized at the English court: she could not play a musical instrument or sing – she came from a culture that looked down on the lavish celebrations and light-heartedness that were an integral part of King Henry's court. Yet none of this would have mattered if her looks had appealed to the king. It quickly became obvious that they did not.

On 27 December 1539 Anne arrived at the port of Deal in Kent. She travelled to Dover, where the duke and duchess of Suffolk officially greeted her and accompanied her to Greenwich. Within four days she had reached Rochester Castle. It was normal procedure, and not a strange fancy of Henry's, for the prince to arrive and see his bride incognito, before their official meeting. As Henry loved such games, it was obvious that he would do so and Anne should have been warned to expect it.

He had not been able to wait to see her and travelled to meet his bride in order to 'nourish love'[1], but when he arrived she did not know who he was – unsurprising as he was dressed down – and paid little attention to him. He told Cromwell on his way out that 'I like her not'.[2] Henry was a romantic. It seems that, in his head, he had built this up, perhaps expecting it to become a love match.

Wotton, the English envoy who had been with Holbein in Cleves, described the paintings of Anne and her sister Amelia as 'expressed their images very lively'[3] – they were good likenesses. Anne was tall, as Henry had requested. She was 'of middling beauty, with a determined and resolute countenance … [with] a steadiness of purpose in her face to counteract her want of beauty'.[4] The description of her looks, 'middling beauty', was used by ambassadors for all four of Henry VIII's English wives, who he had married for love.

What probably repelled Henry most were the scars on her face. Smallpox marks were common, but we have no evidence that Henry knew his bride had this defect until her arrival; there is no sign of it in her official portrait. Anne also looked every inch a German lady, and this style was not admired in England. The French ambassador guessed she was about thirty, although she was only twenty-five. Added to this, Anne's attendants wore such 'coarse and unsightly garb that they would be considered ugly through it even had they any personal attractions'.[5] Her clothes, her inability to communicate with the English and her body odour – according to Henry she had 'displeasant airs' – would have ensured she did not delight her husband at first meeting. But Anne of Cleves was a woman who should have made a good second or third impression. Henry may have never called her a 'Flanders mare', but his opinion was certainly that she was an unattractive woman. (Henry never referred to Anne as such, this was the description used by Bishop Burnet in the seventeenth century.)

On 3 January 1540 Henry formally met Anne of Cleves at Blackheath Common. Henry described his new wife as 'well and seemly [yet] nothing so fair as she had been reported'.[6] He added on his wedding day that 'if it were not to satisfy the world, and my realm, I would not do that I must do, ay for none earthly thing'.[7] For Cromwell, who had arranged this marriage, these confidences were difficult to hear. Henry was hoping that his wily minister could find some diplomatic way out of the marriage, but there was no way to reject her now they had met. The day after the wedding night, Cromwell asked Henry, 'How liked you the Queen?' Henry replied, 'I liked her before not well, but now I like her much worse.'[8]

They were married by Cranmer on the feast of the Epiphany. Henry showed by his reaction that he saw little difference between a wife and a mistress. He had expected to lust after his wife, and their meeting was a bitter blow. Shortly after his marriage to Anne of Cleves, Henry gave Anne Bassett a 'fine horse and saddle'. This indicates that early on in the marriage, it was not a foregone conclusion which of the maids of honour would next be promoted to queen. This gift prompted rumours of an affair between Anne Bassett and the king; there had been gossip about them two years before, when Henry had been looking for wife number four. Anne was described as 'fair, well-made and behaveth herself so well that everybody praiseth her that seeth her'.[9]

She was the daughter of Sir John Bassett and Honor Grenville. John had died while Anne was a young child, and Honor had then married – for love – Arthur Plantagenet, Viscount Lisle, the illegitimate son of King Edward IV. Having King Henry's uncle as her stepfather would have helped Anne secure a position at court. She was born circa 1521,[10] so was approximately eighteen when rumours first began about her relationship with Henry. She and her siblings were brought up in Calais, where Lord Lisle was the governor. Like many noblewomen, Anne spent some time in France, moving there in 1533 to learn the language. Her mother was fiercely ambitious and must have hoped that her daughter would acquire some of the Continental polish of women like Anne Boleyn.

Like many ladies-in-waiting, as soon as Anne arrived at court, she was expected to start campaigning for another relative to be given a position – in this case her sister Katherine. She seems to have found this cringeworthy, and had to justify to her mother why the king had rejected this suggestion, explaining that Sir Francis Bryan and others had tried before her for their own kin, but Anne of Cleves would need fewer ladies than Queen Jane had, as she was bringing several women with her from Cleves. Anne Bassett's letters do not reflect the idea that she had strong influence over Henry in 1539. Yet from the political backwater of Calais, Lady Lisle kept in close contact with her allies at court, finding out all the latest titbits of gossip; there is no mention in their surviving correspondence of a liaison between Anne and the king. Anne did not write her well-known letters to her mother with her own hand, she had a secretary perform this, which indicates that she was barely literate.

She seems to have become ill in 1539, just before the arrival of the new queen and Henry recommended she went to the countryside. There are several reasons other than illness for this taking place shortly before Anne of Cleves' arrival. It could be that Anne Bassett had been his lover and he felt it would be better to send her away before his bride arrived; she may even have been feigning illness to escape ending up as Henry's next wife or mistress. It may be significant that she was staying with her cousins, the Dennys. Antony Denny was arguably the king's most trusted servant towards the end of his reign; he even had a dry stamp with which he could attach the king's signature to any document. Conspiracy theories aside, Anne may have attracted the king's attention, but there is no evidence that this developed into a relationship, despite the repeated rumours over the latter years of his reign.

Poor Anne of Cleve's physical appearance was analysed by Henry – and found inadequate. 'Her body [was] in such a sort disordered and indisposed … [it could not] excite and provoke any lust in him.' She 'had breasts so slack and other parts of body in such sort that [he] somewhat suspected her virginity'.[11] Henry was spending most nights with his wife, but insisted 'she was still as good a maid … as ever her mother bare her'. He informed Dr Chamber and Dr Butts that during the first month of marriage he had had two 'nocturnal ejaculations' but he could not bear to touch his wife. After Henry had apparently tried for four nights, Dr. Butts told him not to 'enforce himself'.

Some have argued that Henry did not consummate his fourth marriage because he was impotent; this seems unlikely, yet he had no mistresses at this time. Henry VIII was a king; he could have anything he wanted and rarely was forced to go against his own inclinations, so to have sexual intercourse with a woman who he personally found repulsive would have been extremely difficult for him. He had his pick of all the young women in the country and with the new queen came many female attendants, who had been missing at court since the death of Queen Jane two years earlier. Henry talked to his doctor about their relationship and the notes from these conversations were used as evidence in the annulment proceedings. Therefore we know that Dr Chamber advised Henry that if he felt that he could not 'be provoked or stirred in that act', then he should not force himself.[12] The king did insist to Dr Butts that he 'thought himself able to do the act with other but not with her'.[13]

Contemporaries seem to have found it impossible to believe that this union was unconsummated – how could it have been after six months of marriage? Richard Hilles wrote at the time: 'Who, judging of the King by his fruits, would ever believe him to be so chaste a character' as to not consummate his marriage. But this was a man who needed to feel attracted to his wife – and fairly or unfairly, Queen Anne disgusted him. Perhaps now that he had a strong, healthy son he had less need to consummate this marriage – yet experience had taught him that one boy was not enough to secure the Tudor dynasty. Henry was not a man who would have sacrificed his desires for the sake of an heir, despite the other lengths he had been prepared to go to previously to sire one.

Henry just did not desire Anne – and he was not subtle about it. Her German clothes, her strong body odour, her slack stomach and sagging breasts all led him to doubt her virtue. The safety of the kingdom depended on a spare to add to the heir, but Henry could not bring himself to consummate the marriage. 'He lamented his fate that he should never have any more children if he so continued, declaring that before God he thought she was not his lawful wife.'[14] His lack of attraction was, of course, a message from God that they were not truly married.

There would have been intense speculation as to the relationship of the king and queen. Her ladies changed the sheets, prepared their mistress for bed and knew the guards who stood outside the bedroom; as there was no real privacy at court, they were aware that the queen was still a 'maid'. Lady Rochford and Lady Rutland apparently spoke to Anne about this. There was only one person at court who seemed unaware that the marriage had not been consummated – Queen Anne herself. During her sheltered upbringing, she seems to have been given no idea how babies were conceived. She insisted to her ladies-in-waiting that

> When he comes to bed, he kisses me and taketh me by the hand and biddeth me 'goodnight, sweetheart' and in the morning kisses me and biddeth me, 'Farewell, darling'. Is this not enough?

Lady Rutland replied:

> Madam, there must be more, or it will be long ere we have a Duke of York.[15]

Some doubt has to be cast on this story, as the queen's level of English was not good enough for these to have been her words.

All the time there had been no queen, there had been no maids of honour to serve her. Now, with Anne of Cleves' arrival, the court was filled with young women who had been selected for their beauty, grace and the courtly skills that Henry admired. He did not wish to take a mistress, he wanted a wife – a companion and consort as well as a lover. Even though he was not attracted to his wife, many thought he could not possibly annul a third marriage; those who knew him well were not surprised at the turn of events. Soon the king had fallen madly in love with the duke of Norfolk's niece, the vivacious teenager, Catherine Howard.

Although Catherine's parents had been poor, she had a very noble lineage and her uncle was both one of the richest men in the kingdom and a loyal servant of Henry's. Norfolk knew the benefits of the king falling in love with one's relative – Catherine was at least the third of the duke's nieces Henry had fallen for* – but he would also have been aware of the dangers. Norfolk had led the jury who condemned Anne Boleyn to her death and had seen the king discard other women along the way, even Henry's own daughters, whose titles and status had been discarded along with their mothers. But the potential for advancement outweighed the risks – and the Howards were unlikely to be so unlucky a second time.

Competition would have been fierce to gain a place as maid of honour to the new queen – and the Howards had managed to secure three of the appointments. Henry wanted only a certain number of ladies attending his new queen, especially as she had brought around a dozen with her from Cleves. He was, however, definite that all ladies must 'be fair and as he thought meet for the room'.[16] Among the queen's other ladies-in-waiting were Anne Bassett (Henry had also been rumoured to have had an earlier affair with a 'Mistress Browne', another member of Anne's family); Bessie Blount; and Bessie's daughter-in-law, Margaret Skipwith, who Henry was rumoured to have considered for his fourth wife; the queen's apartments were littered with the close relatives of her husband's discarded conquests.

As we are unsure when Bessie died, it may have been her husband's second wife who was at court. Henry continued to make grants to Bessie until 9 January 1539. By June 1541 Lord Clinton was married to Ursula Stourton; Bessie died at some point between these dates. Rumours that she died of consumption are unsubstantiated and may be confusing her with her son.

---

*After Mary and Anne Boleyn and probably Elizabeth Carew; Jane Seymour was the duke's cousin and Lady Anne Stafford was his wife's aunt.

By April 1540 Henry had started giving Catherine Howard lands – but he was still married. The examples of Anne Boleyn and Jane Seymour showed the Howard faction what could happen at Henry's court if the king was not enamoured with his wife and his would-be mistress would not consent. Anne of Cleves, though a Catholic herself, represented an alliance with a Protestant dukedom. Henry was moving further away from his initial religious policy of 'Catholicism without the Pope' and adopting some Lutheran practices. The conservative faction, led by Catherine's uncle, the duke of Norfolk, and Stephen Gardiner, bishop of Winchester, needed to win back ground.

Thomas Cromwell knew he was in danger. He was closely matched with his conservative enemies. But they had a trump card that Cromwell, with all his cunning could not beat – Catherine. Cromwell had solved many problems for the king, but confided in his friend, Thomas Wriothesley, that this was irrelevant if he could not solve the main issue – 'The King liketh not the Queen.'[17] The problem was as simple and unchangeable as that.

On 10 June 1540 Thomas Cromwell was arrested during a council meeting. He was accused of treason and 'revealing to a third party intimate secrets about the relationship between Henry and Anne [of Cleves]'.[18] This would have been unforgivable in the king's view; he seems to have confided in Cromwell, who took it upon himself to improve the situation. Cromwell had suggested to Anne of Cleves' chamberlain that he should advise Anne on how to entice the king. There has been a suggestion that Cromwell had the king's permission to speak to Anne herself, but not to her chamberlain, Thomas Manners, earl of Rutland. If either of these scenarios is correct, then Cromwell was lacking his usual canniness – there was nothing that could make Henry attracted to Anne.

Queen Anne would have been worried by this development. Cromwell was an extraordinarily able politician, and an utterly ruthless one. He would always do whatever his king wanted – by whatever means necessary. Anne of Cleves saw Cromwell as an ally and may have worried that she would suffer the same fate. When Henry was in bed with Catherine, he was also 'in bed with' the Howard-led conservative faction. Cromwell was the first victim of the king's attraction to the young maid of honour.

It was Cromwell who could take the lion's share of the praise for achieving Henry's annulment from Katherine of Aragon, and who had got rid of Anne Boleyn when she was no longer wanted. But he had also arranged the marriage with Anne of Cleves. For leaving him stuck with a wife he found unattractive, Henry could not forgive his faithful servant. His shock led to disappointment and great resentment against those he felt had saddled him with this woman. As with Thomas Wolsey, who had not been able to secure the annulment of Henry's marriage to Katherine of Aragon, Henry lived to regret Cromwell's fall, when he was left without a servant who could match him.

On 20 June Anne spoke to the Clevian ambassador, Harst, about Henry's relationship with Catherine Howard[19]. He was already well aware of it, and wrote that that they had been having an affair for months.[20] Four days later, the Privy Council instructed Anne to go to Richmond Palace; the king did not accompany her. Harst wrote that the queen was concerned she would be treated as Katherine of Aragon had been. As witchcraft was often used to explain impotence, and Henry had already accused one wife of sorcery, Retha Warnicke argues that Anne was in danger of more than annulment.

On 6 July messengers arrived to see the queen, and suggested that the marriage's legality should be investigated. She did not agree immediately, as has sometimes been portrayed. She is said to have fainted at the news and the king's men were sent away, returning the next morning. Then they spoke to her servants. Eventually, they received Anne's consent to look into these matters – all knew the conclusion they would arrive at, and all knew of the rumours that his new love, Catherine Howard, was pregnant. On 9 July the Council declared Henry's marriage to Anne invalid.

Henry had to dig around to find a reason why his marriage to Anne of Cleves should be annulled. To a man who believed that marriages were made in the eyes of God, ending his marriage just because he did not desire his bride was not an option. God must be trying to tell his representative in England something – and surely it was that the marriage had been invalid from the start. There was only one possible ground on which to annul the union: Henry knew that Anne had been betrothed to the duke of Lorraine years earlier. A betrothal was considered tantamount to marriage, but royal engagements often fell through. This was a genuinely grey area in Church law that the royal families of Europe had often exploited when they wanted to end their marriages. The annulment, Henry's third, was remarkably easy to obtain.

The long alliance between Spain and France was ending, so the friendship of the German duchies was no longer so important. But most significantly, Anne herself did not object. There were no children and there had been no consummation to complicate matters. She did not attempt to gain power at court and retired to the English countryside where she seems to have spent the rest of her life quietly and happily. Henry provided for his 'sister', giving her precedence over all ladies at court except his wife and daughters. He even gave his former wife Hever Castle, the old family seat of the Boleyns, which had been sold to him on the death of Sir Thomas. Once Henry had annulled the marriage and squared his conscience, he found that he liked Anne, and friendships blossomed from this extraordinary situation, between Anne and her new 'brother' and also between Anne and her replacement, her former servant Catherine Howard.

The psychologist J.C. Flugel argued that Henry VIII unconsciously desired incest, and this both attracted him to, and encouraged him to discard, his wives. This is partly because all of his wives were his distant cousins: Katherine of Aragon was his sister-in-law (so his sister according to the Church) and his fifth cousin; Anne Boleyn was his ex-mistress's sister (so also considered to be *his* sister) and Henry's eighth cousin; Jane Seymour was his fifth cousin and closely related to Anne Boleyn and Catherine Howard; Anne of Cleves was his seventh cousin, two generations removed; Catherine Howard was first cousin to the Boleyn sisters, and Henry's eighth cousin; and Katheryn Parr was his third cousin once removed. We do know that he was related to some of his mistresses as well, such as Lady Anne Stafford, who was his second cousin and also related to him through several other branches of the family tree.

On annulling three of his marriages, he declared the women to be his sisters (Katherine of Aragon, Anne of Cleves and Anne Boleyn; Katherine as she had been married to his brother, Anne Boleyn because he had had sexual intercourse with her sister, and Anne of Cleves he declared an adopted sister). Bearing in mind how numerous the Howard clan was, and how restricted the English aristocracy and European ruling families were at that time, it is unsurprising that Henry ended up marrying his distant cousins. Whether he married abroad or at home, any woman near his status was related to him. There is no evidence that Henry deliberately sought out his relations, and marrying distant cousins could hardly be considered incest.

It is unclear whether Henry, who had not been closely linked to a woman in over three years, made Catherine Howard his lover before the wedding. But there is no doubt that he was truly in love with her. There were reports of Henry travelling across the Thames to visit her, even after midnight,[21] while he was still married to Anne. Henry was soon visiting

Catherine* nearly every day, but most people did not yet realise that she was anything more than another mistress.

Henry VIII had showed his pure motives towards Jane Seymour by ensuring that their relatives were present during his courting of them, and the same seems to have been true of his courtship of the teenage Catherine. A week before the wedding ceremony, there was a rumour that she was pregnant.[22] It is unlikely that Catherine's family allowed her to be left alone with the king until he had proposed, as they knew from experience that she could win a crown. However, once the couple were engaged the family may have been more relaxed. The king was clearly enchanted by his bride-to-be and Catherine is unlikely to have rejected any advances he made. Although she may have been dazzled by him, and was eager to please him, she was probably not physically attracted to Henry.

From the time her cousin had charmed the king so completely, every English lady-in-waiting had become a potential queen-in-waiting. Henry had overthrown the normal order of things – the double life kings were expected to lead. If he fell in love, he married the woman. But if she let him down, he would discard her, almost as easily as he would discard a mistress. Catherine does not seem to have fully understood this.

Catherine's motto was 'No other wish but his'.[23] She seems to have combined the meekness towards her husband that had entranced him in Jane Seymour with the *joie de vivre* and energy of Mary Shelton or Bessie Blount – but without the intelligence of any of his former lovers. The dowager duchess of Norfolk said that 'The King's Highness did cast a fantasy to Catherine Howard the first time that ever his Grace saw her'.[24] This would have been shortly before the arrival of Anne of Cleves.

Marillac, the French ambassador, described Catherine's beauty as '*commonplace*' – the same word he had used to describe Anne of Cleves' looks. Yet he later referred to her as 'a lady of great beauty'.[25] This may have been flattery for the woman who was by then the queen, or her more expensive clothing and jewellery, not to mention her power and title, suddenly increasing her attractions. Unfortunately, we cannot give our own opinions, as there is no portrait that is definitively Catherine Howard; all those which have been labelled as Catherine are suspected to be Jane Seymour's sister,

---

* Catherine tended to spell her name with a K, but I have spelled it with a C here to differentiate her from the many other Katherines in Henry's life.

Elizabeth. (Although in one of these portraits the woman is wearing a necklace we see in a portrait of Jane Seymour, which may indicate that it was part of the royal jewellery collection. However, as Elizabeth was Jane's sister, the necklace may have been passed on to her rather than Henry's later wives.) Catherine appears to have been seductive rather than stunning; not classically beautiful but a vivacious and pretty teenage girl.

The Howards, despite their previous brush with attracting Henry to one of their clan, were elated and saw this as an opportunity to advance themselves. There was talk that Norfolk had encouraged Catherine to attract the king, but she was an attractive woman and Henry would have needed no encouragement to notice her. The Howards simply grabbed the chance when it was offered to them. Anne Boleyn had not seemed grateful to her family – Catherine was much more compliant a character and could be guided by her older and greedier relatives. Henry called her his 'blushing rose without a thorn'[24] and nothing was too good for her. Expensive jewellery, clothes, titles and money were lavished upon the teenage girl, who seems to have loved every minute of this attention from her benefactor. She was also described as inclined to tantrums and difficult to serve.

After the first meeting with Anne of Cleves, where he burst in upon his fiancée imagining he was a dashing suitor and being mistaken for a dangerous intruder, he probably felt rejected. Henry was not a man to allow the disappointment to be blamed on his own actions. And according to the dowager duchess of Norfolk, he was visibly attracted to Catherine Howard the moment he saw her. Anne was not an attractive proposition next to her coquettish and pretty young maid of honour.

Chapter 12

Rose Without a Thorn

'Company is good or ill
But every man hath his free will ...'

Henry married Catherine Howard at Oatlands Palace, Surrey on 28 July 1540, the day of Thomas Cromwell's execution. Their marriage brought renewed energy to the court. Once married to Catherine, Henry was like a child in a sweet shop, celebrating his good luck with constant festivities. He still hunted until he had tired out several horses, threw himself into jousting, tennis and dancing with youthful exuberance, enjoying the admiration of the whole court. A large cloud seemed to be lifted off him. It was said that: 'The King's affection was so marvellously set up on that gentlewoman, as it was never known that he had the like to any woman.'[1]

Henry's frame and height meant that he could carry his extra weight; he was still a physically impressive man when he started pursuing Catherine Howard. This king, who had probably been without a woman in his life for three years, had now fallen madly in love. He was wholly besotted, his behaviour surprising even the courtiers who knew him so well. He does not seem to have been able to keep his hands off Catherine. It was reported that 'the King is so amorous of her that he cannot treat her well enough and caresses her more than he did the others'.[2]

Despite the rumours of impotence, it is unlikely that Henry would have been so happy during his fifth marriage if he had been unable to consummate it. There are many reports from ambassadors of the time explaining how Henry showered Catherine with presents, how the French ambassador had never 'seen the King in such good spirits or in so good a humour'.[3] But there was, after their courtship, not even a hint of a pregnancy. Henry had certainly slowed down and there was no suggestion that he was unfaithful to Catherine Howard.

Catherine's numerous kith and kin were now voracious in their desire for court appointments, and Catherine, although apparently difficult and haughty at times, helped her relatives advance themselves. Her parents were both dead, but she had many siblings, cousins, aunts and uncles clamouring for grants, posts and money. She appears to have been unconcerned about the responsibilities of being queen. She had every possession she desired, and everyone at court was anxious to win her favour. Yet it was only four years since Anne Boleyn's execution and this should have played heavily on her mind. Catherine ensured that her old friends found positions at court. With her wild and unrestricted childhood, bringing to court those who knew her secrets was extremely dangerous.

Catherine could read and write and had received an average education for a noblewoman. A lady should obey her father and then obey her husband; there was no need for her to learn more than was necessary for this. Some women ran country estates and had to be able to perform these duties well, even when their men were away, as they often were, at court or at war. This required organisational and administrative skills, so their academic education often prepared them directly for this and nothing else. Catherine had been trained only for court.

The Privy Council described Catherine as a 'jewel of womanhood'.[4] Henry showered his new wife with diamonds, pearls, rubies, gold and silver in the form of necklaces, gowns and shoes. He satisfied her every whim. This was a relationship which had been promptly consummated, in a way that pleased his conscience (in marriage), and his last wife had faded into the background without causing a fuss. There had been no debates, no papal courts or threats of invasion, little of the emotional behaviour he increasingly disliked in women when this marriage was being annulled; God was finally giving him all he wanted.

Catherine was in a strong position, but it was not one she could take for granted. It was important to make friends in high places, but she seems to have lacked the skills to do so. She argued repeatedly with her stepdaughter, the Lady Mary. The new queen simply wished to enjoy herself at court, dancing and feasting with her young friends. She would have been a good mistress for Henry, but Catherine was even less suited to the dignified and regal role required of the Queen of England than her cousin Anne Boleyn had been. Yet as long as she retained Henry's love, no one at court — not Mary, and not the reformers — could touch her.

It is unsurprising that Henry's daughter Mary, who had become close to Jane Seymour and Anne of Cleves, would have disliked her young step-mother from the start. Not only had Catherine supplanted Anne of Cleves, but she was five years younger than Mary, and her polar opposite. Catherine was also closely related to the woman Mary blamed for so much, Anne Boleyn. The parallels between Henry's fourth wife being replaced by her young maid of honour and Mary's mother being replaced by the new queen's cousin would have been uncomfortably obvious. No one could then have foreseen exactly how similar their stories would be.

The king and queen did argue occasionally — he once refused to allow Catherine to see him for a week. This was dangerous for his wife, as fac-tions could have worked against her during this time. However, overall he was extremely happy in his latest marriage. The only thing that seems to have ended Henry's rejuvenation was illness; his ulcerated leg was again causing him pain and this caused the onset of a period of depression. One clear sign of the king's infatuation with Catherine was his decision to try a 'new rule of living' as the French ambassador called it — trying to lose weight. In 1540 this seems to have improved Henry's health for a short while, before his 'sore legge' incapacitated him again.

In August 1541 rumours were spread that King Henry, who had been seen enjoying the company of Anne of Cleves at court on several occa-sions, was going to set aside his fifth wife to re-marry his fourth. This gossip continued throughout the marriage. On 11 December 1541 Chapuys wrote that Anne 'was known to have gone away in the family way from the King, and had actually been confined this summer'.[5]* The descriptions of the New Year celebrations of 1541 are bizarre: the former queen and her replacement staying up to dance together while the king went to bed early because of the pain in his leg. The rumours were ridiculous — Henry was still captivated by his young queen and felt no sudden attraction to her predecessor, yet the gossip shows just how cordial his third annulment had

---

* Chapuys' reports always need to be taken with a pinch of salt, especially when they concern Anne of Cleves, who he disapproved of.

been. Henry wished to show Anne favour, for she had done as he wished without arguing – such a pleasant contrast to Katherine of Aragon. Yet there were indications in 1543 that Anne herself was hoping for a reconciliation.

Henry was almost the same age as Catherine's father, Lord Edmund Howard. Despite presumably growing up at court together, Henry and Edmund were never friends. Several letters show that the king did not respect the duke of Norfolk's younger brother and did not offer him the lucrative positions that he was so desperate for. Edmund was constantly crippled by debt. He had even been to court charged with using his office of provost-marshal of Surrey to rule in favour of his relatives, who had given him a large gift. The king had no sympathy with this medieval, feudal behaviour, at least not in Edmund's case. The Tudors had worked hard to limit the power and corruption of the nobility.

Catherine's father was judged to have been a pathetic failure by most people's standards, including the king's. Yet Henry would have given many of his possessions for Lord Edmund's fertility – Catherine was the youngest of his ten children. Edmund himself was one of twenty-three siblings, who included Elizabeth Boleyn and the duke of Norfolk. Her mother, Joyce Culpeper, had died when Catherine was a young child. Catherine must have been chosen out of the Howard clan for her position at court because she was attractive and showed promise, as there were many Howard girls and only so many places to be filled.

Catherine was poor, but she still had her noble blood, and as such she was sent away to an aristocratic household to be brought up. She went to the estate of Agnes Howard, dowager duchess of Norfolk, one of the most high-ranking women in the country and young Catherine's step-grandmother. Although Catherine was the niece of the first peer of the realm, she had to share a dormitory with many other girls. These girls were from various noble and gentle families who had connections to the Howards, and many of them were of a similar rank to her. Her father died in 1539, and by the time she became a maid of honour she was an orphan, just another Howard mouth to feed among many.

Castillon, the French ambassador, had described her as eighteen in 1539 when she was first appointed at court.[6] Although some historians have suggested she was younger, we have no evidence to back this up. She had already been involved in two sexual relationships and, in a time when puberty was later than it is today, an earlier date sounds unlikely, especially as her relationship with Francis Dereham was long term. Therefore, we can assume that she was born around 1521.

Catherine showed, by all accounts, no interest in any form of reading or studying. This might have annoyed the intellectual Henry at a younger age, but now he was happy to watch her light up the court, enjoying all the festivities and receiving the homage she was due as the woman he loved. The forty-nine-year-old king, obese and suffering from other health problems, appears to have enjoyed something of a second youth while married to the light-hearted Catherine. She was interested in music, dancing and games, was from a very aristocratic family and was very attractive. So what if while she had been learning to play music she had allowed her music teacher to become more familiar with her than he should?

In November 1541 the party came to an abrupt end. It had been going so well, and after sixteen months of marriage Henry was still clearly infatuated with his young wife. Then a report was made to the Council by a man called John Lassells. John's sister, Mary, had told him that Catherine had been sexually involved with young men before her marriage. Mary had shared a dormitory with her while they were under the guardianship of the dowager duchess of Norfolk. Once in possession of such information, it could be considered treason not to alert the king; either way, Lassells was in a dangerous but powerful position.

This may have been part of a wider plot. John Lassells was a Protestant, who was burnt at the stake for his religious beliefs four years later; he may have sought to bring down the influence of the conservatives and the Howards were leading advocates of the old ways. Catherine had the capacity to be a significant influence on Henry, and her relatives were now entrenched in the important positions at court. We have no record of Catherine's personal beliefs, but regardless of her own views, she was a figurehead of the conservative faction at court.

Thomas Cranmer, archbishop of Canterbury, was the unfortunate man who was responsible for giving Lassells' report to his king. He only dared do so in a letter, and reluctantly. Although he was a Protestant whose position was in danger from the ascendancy of the Howards, Cranmer was not a man to gloat at the misfortune of others. At this point, he was simply revealing the queen's past with Henry Manox, the music teacher, and Francis Dereham. A queen could never be even *suspected* of loose morals – if she became pregnant, there could not be the slightest doubt that the child was the king's. At first, Henry did not believe the stories. He ordered Catherine to be kept to her apartments while he tried to track down the malicious gossipmonger and disprove the lies. But it did not take much digging to find several witnesses to corroborate Mary Lassells' story. On 12 November 1541, Catherine was arrested.

The whole story was repeated to Henry – of how her paramour, Francis Dereham, had begun visiting the dormitory to see Catherine's friend, but soon moved on to Catherine herself. Some of the girls in the dormitory were visited by their husbands or lovers. Married couples rarely had their own bedroom; this was a luxury only the king and queen regularly enjoyed. Gentlemen from the duke of Norfolk's household, including Dereham, would often come over to spend time with the girls and this led to many love affairs. Like many of the young people involved, he was a distant cousin of Catherine's. Her family knew of the nocturnal visits to the ladies' apartments, but did nothing to prevent the young girl embarking on a sexual relationship.

The dowager duchess of Norfolk, a shrewd but at times reckless woman, did not intervene. She boxed their ears with her fists and with her words when she caught them, but she seems to have been aware, for many months, of Dereham's frequent visits to Catherine's bedroom; she only became angry when it was out in the open. They bought each other presents; Dereham gave Catherine fine materials for dresses and caps and she sent him a band to wear upon his sleeve. Alice Restwold, one of Catherine's roommates, insisted that she had been disgusted with Catherine's behaviour because 'she was a married woman and wist what matrimony meant and what belonged to that puffing and blowing'.[7] In fact, Alice seems to have been one of the leaders of the conspiracy.

There had been talk of marriage. Catherine later insisted she had never considered this as more than role play, although she and Dereham had openly referred to each other as 'husband' and 'wife'. He was near her social level, but not near enough that she would consider marrying him. And this was not Catherine's first love affair. Henry Manox, although a gentleman, had only been able to obtain a place at the dowager duchess's residence as a music teacher. Catherine may have been around fourteen at this time. They had made each other promises of marriage and could be considered, once they had consummated their relationship, legally married. These relationships often occurred, and often ended. But any subsequent marriage they made was legally doubtful.

Catherine did not give Manox the little love tokens that she was later to give to Dereham – she told him clearly that 'I will never be naught with you and able to marry me you be not'.[8] They could only have married if they had eloped, to lead an impoverished life. In an age where a woman might starve to death if she married a man of little means, Catherine was understandably aiming for someone who could keep her and her future children in luxury. Neither she nor Manox seem to have considered this an option; he insisted to Mary Lassells that his intentions were not honourable.

Catherine confessed that she 'suffered him [Manox] at sundry times to handle and touch the secret parts of my body'.[9] She also admitted that Dereham 'lay with me naked and used me in such sort as a man doth his wife many and sundry times'.[10] She had then made Dereham her private secretary and usher of her chamber once she was queen. This looked extremely suspicious now that the truth had been revealed, and led to speculation that their relationship had continued after her marriage. This does not seem to have been the case – as Catherine had moved on to Thomas Culpeper.

To betray Henry was an incredibly dangerous move. Yet it was a vicious, violent world and adultery was the least of many people's worries. For sixteenth-century English people, life was too short for moderation and this extended to love affairs and marriages. Life had been too short for Henry to stay married to women who repulsed him when their attendants were so attractive. And life was too short for Queen Catherine to stay faithful to her king – she had to enjoy every moment, and that meant with attractive and exciting young men, not her old, obese husband.

There remains one letter that Catherine sent to Culpeper, showing that they were not careful to destroy their incriminating correspondence:

Master Culpeper,

I heartily recommend me unto you, praying you to send me word how that you do. It was showed me that you was sick, the which thing troubled me very much till such time that I hear from you praying you to send me word how that you do, for I never longed so much for a thing as I do to see you and to speak with you, the which I trust shall be shortly now. That which doth comfortly me very much when I think of it, and when I think again that you shall depart from me again it makes my heart die to think what fortune I have that I cannot be always in your company. It my trust is always in you that you will be as you have promised me, and in that hope I trust upon still, praying you that you will come when my Lady Rochford is here for then I shall be best at leisure to be at your commandment, thanking you for that you have promised me to be so good unto that poor fellow my man which is one of the griefs that I do feel to depart from him for then I do know no one that I dare trust to send to you, and therefore I pray you take him to be with you that I may sometime hear from you one thing. I pray you to give me a horse for my man for I had much ado to get one and therefore I pray send me one by him and in so doing I am as I said afor, and thus I take my leave of you, trusting to see you shortly again and I would you was with me now that you might see what pain I take in writing to you.

> Yours as long as life endures,
> Katheryn.

One thing I had forgotten and that is to instruct my man to tarry here with me still for he says whatsomever you bid him he will do it.

Catherine clearly found writing difficult, but she later wrote to Henry begging forgiveness and insisting that her past faults were in the past, that when she married him she 'intended ever during my life to be faithful and true unto your Majesty after'. A promise she had not kept, as he was soon to find out. It was discovered that Catherine had been secretly meeting Thomas Culpeper. She admitted the rendezvouses but denied she had committed adultery. The energetic athlete for whom women had swooned in his youth was long gone – Henry had to face the fact that the woman he was completely besotted with had preferred his younger, more virile friend. Catherine Howard found Thomas Culpeper, a convicted rapist and murderer, more enticing than the omnipotent King of England.

The Howard clan had managed to keep their position after Anne Boleyn's fall, but they must have made Catherine aware of how difficult this had been. The duke of Norfolk had condemned Anne Boleyn – his own niece – to death and there was no doubt that he would do the same for Catherine if he had to. He could do little else; 'the wrath of the King meant death.'[11]

She had promised to 'take thee, Henry, to my wedded husband, to have and to hold, for this day forward, for better or worse, for richer and poorer, in sickness and in health, to be bonair and buxom in bed and at board, till death us do part'. Perhaps the vows needed to have specified with whom she was to be 'bonair and buxom in bed'. This letter shows that she felt passionately for Culpeper, who she called her 'little sweet fool'.[12] There is little evidence that this was a tragic love affair though; she was later happy to insist he had tried to force himself on her. The king was still an attractive man to a few observers, but he was not enough for Catherine. The man who caught her eye, Master Thomas Culpeper, was a distant cousin on her mother's side*, a gentleman of the Privy Chamber. According to Marillac, the King trusted Culpeper enough that he 'ordinarily shared [Henry's] bed' but it seemed he had 'wished to share the Queen's bed too'.[13]

Henry had not only to accept that the woman he loved passionately had conducted a sexual relationship before he had met her, he also had to face the fact that she was arranging lovers' meetings with a charming, handsome and – most hurtful of all *–young* coutier. He must have realised that, crown or no crown, Catherine did not really desire him as a man. He was obese, irritable and often ill – most of all, he was old. In his head, their relationship had been love's young dream; he now had to confront the reality that he was simply a man well past his prime, lusting after a teenage girl who had only married him for his crown. He does not seem to have ever fully recovered from this realisation.

It was soon revealed that Catherine and Culpeper had regularly exchanged gifts and notes, arranging clandestine rendezvouses. He had often visited her room at night and Catherine was said to have looked at him lovingly in front of one of her women. At court, where people lived in each other's pockets, it was only a matter of time before their conduct was reported to the king. It was noticed that Queen Catherine was not interested in having guests in the evenings anymore, although no one at first realised who she had started entertaining.

Catherine had been married to Henry for over a year when she began her midnight meetings with Thomas Culpeper. There was an expectation – particularly as pregnancy rumours had started before the marriage – that she would bear Henry a child. There is the possibility that Catherine was hoping she would conceive with Culpeper. As a teenage queen, to an old and unwell king, she was likely to outlive her husband. As the mother of a prince, she would have been in a powerful position. Then it would have been difficult to have had her executed, or to sideline her when the young Prince Edward ascended the throne. A son would have given her security. Yet there is no proof that Catherine and Thomas were motivated by anything other than lust and a taste for adventure.

---

* Her sixth cousin, so they were not closely related; King Henry was her eighth cousin.

According to Culpeper's confession, Catherine had warned him not to tell anyone about their affair, not even a priest at confession. Both would have believed that if they died with the guilt of adultery unconfessed, they would go to Hell, but Catherine was also aware of the risks of confession to her mortal life. This was a period when many boys went into the priesthood just for steady employment. There were constant complaints that there were too many priests and that many of them could not read or write even in English, never mind in Latin. Therefore, throughout the mass, which was entirely in Latin, many priests were probably talking nonsense – not that any of the congregation would be likely to notice. Only around court and the universities of Oxford and Cambridge would there be found someone who could correct a priest's Latin.

Catherine felt that Henry would definitely find out about their affair if Culpeper confessed to a priest, as the king was the supreme head of the Church. She may have meant that as the king was almost a demigod in his subjects' eyes, he would know the content of all people's confessions. But she also may have realised that although priests swore oaths that they would never tell what was mentioned in the confessional, it would put the priest in a difficult position if he knew the truth – and in a potentially powerful one. But such a relationship could only be kept secret for so long.

Culpeper was reckless and rash; he was also a rapist and a murderer. It was only his friendship with Henry that had saved him from the death penalty. He was around ten years older than Catherine and twenty years younger than her husband. Catherine wrote to Culpepper: 'It makes my heart die to think I cannot be always in your company.'[14]

Yet when Catherine was confronted, she put the blame wholly on the scheming Lady Rochford and the pestering Thomas Culpeper. Jane Rochford was shocked by this and told what she believed to be the truth – that 'considering all the things that she hath heard and seen between them' she was sure that Catherine and Thomas had been lovers. It is surprising that Catherine's accomplice in this affair was Lady Jane Rochford, the widow of George Boleyn. She should have been fully aware of the danger Catherine was placing herself in just by spending time alone with a young man; Lady Rochford should also have known of the dangers to herself. Culpeper, like Catherine, denied that they had actually had sexual intercourse, but said that 'he intended and meant to do ill with the Queen and in likewise the Queen so minded to do with him'.[15] Dereham was, at this point, in the clear. Then someone came forward and said that they had heard Dereham say he might marry the queen if the king died.

Chapuys remarked on how Henry had been almost triumphant when it was 'discovered' that Anne Boleyn had committed adultery; but with Catherine it was very different indeed. He was madly in love with his wife and deeply saddened that he had been tricked. He had worked his way through five brides and was single once again. For an old romantic and a traditionalist at heart, this would have been devastating; from that time on, Henry appears to us as an old and increasingly dangerous man. Chapuys wrote that Henry's

> case resembles very much that of the woman who cried more bitterly for the loss of her tenth husband than she had on the death of the other nine put together: the reason being that she had never buried one of them without being sure of the next, but that after the tenth husband she had no other in view.[16]

The situation was replicating the fall of the queen's cousin Anne, but this time the allegations were true. Henry's wife really had committed adultery, and had really had sexual intercourse with more than one man. The marriage truly was invalid. All the key players were guilty of treason. Francis I, who had married women he was not attracted to, commented that Catherine 'hath done wondrous naughty' and sent his rival Henry a letter of condolence.[17] Henry had been publicly humiliated by this – all of Christendom knew him to be a cuckold, twice over. Henry seems to have taken some time to accept that this had really happened.

In a rage he 'shouted for a sword with which to slay the girl who had betrayed him, and he swore aloud that she would never have "such delight in her incontinency as she should have torture in her death"'.[18] The monarch then broke into a cringeworthy display of weeping, while his Council stood there, unsure what to do. He then bizarrely claimed that the Council were responsible for 'this last mischief' and felt he had suffered 'ill-luck in meeting with such ill-conditioned wives'.[19] This time he had no pretty maid of honour to sweep off her feet – indeed, he could barely walk on his own; this time, he was still madly in love with his wife; this time it was all true.

He embarrassed his courtiers by openly weeping, not bothering to hide his desolation. For days this continued, and then Henry realised that the show must go on. He began flirting with the ladies of the court. Henry was finally informed that Catherine had admitted most of the accusations against her and he described her as 'that wicked woman'.[20] Like the other three wives he had discarded, he did not say goodbye. Catherine lamented the 'gracious and loving prince I had' to Cranmer.[21] He had been so in love with her that his councillors were determined to ensure that she did not see him again, as they believed she may win him round.

Catherine's family and friends, those who had been leaching off her for the last two years, quickly distanced themselves from the fallen queen. Most of her close relatives had been sent to the Tower. The duke of Norfolk denounced Catherine publicly, but as his family were in danger, it is understandable that he wished to disassociate himself from his niece; he was in fear of his life. He went so far as to declare that Catherine should be burnt alive.[22] A power vacuum was being created at court – the Howards remain an aristocratic family to this day, but they never quite recovered the influence they had during Henry VIII's reign.

Adultery was a king's birthright; fidelity was a queen's obligation. It was a double standard, but it made sense. If Henry had an affair during marriage and fathered a child, it was unlikely to damage the monarchy. The child would be well provided for, and so would the mother. If a queen had an affair during marriage and conceived, then somebody else's bastard could inherit the throne of England. In an age where people believed in the divine right of kings, this situation would have been against God's ordained social order and therefore a challenge to God's authority. It was unthinkable for a queen to allow any hint of scandal about her; she must be completely and utterly above reproach.

Yet Catherine Howard was a queen who dared to play the role of a mistress. She was only the second queen in English history who historians believe was unfaithful to her royal husband. (The first was Isabella the 'She-Wolf', Edward II's wife; and she had far greater provocation, as her husband neglected her in favour of his homosexual lovers. Historians are almost unanimous in considering Anne Boleyn innocent of adultery.) The example of Anne Boleyn should have been foremost in the mind of any woman agreeing to marry Henry, and for Catherine it should have been more so as Anne was her cousin. She has been portrayed as a stupid slut and as a romantic heroine. The truth seems to have been that her affair was based on lust, not love; she was happy to blame Culpeper for the whole sorry mess.

Dereham was disembowelled and castrated while conscious; he suffered the death the law demanded of a common traitor. Culpeper – the king's former friend and from a more genteel family than Dereham's – was beheaded. Then, in an eerie repeat of her cousin's fate six years before, Catherine Howard's marriage was annulled two days before her execution. She was beheaded on the same block, in the same place, before being buried beside Queen Anne in St Peter ad Vincula, Tower of London, condemned for having led 'an abominable, base, carnal, voluptuous and vicious life' and having behaved 'like a common harlot with divers persons'.[23] She was executed on the eve of St Valentine's Day, 13 February 1542, three months after she had been arrested. They may have waited this length of time to see if she was pregnant, although the paternity would have been in doubt. She was very weak and upset but managed to compose herself.

Henry was a shattered man; the wife who had given him a renewed zest for life had betrayed him. It was enough to smash anyone's ego to smithereens, and as Henry's ego was bigger than most, it had a devastating effect on him. This whole fiasco did nothing for his chances of marrying a foreign princess. Christendom was shocked by the English king's behaviour – a prince was expected to marry, maybe annul *one* marriage if the woman was sterile, and to have mistresses. He had now annulled four of his five marriages and executed two of his wives. The slim chance he had previously had of marrying a princess had turned to nil. If he married again – for a *sixth* time – it would have to be to an Englishwoman again and he had had little success with his choice of English aristocrats so far.

On the day that Catherine was condemned, 29 January 1542, Chapuys wrote to Charles V: 'The King has shown no inclination whatever to a fresh marriage nor paid attention to any lady of his court.'[24] Yet this soon changed. In February it was reported that

Since he was informed of the trial and subsequent condemnation on the 29th [January], he has considerably changed, for on the night of that day he gave a grand supper, and invited to it several ladies and gentlemen of his court … the lady for whom he showed the greatest predilection on the occasion was no other than the sister of Mr Cobham, the same lady whom Master Wyatt did some time ago repudiate on a charge of adultery. She is a pretty young creature and has sense enough to do as the others have done should she consider it worth her while. It is also rumoured that the King has taken a fancy for the daughter of Madame Albart, the niece of the Grand Esquire, Master Anthony Browne, and likewise for a daughter by the first marriage of the wife of [Lord] Lisle* This last attachment of the King, as the report goes, is founded on the fact that the above-mentioned official, who for the last two years has been kept a prisoner at the Tower, has all of a sudden obtained his liberty.[25]

The whole court was on the lookout for the woman Henry would choose as his sixth wife.

As Henry slowly evolved into an obese and bald monarch who had to be carried around in a sedan chair, his leg oozing pus, he no longer maintained mistresses. His fifty-seven-inch chest and fifty-four-inch waist were not as alluring as in his younger days, but Henry did not give up trying to impress the ladies. Two beautiful ladies-in-waiting, each an intelligent and amiable woman, missed out on the booby prize. Anne Bassett was a popular, shy and well-respected maid of honour who did not, as far as we are aware, accept the king's advances; Elizabeth Brooke was the opposite, a married woman notorious for her adultery. It was understood that if another woman entranced him, it would mean a crown.

Anne of Cleves herself seems to have hoped that Henry would take her back after the execution of Catherine Howard; she is said to have given way to 'great grief and despair' when he did not.[26] Her brother, Duke William, clearly believed this to be a possibility; he pursued this to an embarrassing extent, forcing the Council to issue a formal rebuff. This was surprising; Anne had not demurred when she had been discarded, and two years on Henry was an even less enticing prospect, having executed another wife. It is likely that it was her family who were pushing for this, and not Anne herself.

---

* Elizabeth Brooke was described by Chapuys as a 'pretty young creature'. She had first given birth in 1521; her eldest son was twenty-one years old. Even if she was then only thirteen (which is unlikely) she would have been thirty-four when she was described as 'young'. The details given by Chapuys clearly indicate Elizabeth Brooke, who was both the sister of Lord Cobham and the wife of Thomas Wyatt. The use of the word 'young' could be argued to indicate that this was another Elisabeth Brooke, Elizabeth Brooke Wyatt's niece. She was a beautiful woman; however it probably suggests that Elizabeth Brooke Wyatt was simply youthful-looking. As Anne Bassett was both a close relative of Anthony Browne and the daughter of Lady Lisle, it is likely that these rumours were both referring to her.

There were fewer women at court after Catherine's execution. All the ladies-in-waiting were sent home, some had been sent away even earlier to attend to the queen in her last days. Henry kept only one maid of honour at court: Anne Bassett. She was paid even when there was no queen to serve, and later impressed Queen Mary enough to be made a lady of the Privy Chamber in her reign.[27]

Although Henry had been fond of his uncle, Anne's stepfather Lord Lisle, he had been under suspicion of plotting to betray Calais to the French and had been languishing in the Tower since March 1540. The family were lucky that Henry allowed Anne to stay and serve Catherine Howard and Katheryn Parr, as well as to bring her mother and sister to court. Henry was apparently arranging a marriage for her, as she had no male relative to do this for her. It is possible that Henry, ever wanting to have another woman lined up, was considering Anne for himself.

When Jane Seymour was pregnant, Lady Lisle had sent her some quails, which she had been informed that the queen was craving. Jane took the not-so-subtle hint and invited the two Bassett girls to court, to choose one to be her lady-in-waiting. She chose Anne, aged around sixteen, rather than her sister Katherine. Although she was required by Jane to dress conservatively, Anne was described as a 'pretty, young creature', 'fair, well-made and behaveth herself so well that everybody praiseth her that seeth her'. The king had apparently commented that she was *'far fairer'* than her sister.[28] She set off for her new glamorous position at court, and arrived in time for the queen's funeral. It was then back to her parents' home in Calais, as there was then no queen to serve.

If Henry did consider marrying Anne Bassett, she may have had her family's previous mistakes counting against her. As well as her stepfather's alleged treason, there was her sister's indiscretion. Elizabeth Bassett had acquired a position as maid of honour to the king's 'sister', Lady Anne of Cleves. She was reported and imprisoned for her comments on the king's love life. She and her friend Jane Rattsey were said to have discussed Queen Catherine's execution, wondering 'Is God working his own work to make the Lady Anne of Cleves queen again?' and Elizabeth commented, 'What a man is the King! How many wives will he have?'[29]

Anne Bassett was Henry's first cousin (by marriage) so he would have needed another dispensation if he had wished to marry her. One concern about Henry marrying Anne would have been her age. He had married a vivacious teenage lady-in-waiting two years before and it had ended in degradation and decapitation. He did not wish to repeat this fiasco. He seems to have made this decision then with his head rather than his heart when he instead chose a sensible and intelligent woman, Katheryn Parr, as his companion through old age.

Anne Bassett remained single until 1554, when in her early thirties she married Sir Walter Hungerford, who was twelve years her junior.[30] He regained the title of baron, attainted when his father had been the first person to be executed for homosexuality in England, in 1540. Anne died in 1557. We do not know whether Henry chose to pursue his attraction to Anne Bassett or Elizabeth Brooke further. It was probably too soon for Henry to do more than show some interest in other women; he was, understandably, still devastated by his wife's betrayal. Henry had ordered Wyatt to take his adulterous wife back shortly before. But either lady would have made a very interesting Queen of England.

The king passed a new law; if a woman was to marry the king she had to declare everything about any past sexual affairs. For her not to do so was treason. Even more damning, anyone who knew anything untoward about the woman and did not inform the king was also guilty of treason. The courtiers had made careers out of attracting the king's attentions to their family members; now it was clearly a dangerous gamble. Few women at the English court had not had some relationship that could be considered a precontract, or had not been involved in a sexual affair; even if they had not, one could easily be fabricated and all her friends and family brought down with her. It is significant that all the women Henry was attracted to from this point onwards seem not to have been interested in him.

Chapter 13

How Many Wives
Will He Have?

'Virtue to use;
Vice to refuse
I shall use me …'

Just over a year after Catherine's execution, to many people's surprise, Henry married for a sixth time. On 12 July 1543 the king wed Katheryn Parr[*] with only seventeen people present. The only fitting end to the matrimonial career of England's most-married king was for him to make Katheryn the nation's most-married queen. She had been married twice before and would go on to marry for a fourth time after his death. Katheryn had all the skills needed to be queen to the ailing English king – but she would be in danger every day of their marriage.

At the end of 1542, Katheryn and her elderly husband, Lord Latimer, had based themselves in London, where he appeared to be slowly dying. Katheryn nursed him until the end, and visited court often, but did not have an official position there. Her uncle, brother and sister – all of whom she

---

[*] I have chosen to use this spelling of her name because she always wrote it herself as 'Kateryn' or 'Katheryn'. I also wish to limit any confusion with the many other Katherines to be mentioned here – Queen Katherine of Aragon, Queen Catherine Howard, Catherine Carey and Katherine Willoughby – I have varied these spellings only to differentiate between these women.

was close to – served the king and queen, and during this time she would have had the opportunity to see Henry. After her husband's death, Katheryn became the lady-in-waiting of Henry's daughter, Mary; they knew each other from childhood as their mothers had been close friends. Soon there were reports that the king had begun to visit Mary more often.

Unlike ladies in the past, Henry's final wife did not have to help overthrow her predecessor to get the position of queen; Henry made it very clear from the beginning that she had been selected not merely for the role of mistress, but for advancement to the throne. We have records of Henry sending gifts to Katheryn from 16 February 1543 – a fortnight *before* her husband died. He had not married one of the seductive maids of honour who had attracted him the year before, and no doubt there were others during 1542 and 1543. It was now a year, almost to the day, since Catherine Howard had been executed, and Henry was ready for a new wife – but he did not want to repeat the mistakes of the past.

It was, for Katheryn, a case of being in the wrong place at the wrong time. Henry had now recovered from his last wife's betrayal and the idea of another Queen Katheryn did not disconcert him; it was after all an age where nearly every lady at court was named Anne, Elizabeth, Katherine or Mary. Henry had also, again, chosen the antithesis of his last love. Mistress Parr was sensible and serious where Mistress Howard had been flirty and fickle; Katheryn was someone with whom Henry could enjoy entertainments and dancing, or discuss academic and religious issues. She was not a woman who would recklessly take a lover while married to the king. She seemed the perfect choice.

But not so in Katheryn's eyes. Having done more than her duty in marrying twice for her family, and having just finished nursing a very ill old man, she felt that she deserved some happiness. Katheryn seems to have fallen for the very charming Sir Thomas Seymour. Her feelings were clearly reciprocated; although Lady Latimer was a widow of some means, the uncle of the future king was a man who could aim for a better match. Seymour had to stop courting her the minute Henry made his intentions clear, but Katheryn's feelings for Seymour do not seem to have completely disappeared.

Henry had been six foot two inches tall with a thirty-five-inch waist around the time of his affair with Bessie Blount.[1] By now, he had a fifty-seven-inch chest and fifty-four-inch waist. Katheryn is said to have remarked 'Better to be his mistress than his wife'.[2] This was very different to Anne

Boleyn's attitude that 'your wife I cannot be, your mistress I shall not be', but then Katheryn had learnt lessons from the examples of Anne and her three successors and this showed clearly in her marriage. Katheryn was also no longer in her prime. At thirty-one she was considered to be at the end of her childbearing years. She had also been married twice without having a child; it was therefore widely assumed that she was infertile – but Henry had not got a woman pregnant since 1537, six years earlier.

Katheryn may have been horrified at the thought of marrying Henry, but there was one woman who allegedly *did* desire it. He

> heard in a good quarter that the said lady [Anne of Cleves] would like to be in her shirt (so to speak) with her mother, having especially taken great grief and despair at the King's espousal of this last wife, who is not nearly so beautiful as she, besides that there is no hope of issue, seeing that she had none with her two former husbands.[3]

Anne may not have seen the attraction, but Katheryn's appearance was obviously far more to Henry's taste than hers had been. She was around five foot two inches or so tall, with curly red hair.[4] She even took regular baths, unlike Anne of Cleves. It was Katheryn's personality that drew the compliments; we do not have one compliment on record for her looks.

Anne of Cleves seems not to have given up hope of re-marrying Henry and being reinstated as Queen of England. Even after Henry's death, Anne petitioned Queen Mary for acknowledgement of her position as dowager queen. Katheryn Parr, who had held this title, was then dead, but to be given this name – and the pensions and position that would come with it – would be declaring Anne's marriage to Henry had been valid after all. The Council fobbed her off, claiming that they were too busy to discuss it. Anne died on 16 July 1557, probably of cancer and was buried at Westminster Abbey.

Henry does not seem to have noticed, or cared, that Katheryn was less than swooning at the idea of marrying this grumpy old man. Perhaps he mistakenly thought he was more attractive than he was – perhaps he simply did not see her feelings as relevant. It is unlikely that he was passionately in love with her although he did find her attractive. She was nothing like Catherine Howard, who had oozed sexuality, but she was charming, intelligent and trustworthy – and as time went on, he would have appreciated her good company and nursing skills. The reports from their early marriage show a couple who complemented one another well, but whose relationship was founded on respect and friendship, not passion.

Within a month of Lord Latimer's death, Katheryn's family were reaping the benefits of Henry's interest. Her brother, William Parr, and soon afterwards her brother-in-law, William Herbert, were showered with favours. The Boleyns and the Howards had benefited in the short term from Henry marrying into their family, and the Seymours were firmly established as the relatives of the Prince of Wales; the Parrs would have coveted this. The family pressure on Katheryn to encourage Henry's advances would have been very strong.

Although Henry VIII inherited a solvent estate, his father had damaged the fortunes of many noble families to make this possible. One of the victims of Henry VII's economic policies had been the Parr family. They owed nearly £9,000 to the king by the time he died because they had been asked to pay for the privileges they had enjoyed free of charge for generations. Their family estates, including Kendal Castle in Westmoreland, could not pay off the crippling debt, as it only earned them around £150 per year.[5] Katheryn's family were unable to arrange glittering marriages for all three of the children. Maud Parr had had to call in every favour she could to secure the highly eligible Lady Anne Bourchier for her son, and it seemed at the time that her two daughters, Katheryn, future queen, and Anne, future countess, could expect to struggle to marry at all. In the end, because Katheryn appealed to the king, no dowry was necessary.

Katheryn did her duty and married the now old and very irritable King Henry. They wed at Hampton Court four months after her second husband's death, with a select few people present. These included two of the king's previous brothers-in-law, Edward Seymour, brother of the late Queen Jane, and Edward Baynton, brother-in-law of Catherine Howard; as well as Thomas Cranmer, a close family friend of the Boleyns, and Sir Anthony Browne, whose sister and niece were rumoured to have been mistresses of Henry's. It also included at least one woman who would attract his attention later in the reign.

The new queen showed herself to be a deeply religious woman who loved learning, but she was also energetic and enjoyed dancing and fashion. She had a temper – she once wrote of her brother-in-law: 'It was fortunate we were so much distant for I suppose else I should have bitten him.'[6] She was affectionate towards the rest of her family and fiercely loyal. But while she was married to Henry, she had to be very, very careful that the more forceful parts of her personality were kept under wraps. She may not have been constantly at court during his other marriages, but she was well aware of the danger she was now in.

Katheryn was thirty-one, unostentatiously attractive and a popular choice with ambassadors, commoners and courtiers alike. She was well-liked by her three stepchildren, who seem to have felt secure with her. Under the reign of Anne Boleyn, Princess Mary had been treated badly. Jane Seymour had been kind to Mary, but her marriage had stripped Elizabeth of her status. Anne of Cleves had only reigned for a few short months and Catherine Howard had been at loggerheads with Mary, while seeing little of Elizabeth. Katheryn Parr finally united all of Henry's children, and helped make the Tudors a family for the very first time, living up to her motto, to be 'useful in all I do'.

Katheryn ensured that Elizabeth was treated well and was influential in securing the young girl, by now ten years old, a first-class education, which helped prepare her for running the country. Katheryn is thought to have appointed the renowned scholar John Cheke as principal tutor to Prince Edward. Cheke was a Protestant and is widely thought to have influenced Edward to adopt the 'new ways'. It is clear that all three stepchildren greatly loved and respected Queen Katheryn. For the first time, Henry had chosen a woman with experience of marriage, running a household and stepchildren.

Anne and Mary Boleyn, Mary Shelton and Katheryn Parr, all benefited from a far greater education than women of the generation before them. In the cases of Anne and Katheryn, the king was probably attracted to them because they were cultured and clever. Katheryn Parr spoke English, Latin, French and Italian, and had books in all these languages; she also began to learn Spanish in 1546. Her group of friends, including women Henry was linked to such as Katherine Willoughby and Mary Howard, spent much of their time in theological discussions and study, not just in doing the intricate embroidery that had been the main pastime during the reigns of previous queens. This gave the women, with their understanding of religion and politics, more scope to influence the king, if they knew how to persuade him that it had been his idea all along.

Katheryn's sister, Anne Parr, had worked in the household of all Henry's queens and so would have been a valuable chief lady-in-waiting. She had seen the terrible effect Henry's cruel treatment had had on Katherine of Aragon; his flaunting of Anne Boleyn before the court and then his brutal disposal of her; his search for a fourth wife before Jane Seymour was cold in the ground. She had also witnessed his distasteful treatment of Anne of Cleves and had served Catherine Howard in the palaces and in the Tower while she was awaiting execution. Anne may have advised Katheryn on the mistakes of Henry's first five wives – certainly Katheryn, of all his queens, demonstrated an excellent understanding of how to handle her husband.

Both Katheryn's parents, the charming Thomas Parr and his wife, the independent and extremely capable Maud Parr, had been at court during the celebratory beginning to Bluff King Hal's reign. Maud could easily be called a 'modern woman'. Unusually for the sixteenth century, she appears to have been close to her children. As her mother spent much of her time at court, Katheryn may have been there as a child and so met Henry. She is thought to have shared some of her early education with Princess Mary, although much of Katheryn's learning was developed as an adult and it is unlikely she had a first-rate education.

Maud has impressed historians, not just for the way she gave her daughters as fine an education as she gave her son, but for her independence. She managed her estates efficiently and chose to remain a widow although she was still an attractive young woman when her husband died. Maud was chosen to be a lady-in-waiting to Katherine of Aragon and became close to her. Although she was seven years younger than the queen, she nevertheless would have been a woman deserving of her friendship and respect. Outgoing, strong-willed and committed scholars, they would have had much in common. It is also likely that, as queen, Katherine of Aragon would have been the godmother to her lady-in-waiting's first surviving child, who was born in 1512. It was usual to name children after one of the godparents. It is likely that the first of Henry's Queen Katherines was the godmother to his last Queen Katherine.[7]

Her first marriage was to Edward Borough when she was only fifteen. They lived in Lincolnshire, which Henry referred to as 'one of the most brute and beastly [shires] of the whole realm'.[8] Their marriage lasted four years, until his death in 1533. She secured a significant inheritance after the death of her husband and so had been in a position to negotiate a good second marriage. When Katheryn decided to marry again, she had no parents alive to help her and seems not to have needed the assistance of her substitute father, her uncle Sir William Parr of Horton. A few months after Borough's death, Katheryn married Lord Latimer of Snape, Yorkshire, a kinsman of hers. This was a step up – she was now Lady Latimer and only one of her female relatives and ancestors had managed to get herself a title; Katheryn had now already married slightly above her station.

During the Pilgrimage of Grace in 1536, Lord Latimer had showed himself to have none of the strength of mind his wife possessed. Virtually kidnapped by the rebels who were gathering numbers in the north of England in protest at the dissolution of the monasteries, Latimer became a spokesman for the malcontents who were marching against the king's 'evil advisers' who had caused him to break with Rome. His level of involvement is debated – whether he led the rebels as a frightened figurehead or out of a genuine commitment. He certainly agreed with the complaints of the common people who were showing no sign of disbanding quietly; but he did not want to risk everything he had by joining the protest. Katheryn's ex-father-in-law, Lord Borough, had also been kidnapped by the marchers, but he had managed to escape – the king was very suspicious as to why Lord Latimer had not done the same. Latimer was known to be a conservative, and so was now at grave risk of execution for treason, and of having all his property confiscated.

The rebels sent Lord Latimer to Henry as their figurehead; he was to pass on their demands. When he arrived, he threw himself on the king's mercy and condemned the rebels, declaring that he had been too in fear of his life to denounce them earlier. When the rebels heard of Latimer's defection, they kidnapped Katheryn and her stepchildren. Their house was burgled, and they were held hostage – Latimer had to return to Yorkshire and sweet-talk the rebels into leaving his family home.

Latimer's involvement in the Pilgrimage of Grace left Katheryn unsure of the roof over her head and in fear for her and her stepchildren's lives. If he was judged a traitor, all his belongings would be forfeited to the crown; Katheryn would be reduced to relying on her family's charity. Two of Latimer's brothers were declared traitors and executed, as were several of his friends and kinsmen. Katheryn was lucky that her brother and uncle, as northern lords, were trusted by the king to march against the 'pilgrims' with the duke of Norfolk. It was Norfolk who was charged with providing evidence of treason against Katheryn's husband. Despite Cromwell saying that the king expected, and so wanted, Lord Latimer to be found guilty,[9] Norfolk insisted he saw no evidence – in fact the evidence was very similar to that against his condemned brothers.

Although the widow of a suspected rebel, Katheryn does not seem to have had her own reputation damaged. The king, as with each of his wives except Anne of Cleves, was eager to give Katheryn all she wanted and was clearly very fond of her. However, he was not a man to be depended upon. It was also a dangerous time for those who had been close to Katheryn previously. It is likely that if Thomas Seymour had not kept himself away from court, then rumours would have abounded that Katheryn had been as adulterous as the last Queen Catherine. By sixteenth-century standards, Katheryn, the author of bestselling books and a woman who acted as if she was equal to men, was clearly unable to control her own behaviour and was guilty of upsetting God's ordained social order. Seymour had wisely spent much of Katheryn's reign abroad. While she was queen, no hint of such scandal was made, but as soon as Henry died, this changed.

Henry is widely perceived to have been almost infertile, yet his wives and lovers conceived many times. He had at least two sons and two daughters who survived to adulthood, a perfectly respectable tally for a sixteenth-century man. Many people had large families but many also did not; Henry was not seen by his contemporaries as anything more than unlucky. The only reason people expected more of Henry was because he had had so many different partners – and three out of his six wives never conceived by him at all.

If Henry was fertile but unlucky up until then, he seems to have been infertile by the time he married his next lover, Catherine Howard. Her previous sexual experience, with at least one man, had not resulted in pregnancy, but during her relationship with Dereham she had boasted to her friends that she knew how to prevent a pregnancy. It is extremely doubtful, however, that she would have wished to prevent conceiving the future King of England. Henry, also, was forty-seven years old by the time of his fifth marriage and would be unlikely to be as fertile as in his youth.

It is likely then that by the 1540s Henry was infertile. There was never so much as a rumour that Queen Katheryn was with child and there were no high expectations of the new queen bearing a duke of York. Catherine Howard had married Henry when he was forty-seven and she was a teenager; she did not conceive, but then, as we know, she had not from her earlier relationship either. Katheryn Parr had not conceived by her first two husbands and was thirty-one when she married Henry, yet she did conceive after his death, aged thirty-six and soon into her fourth marriage.

There were still banquets and dancing, but Katheryn created a social life for Henry that suited the ageing monarch – conversation and music with her trustworthy friends in her own apartments. History showed she must watch her ladies-in-waiting like a hawk, to see if one would become the figurehead of a faction to have her overthrown. Katheryn, for all her abilities, and with Henry now aged fifty-two and not so quick to run after the latest pretty girl at court, still needed to keep an eye out for predators. Katheryn's ladies wore black, conservative outfits which were probably designed to present a virtuous exterior and not to attract attention. A letter from Henry to Katheryn in 1544 shows that she had asked his approval to appoint new ladies-in-waiting, to replace some women who were ill. Henry felt that the women Katheryn had chosen were too old and dowdy but accepted that it was her decision.

Her friends included her sister-in-law, the beautiful Elisabeth Brooke (not to be confused with her aunt, Elizabeth Brooke, the wife of Sir Thomas Wyatt who attracted Henry in 1542), and other attractive women such as Joan Champernowne. Joan, although married, was renowned for her beauty and brains, which Henry must have noticed. He was linked to two of Katheryn's other friends during their marriage: Katherine Willoughby, duchess of Suffolk, and Mary Howard, duchess of Richmond and Somerset. These women had all the qualities to entrance Henry if they put their mind to it. They would also have had a powerful support network behind them. But they were loyal to Katheryn and it is them she surrounded the king with.

Katheryn played the role of consort well, but slowly Katheryn Parr began to make enemies at court. One reason for this was her increasingly obvious heretical views; many conservatives were concerned that a woman suspected of Lutheran leanings had such influence over the king, the Prince of Wales and both princesses; all four royals clearly loved her and respected her opinion. She was not the traditional idea of a Christian wife and mother; she wrote books, she studied, she rejected the traditional feminine pastime of embroidery. The increasing opinion among the conservatives was that the queen was a shrew – and if she was capable of going against what a woman should be to this extent, then what else was she capable of?

Katheryn was given many reminders that her position was vulnerable. In 1545 Henry commissioned portraits to depict the mighty Tudor dynasty. He had three healthy children, and a loyal wife. The dynasty looked more secure. One painting showed King Henry, the queen, and his parents, Henry VII and Elizabeth of York. Another showed Henry and the queen with Edward, painted as if the three of them were the Holy Family, with Mary and Elizabeth on the edges of the portrait; their mothers did not feature.

But the queen by Henry VIII's side in these pictures was not his dedicated wife of two years, Katheryn Parr; it was a woman who had died eight years earlier – Jane Seymour.

Henry later referred to Jane as his 'true wife', 'entirely beloved', and with the passing of the years she was put onto a higher and higher pedestal in Henry's mind. Katheryn was not considered part of the Tudor dynasty, as she had not given him a son. Henry blamed his wives, as was the belief then, for his lack of offspring – therefore Jane's memory was elevated higher and higher after her death as she was the only successful one – and as God decided who would have children, she was the only union which God had approved of – giving birth to girls did not count. And Katheryn Parr had not even given him that. Within a few months, rumours spread throughout Europe that Henry had fallen in love with one of Katheryn's ladies-in-waiting.

Chapter 14

Queen Katherine the Fourth?

Katherine Willoughby was aged around twenty-five at the time of Henry's sixth marriage. She was the daughter of William, Lord Willoughby d'Eresby and Maria de Salinas, the woman 'whom she [Katherine of Aragon] loves more than any other mortal'.[1] Katherine Willoughby was brought up at Grimsthorpe, Lincolnshire, until William died in 1526. Her mother was a close friend of both Katherine of Aragon and Henry's sister, Mary the French Queen. Henry had liked Maria enough to name a ship after her and Katherine had been the second mourner at Katherine of Aragon's funeral due to the close connections between the families and Willoughby's high rank.

Her father had been very wealthy and most of his estate was left to his only child. Katherine thus became the 12th Baroness Willoughby d'Eresby and owner of much of Lincolnshire when she was only seven years old. Her wardship automatically belonged to the king and he sold this to Charles Brandon, 1st duke of Suffolk, who initially betrothed her to his son and heir, Henry Brandon, earl of Lincoln, the nephew of Henry VIII. This would have placed her children in the line of succession.

Yet in 1533, within three months of his beloved wife's death, Suffolk had married his young ward himself. The earl of Lincoln died soon after, according to Anne Boleyn, of a broken heart. Despite the thirty-five-year age difference, it was a successful marriage and they had two sons, Henry and Charles. Suffolk was the king's closest friend, which is why he rose to a dukedom within five years of Henry's accession, despite not coming from an aristocratic family. The knight's son had gone on to marry

Henry's sister, Princess Mary. Katherine Willoughby, duchess of Suffolk, had not only been married to Henry's brother-in-law, but was Katherine of Aragon's goddaughter. In an age where sister-in-law meant literally that the law regarded that woman as your sister, connections between in-laws and between godparents and their godchildren were grey areas and considered semi-incestuous.

It is ironic that as Henry aged, many of the women he became attracted to were named after his first wife. It was customary for courtiers to name a daughter after the reigning queen, and therefore many women a generation younger than Henry were named Katherine. Like Katheryn Parr, Katherine Willoughby's mother had been a close friend of Katherine of Aragon. Maria de Salinas, who had come from Spain to serve Katherine of Aragon before she married Henry, had married the English Lord Willoughby and so never returned to her homeland.

Katherine Willoughby seems to have been an independent woman; after Suffolk's death in 1545, we have no talk of the very eligible duchess trying to arrange a new marriage for herself. Around the time of the rumours that Henry intended to marry her, she was beginning a relationship with her master of the horse, who she went on to marry.

Known for her sharp tongue, intelligence and strong religious views, Katherine Willoughby was a force to be reckoned with. If she had chosen to pursue Henry, Katherine would almost certainly have taken Katheryn Parr's place, with her friend perhaps ending up on the executioner's block. If her husband had died two years earlier, before Henry married his sixth wife, Katherine might have become Queen of England then. There is much in the imperious determination, wit, fearlessness and fierce intelligence of Katherine that is similar to the character of Anne Boleyn.

Katherine named her dog Gardiner after the bishop of Winchester and was not afraid to publicly show her hatred of such a powerful man. The influential councillor would happily have had her sent to the block. It may have been Gardiner's attempt to disconcert the queen and her friend that led to the rumours that Henry was planning to rid himself of Katheryn Parr in favour of Katherine Willoughby. As the leader of the conservative faction he may have supplied information to the Imperial ambassador, including reports about Henry's attraction to the duchess.

At this time, Katherine Willoughby was the most powerful unmarried woman in the country. She was not only described as 'a lady of sharp wit and sure hand to thrust it home and make it pierce when she pleased', she also received the ultimate Tudor accolade from John Parkhurst – as equal to 'men of the highest distinction'.[2] She was an ardent Protestant who allegedly converted her husband before he died in 1545. Bishop Gardiner, the man most desperate to arrange the downfall of Queen Katheryn Parr, was trying hard to bring down all the influential Protestant ladies at court. He hated Katheryn Parr, but he hated Katherine Willoughby even more. In 1555, during the reign of Queen Mary, Katherine and her new husband had to go into exile to avoid Gardiner's wrath.

In June 1546 a man named Robert Parker made a prophecy that there would soon be a new queen – these prophecies were common, but probably reflected local rumours. In this year, there were even rumours that Anne of Cleves had given birth to two children by the king. But towards the end of his reign, Henry arranged for his sixth wife to be arrested. Perhaps he genuinely believed she had committed treason, perhaps it was simply force of habit. Either way, Katheryn managed to beg the king for forgiveness and seduce him out of his dangerously bad mood. Although it was now clear that the dangers of attracting the king were even greater, so were the rewards.

In February 1546 Van der Delft, the Imperial ambassador, wrote:

> I hesitate to report there are rumours of a new queen. Some attribute it to the sterility of the present Queen, while others say that there will be no change during the present war. Madame Suffolk is much talked about and is in great favour; but the King shows no alteration in his behaviour to the Queen, although she is said to be annoyed by the rumour.[3]

Katheryn Parr may have been relieved that it was her principled friend who had allegedly attracted the king, rather than an unscrupulous woman of the court. His wife and her possible replacement were such close friends that when Queen Katheryn's daughter was orphaned in 1549, it was the duchess of Suffolk who took in the child and paid all expenses; she had even been one of the few to attend Henry's sixth wedding. Even so, there was still danger – whether Katherine encouraged the king or not, he made the decisions and if he had become determined to have her, he would have done so.

There was almost as much evidence to arrest and execute Katheryn Parr as there had been for Catherine Howard, and far more than against Anne Boleyn. Rumours of witchcraft had abounded about Anne, but Katheryn Parr knew many traditional treatments using herbs and natural ingredients – knowledge of healing could easily attract accusations that a woman was a witch. She also owned forbidden Protestant books which her husband had made illegal – the man she had sworn to obey, both as his subject and as his spouse. Although Katheryn was intelligent and diplomatic, Henry expected, like most men of the time, complete obedience from his wife. Henry allegedly complained about Katheryn: 'A good hearing it is when women become such clerks, and a thing much to my comfort, to come in mine old days to be taught by my wife.'[4]

Men in sixteenth-century England believed that 'Woman in her greatest perfection was made to serve and obey man'.[5] There was a certain way for a woman to be; this was a land of black and white, God and the Devil, and nothing in between. It was completely ingrained in Tudor society that women were the weaker sex in every way. They were liable to do whatever others influenced them to do; they had no moral courage and were naturally more inclined to follow the Devil's path. This was not just the opinion of men; women agreed. Even Elizabeth I, one of the greatest monarchs in English history, did not consider other women capable of her achievements.

On 4 July 1546 the Privy Council asked Katheryn's auditors to bring in her accounts, showing all that she owned; they were clearly anticipating her belongings being confiscated.[6] The king later told Dr Wendy of the plans. Whether at the king's instigation or on Wendy's own initiative, documents detailing the planned arrest were left just outside the queen's apartments. Katheryn seems to have thought quickly. She proclaimed that she was ill and called Henry to her in a bid to win back his affection. Where many might have been too petrified to think their way out of it, Katheryn acted decisively.

Henry began a theological discussion with his wife and she allegedly replied: 'Being made after the image of God, as the women were after their image, men ought to instruct their wives, who would do all their learning from them', and so would not debate with him. But Henry was not quite ready to let his wife off.

'Not by St Mary. You are become a doctor [of theology] able to instruct us and not to be instructed by us.' Here Katheryn Parr showed why she was, apart from her religious opinions, the perfect queen consort. Her inspired answer was that she had never believed the radical opinions she had set forth in their discussions. Se had only hoped to distract the king from his pain by debating with him and to benefit from his learned replies. She insisted she had been honoured 'to be taught by his Majesty, who was a prince of such excellent learning and wisdom'.

'And is it even so?' replied Henry. 'Then Kate, we are friends again.'

Wriothesley and forty guards came to arrest her at the appointed time. When they arrived at the queen's apartments, they were surprised to see that Henry was present.[7] Katheryn had chosen a good strategy – appealing to Henry's vast ego. The councillors were berated by the king and sent away with their tails between their legs.

Katheryn's intelligence had given her a vital advantage. At the beginning of the sixteenth century, a humanist education had become very popular among English aristocrats, and they arranged for their children to study languages, mathematics and philosophy. The influence of having a highly educated *female* heir to the throne was undoubtedly felt in the upper classes' fashion for giving their daughters the same tutors as their sons. There was no suggestion that their daughters would go to university (which would have been illegal) or work for a living (a ridiculous idea) but they could entertain and interest their husbands and help in the education of their own children, so they too could fit into court society. Literacy and numeracy skills would help in running the family's estates, but they did not want their daughters to become clerks.

The women of the court, like all Tudor women, could not vote for Parliament and were usually considered to be the property of their husbands or fathers. But with an amenable husband, life was good. Widows were often admired for the freedom they had, but there was one other way to be a free individual – by becoming the king's main mistress. One's income depended on the whim of the monarch, but a clever and attractive woman could acquire many expensive gifts during that time. These could then last her for many years. She could later negotiate a marriage on her own terms, if she wanted to, as she would be a woman of means. Yes, some of the most high-born families might shun the king's cast-offs, but she could make an excellent marriage if the dowry was large enough; only Bessie Blount managed to gain many of these benefits.

Henry clearly loved to display his allegiance and devotion to those he married – while they pleased him. He had his initials entwined with Katherine's, then Anne's, then Jane's, then another Anne's and two more Katherines' on the walls of each of his palaces. He publicly showed affection, love and respect for his wives. He tried to set up a culture of chivalry and courtly love to rival France and Burgundy and he was usually discreet in his infidelity. Yet Henry was a man of his time, who considered women inferior to men. When his daughter Mary finally agreed that she was illegitimate, the child of an incestuous union, and grovelled before the father who had done her so much wrong, Henry replied that it was 'the imbecility of her sex' that had led his daughter to disobey him.

As Katheryn found, the idea of a marriage where both parties took an equal share in the decision-making was alien to the sixteenth century. Men were the leaders, of every country and every household; exceptions were not seen to disprove the rule. Women were naturally inferior and could, like Eve, lead men to the Devil. Many quotes from the Bible were used to illustrate that this was the way God had ordained it. During Henry's reign it was illegal in London for a man to beat his wife after nine o'clock in the evening – not because it was immoral, but because people had been finding it difficult to sleep.

At the beginning of Henry's reign he had appreciated feisty females, but as he became more autocratic, his attitude to women hardened. Henry was a man more comfortable in the company of other men; although he clearly enjoyed women's company, there are no reports of real friendships with women. Katheryn Parr, on the whole, knew how far to push her husband. Once she was established as his wife, she became less cautious. And when she did, it led others to believe that Henry might be looking for a mistress or another wife.

It seems amazing that the Howards would still, four years after the execution of Catherine Howard, and eight years after the execution of Queen Anne Boleyn, consider attracting the king to their women as a recipe for the success of the clan. Yet the earl of Surrey encouraged his sister Mary to make herself the king's mistress, for the sake of the family. It is understandable that he felt she had a chance – her personality was similar to that of her cousin, Anne Boleyn, and Henry's attraction to members of the Howard family has been well documented. But this was not the 1520s and Henry was not an attractive prospect. Nor, after the execution of two Howard women, was attracting his attention risk-free.

Lady Mary had been born in 1519, and was twenty-eight when her family felt she may become Henry's next lover. The family had not fallen when Queen Catherine had been condemned and executed, but Henry was not one to forget such a humiliation. The king was well aware that he may not live to see his nine-year-old son reach adulthood, and any male with too much influence and too much royal blood was in danger at this point. Henry, earl of Surrey, was not only a Howard; he was also the grandson of Edward Stafford, duke of Buckingham, who had been executed for similar reasons in 1521.

On 2 December 1546 Surrey was arrested, and Norfolk was soon charged too; evidence was being gathered against them. Rumours were uncovered that the Howards were plotting to control young Edward when he became king; and there were reports that Surrey might be aiming for the throne himself. Surrey had used the arms of Edward the Confessor, from whom he was not descended – the Confessor had died childless – but his family had been granted permission to bear this, and they had done so for generations without controversy. This was now enough to be turned into a case of treason. And whether she meant it or not, the answers Mary Howard gave when she was questioned helped seal their fate.

Mary is not thought to have been close to either her brother or her father. She could not deny the family's plans to make her Henry's mistress, because she had told other courtiers about it at the time. Sir Gawen Carew reported:

> I have heard by the report of the Duchess of Richmond that the Earl of Surrey should give her advice, upon consultation had for the marriage of Sir Thomas Seymour and the said Duchess of Richmond, that, although her fantasy would not serve to marry with him [Seymour], yet, notwithstanding, she should dissemble the matter, and he would find the means, that the King's Majesty should speak with her himself; but that she should in nowise utterly make refusal of him, but that she should leave the matter so diffusely that the King's Majesty should take occasion to speak with her again; and thus by length of time it is possible that the King should take such a fantasy to you that ye shall be able to govern like unto Madame d'Étampes. Which should not only be a mean to help herself, but all her friends should receive a commodity by the same. Whereupon she defied her brother, and said that all they should perish and she would cut her own throat rather than she would consent to such a villainy.[8]

And it would have been villainy, for many reasons. Henry had conducted relationships with many of Mary's relatives, and she was his son's widow. The marriage may not have been consummated, but it would still make a relationship between her and the king complicated. She had been close to Anne Boleyn and had been of an age with Catherine Howard – both were her first cousins and people she spent most days with, and whose deaths must have touched her deeply. She was also a lady-in-waiting to the present queen, Katheryn Parr. Although Mary was not in Katheryn's closest circle, the two women shared much in common, including their increasingly Protestant views.

Mary, perhaps having seen two of her cousins beheaded after marrying the monarch, perhaps out of morality or perhaps because he was unattractive to her, was horrified. She reported the conversation when questioned about her brother and this helped seal his fate – he had already been arrested for comments he had made against the king and was executed soon after. By this point, Henry was so obese and diseased he had to be carried around in a sedan chair. She would have seen the dangers if her family did not – Norfolk once described his daughter as 'too wise for a woman'.[9] If ever there had been a doubt that acting as a pimp for the king was dangerous, Surrey's execution made this very clear. The likelihood is that she was scared for her own life. She would have been aware that Henry had his spies throughout the court and if she held back any information, this could be considered as treason.

It was the duchesse d'Étampes that Surrey had wanted his sister to emulate. The duchesse not only had a huge influence over the King of France, she was, like Mary Howard and the earl of Surrey, a Protestant. This was a much more dangerous theological position in Catholic France than it was in vacillating England. Yet Madame knew well how to manage her king and could protect those of a similar religious outlook. This may have been what Surrey was hoping for.

From 1529, the duchesse d'Étampes had been very influential on French foreign policy and had encouraged Francis to make peace with the German emperor. Anne Boleyn had encouraged Henry to try to make peace with France, but even Henry would have perceived that this was his best option when wishing to get the annulment to Katherine of Aragon sorted. The policy would most likely have been in place without the influence of Henry's prospective bride. Francis eventually stated that his mistress had too much influence over him.[10] Henry was never to make this mistake.

In the spring of 1546, a marriage had been proposed between Sir Thomas Seymour, the chancer who had caught Katheryn Parr's heart, and the duchess of Richmond. Allying themselves with a gentry family of low pedigree was a big comedown for the rapacious Howards. The Seymours may have provided Henry with a wife, but the Howards were a ducal family, and they had provided him with two. According to the reports, Mary said the marriage negotiations were in order for her to get close to the king and then become his mistress, to 'better rule here as others had done'.[11] They could have aimed her for a crown. But they were not even suggesting she aimed as high as her cousins Anne and Katherine, but merely as high as their other cousin, Mary Boleyn.

The king was understandably furious to hear that the Howards were trying to manipulate him. He prided himself on his Machiavellian manipulation of other people, ensuring that all court factions, all courtiers, were kept on their toes. He felt himself beholden to no man (or woman) and these reports would have brought back unpleasant memories of the disappointments he had suffered in the past. They considered Henry an old man who could be led around by the nose by a pretty woman. After Henry's besotted behaviour with two of Surrey's cousins, this was bound to hit a sore spot if repeated to the king.

In the Tower, Surrey wrote some of his best poetry, including on his closest friend who had died eleven years earlier: Henry Fitzroy, duke of Richmond and Somerset, his sister's late husband. Surrey wrote:

> With dazed eyes oft we, by gleams of love,
> Have missed the ball and got sight of our dame,
> To bait her eyes, which kept the leads above. [12]

Emphasising his relationship with Henry's beloved son did not help Surrey either.

Henry read through and underlined parts of the report of the interrogation of the duchess of Richmond. These included: 'If a man were to advise his sister to become a harlot thinking thereby to bring it to pass and so would rule both father and son.' [13] Henry was not a man to be ruled – and Surrey and Norfolk were sentenced to pay for their presumption, and with their heads. On 13 January 1547 both men were sentenced to death. Surrey was beheaded on 19 January 1547, but fate intervened for Norfolk, as the king died before he could suffer the same fate. He languished in the Tower until the reign of Queen Mary.

Just before Christmas 1546, Henry had sent his wife and children to Greenwich; he did not see them again. As when he had been gravely ill while married to Catherine Howard, he did not want his wife with him while he was in this state, despite Katheryn's excellent nursing skills. We cannot be sure whether Henry desired to see Katheryn over this time and his closest servants denied him, or if, as with all his other wives, Henry did not feel the need to say goodbye. Katheryn must have been desperate to see him – out of duty, and perhaps love, as well as hoping to secure the role of regent during the nine-year-old Edward's reign.

The king died on 28 January 1547. He was an obese fifty-five-year-old, who had been in intolerable pain for the last twenty years or so. We are unsure of the cause of death as he had been ill with several ailments for many years. It has been suggested that it was a pulmonary embolism, caused by the thrombosed vein in his leg which he had been suffering from for many years. He was buried, as he had requested, in St George's Chapel, Windsor, next to 'our true and loving Wife Queen Jane'.[14]

Elizabeth I described Sir Thomas Seymour as 'a man of much wit and very little judgement'.[15] When it came to Seymour, it seems Katheryn Parr had little judgement as well. Three months after Henry's death, the dowager queen married the new king's uncle, whose brother was now the Lord Protector, effectively running England until Edward VI was old enough to govern himself. Surprisingly, for such a sensible and religious woman, Katheryn seems to have become the lover of Thomas Seymour within weeks of her husband's death.

When Henry VIII's sister Mary was widowed in France, she was kept segregated in a palace until they could be sure that she was not pregnant with the king's child. No such tradition existed for English queens, and at thirty-five and childless, most of the English court assumed that she was barren. If Katheryn had been pregnant by Henry, she may not have known this until a few months after his death. The fact that within a month of his death, Katheryn was exchanging love letters and arranging midnight liaisons with her past paramour, could have endangered the Tudor dynasty. Katheryn seems to have become pregnant in November 1547, ten months after the king's death and around five months after her marriage to Thomas Seymour. She was by then thirty-six, unusually and dangerously late to be having her first child in the sixteenth century. She died of puerperal fever – as Jane Seymour and Elizabeth of York had – after giving birth to their daughter, Mary, deliriously blaming her husband.

Conclusion

Many kings had more wives than mistresses and Henry VIII has mistakenly been considered among them. Monarchs including Henry's father, were famed for their fidelity; Edward the Confessor refused to touch his own wife as he felt it was too sinful. Henry also had at least six mistresses that we are sure of, enough to at least equal his string of wives – Lady Anne Stafford, Bessie Blount, Mary Boleyn, 'the handsome young lady' of 1534, William Webbe's lover and Mary Shelton. One can confidently add to that list Étiennette de la Baume, Elizabeth Amadas and probably Jane Popincourt, Elizabeth Carew and Margaret Skipwith. There were undoubtedly many, many more.

When Henry died, he was a far cry from the young man who had made the maids of honour swoon. His impressive height remained, but his fifty-four-inch waist made him nearly as wide as he was tall. The former inexhaustible athlete now had to be carried around in a sedan chair. He was in constant pain from a variety of chronic ailments; he may have suffered from impotence and he was probably infertile. But this was only in the last ten years of his life.

Readers often forget this dangerous and irritable old man was once described as 'the handsomest potentate I ever set eyes on'. He was clever, cultured, good-looking and charismatic. He has been portrayed as an unpredictable character, eager to remove the heads of his friends and wives as soon as they displeased him. There are elements of truth in this caricature, but he was also a devoted lover, providing for some of his mistresses well after their liaison had ended and moving heaven and earth to be with the lady he loved.

It has often been repeated that around Francis I's deathbed, some courtiers were jubilant, declaring that 'the lady-killer is going'.[1] Henry was not judged so. His subjects were in fear of him, but also loved him. He remained popular throughout the country, loved for his childlike enthusiasm and

> nor would any of them endure hearing any thing disrespectful of the King, through the honour they bear him; so that the most binding oath which is taken by them is that by which 'the King's life' has been pledged.[2]

He was also, despite his numerous affairs, not considered a 'lady-killer' as he was reasonably discreet.

He seems to have, in the latter half of his reign, mistaken his attraction to a woman for a legal right to marry. He married five of his wives mainly because he was attracted to them. When they no longer appealed, he felt that his conscience was telling him that he was not truly wed. In an age where marrying for love was considered madness, a prince was expected to have a dutiful wife and beautiful mistresses, and Henry did so for the first eighteen years of his reign. Yet he felt that without love, or at least the possibility of it, there was no marriage. He was a devout man who seems to have considered adultery to be sinful, but believed that his actions were beyond fault; therefore if Henry wanted another woman, it was probably his wife's doing. Blaming the queen made him feel less guilty about his actions.

Edward Hall reports Henry as saying that 'if I know a man which liveth in adultery, I must judge him a lecherous and carnal man'.[3] Yet Henry VIII conducted many affairs throughout his first two marriages, until he was forty-six years old. One criticism that has been levied at Henry time and time again is 'hypocrite'. He condemned his sister Margaret for divorcing her husband to marry the person she loved, yet he did the same soon afterward. He was an idealist who expected immediate gratification, but he also genuinely believed himself to be right in almost all matters.

We have no evidence of Henry feeling that he had ever committed a sin; all the tragedies of his life were God's punishment for somebody else's offences – the Pope for giving permission for him to marry his brother's widow, Anne Boleyn for bewitching him, his ministers, each in turn, for implementing his policies yet not always succeeding. His famously flexible friend, his conscience, seems to have disliked the idea of adultery. All sex outside marriage was against the law of the Church and the laws of the land, yet it was the norm at court. He executed two of his wives on suspicion of a crime *he* had committed: adultery.

Absolute power corrupts absolutely – which is an apt description of Henry as a king and as a lover. Initially, in his first relationship with Katherine of Aragon, he was eager to please, was loving and chivalrous, but he changed over time. He became well aware of what he was able to achieve, and 'Where the word of a king is, there is power: and who may say unto him, "What doest thou?"'⁴ This left his queens and his mistresses concerned for their positions. And annulling his marriage to wed his wife's servant – three times – certainly gave a new spin to the term 'lady-in-waiting' and changed the dynamics of the court.

In the seven years prior to his death, Anne Stafford, Bessie Blount and Mary Boleyn had all died. He had seen four of his wives go before him, including the two he had dispatched before their time. Mary Shelton, Anne of Cleves and Katheryn Parr had all survived him. Only the mistresses he did not choose to marry left Henry's bed completely unscathed. Of all the kings in history, Henry VIII of England must have been one of the most dangerous to have fall in love with you.

Bessie Blount benefited hugely from bearing him a son, but does not seem to have attempted to secure power at court; Mary Boleyn had great opportunities after both her royal affair and his relationship with her sister, but does not seem to have been tempted to advance herself. Anne Stafford attracted scandal with her liaison with the king, but did not care much for her reputation either, later being prosecuted for adultery with a man who was low-born, even if he was very close to the king. Jane Popincourt was not averse to notoriety, continuing her relationship with a French duke after she had finished with Henry VIII. Mary Shelton continued to be linked to other men; Elizabeth Brooke, Anne Bassett and Katherine Willoughby seem not to have been affected much by his interest. Mary Howard and her family suffered for the mere suggestion that he would be attracted to her, when it was used as evidence against her father and brother; she was left to bring up the children of the executed earl of Surrey. Surprisingly, out of the lovers he did not go on to marry, only Elizabeth Amadas, the 'witch and prophetess' seems to have been left bitter, and this was probably due to her husband leaving her as much as to the king's behaviour.

Those he wished to marry did not fare so well. Katherine of Aragon, arguably his first love, was rejected once she was no longer attractive. He had defied Christendom for Anne Boleyn, but she was dispatched for reasons which are still unclear. Jane Seymour also suffered death through her relations with Henry, although in the noble act of bearing a future king. Anne of Cleves was left with limited opportunities to marry or return to her homeland and Catherine Howard was executed, probably before her twentieth birthday. Katheryn Parr is seen as the triumphant survivor, but after three and a half years of trying to keep Henry's love, she was drawn into the bitter factional fighting of Edward VI's reign, dying in childbirth months before her fourth husband was executed. It was clearly better, if only in the reign of this English king and no other, to be a mistress than to be a queen.

King Henry's treatment of women cannot have failed to influence his two daughters, both of whom grew up to have unhealthy attitudes to men. Mary lavished all her repressed and rejected love onto her husband, Philip II of Spain, leaving many deeply concerned that England would become a Habsburg province. Although dutiful, Philip did not reciprocate her strong feelings. Elizabeth never married despite the ambiguity as to who would succeed her, leaving the country in danger of civil war. After Henry's treatment of their mothers and stepmothers, this is unsurprising.

Elisabeth-Charlotte, duchesse d'Orléans and sister-in-law of Louis XIV, wrote:

> I believe that the histories which will be written about this court after we are all gone, will be better and more entertaining than any novel, and I am afraid that those who come after us will not be able to believe them and will think that they are just fairy tales.[5]

This sums up the court of Henry VIII well. His story has been portrayed in fictional television programmes, films and books many times with many embellishments, but there is no need for invention – the bare facts are enthralling enough.

Unlike a queen, a royal mistress had no clear status, no security and no guarantees about her future. She had to constantly work to keep her position – to be the wittiest and the prettiest, to keep her lover interested once the initial lust had faded. Everything in her life was dependent upon his whim and so she had to be sure that she pleased her king at all times. He was expected to have affairs and could choose anyone he wanted, so his lover's position was under constant threat from others – but it was a prize worth pursuing. The influence of the women close to the king, both queens and queans, should not be underestimated. We are all swayed by the opinions of those we hold dearest.

However, it is not the political importance of these women that drew the author to write their stories, but their personalities and their own captivating tales. The women in this book, queens and mistresses, short-term pursuits or long-term lovers, were completely at the mercy of King Henry VIII. Despite this, many of them showed great resilience, determination and character and defied the conventions of their age. These ladies carved out extraordinary lives in a man's world, and emerge clearly through the mists of time as individuals worthy of our attention. The mistresses of Henry VIII were learned or illiterate, plain or pretty, younger or older, spirited or submissive, but they were, without exception, worthy of the attentions of the most intriguing king in English history.

References

Introduction: Henry and His Women

1. *L&P*, XI, no.923
2. Cit. Baldwin Smith, *Henry VIII: The Mask of Royalty,* p.34

Chapter 1: The Teenage King

1. *Calendar of State Papers, Spanish,* 449
2. Da Lodi, contemporary; cit. Erickson, *Great Harry*, p.91
3. Cit. Fraser, *The Six Wives of Henry VIII*, p.60
4. *Thomas More, B.L. Cotton MSS*; cit. Weir, *Henry VIII: King and Court*, p.2
5. Cit. Weir, *The Six Wives of Henry VIII*, p.79
6. Cit. Mattingly, *Catherine of Aragon*, p.92
7. Cit. Weir, *Henry VIII: King and Court*, p.10
8. Cit. Weir, *The Six Wives of Henry VIII*, p.106
9. *L&P*, VI, p.168
10. *L&P*, II, pt. II, p.1490
11. *L&P*, XV, no.229
12. Cit. Fraser, *The Six Wives of Henry VIII*, p.42
13. *CSP, Spanish*; cit. Weir, *Henry VIII: King and Court*, p.123
14. *Ibid.*
15. *CSP, Venetian*, II, p.5611
16. *L&P*, IV, no.6084
17. *L&P*, XIII, no.732; in 1538
18. *L&P*, IV, pt. II, 4442

19. *L&P*, IV, pt. II, 4442
20. Murphy, *Bastard Prince: Henry VIII's Lost Son,* p.13

Chapter 2: A French Affair

1. *CSP, Spanish supplement*, p.25
2. Weir, *The Six Wives of Henry VIII,* p.115
3. Hall, *Hall's Chronicle,* p.567; cit. Mattingly, *Catherine of Aragon,* p.123
4. *L&P*, I, pt. II, no.3163: 17th August 1514; *CSP, Spanish*, III, pt. II, no.854
5. *CSP, Venetian*, II, p.139
6. *Ibid.*, p.152
7. Cit. Weir, *The Six Wives of Henry VIII,* p.121
8. *Ibid.*
9. *King's Jewel Book*, pp.169, 171 and 174; cit. Fraser, *The Six Wives of Henry VIII,* pp.70–1
10. Byrne (ed.), *The Letters of King Henry VIII*, p.42
11. Charles, earl of Worcester to Cardinal Wolsey
12. *L&P*; cit. Weir, *Henry VIII: King and Court*, p.175
13. TNA, E36/215 f.449

Chapter 3: The Beauty of Her Time

1. Cit. Weir, *Henry VIII: King and Court*, p.xiii (the Venetian papal nuncio, Francesco Chieregato, 1517)
2. Hall, *Hall's Chronicle*, I, p.49
3. Murphy, *Bastard Prince: Henry VIII's Lost Son*, p.7
4. *L&P*, II, pt. II, no.1461
5. Cit. Hobden, *Tudor Bastard: King Henry VIII's Son, Henry Fitzroy, duke of Richmond and Somerset and His Mother, Elizabeth Blount,* p.5
6. *CSP, Spanish*; cit. Weir, *Henry VIII: King and Court*, p.124
7. Fraser, *The Six Wives of Henry VIII*, p.71
8. Murphy, *Bastard Prince: Henry VIII's Lost Son*, p.25
9. James, *Kateryn Parr*, p.71
10. *CSP, Venetian*, I, p.83 (Pasqualigo, Venetian ambassador)
11. *CSP, Spanish*, 1531–33, no.967
12. Herbert of Cherbury, *The History of England under Henry VIII*, p.70
13. *Ibid.*
14. Cit. Weir, *The Six Wives of Henry VIII*, p.123
15. Hobden, *Tudor Bastard: King Henry VIII's Son, Henry Fitzroy, duke of Richmond and Somerset and His Mother, Elizabeth Blount*, p.7
16. *L&P*, III, pt. II, no.224

17. *L&P*, III, pt. II, no.2356
18. Act of Parliament 14 Hen.8 ch.34, 1522
19. Burke, *Historical Portrait of the Tudor Dynasty*, 1879, I, p.178

Chapter 4: The Boleyn Girls

1. *L&P*, VI, no.923; *L&P*, VIII, nos.565 and 567; *L&P*, XII, no.952
2. Bruce (ed.), *Correspondence of Matthew Parker*, p.400
3. *L&P*, II, nos.1500–2
4. *CSP, Spanish*, 1529–30, p.422
5. Cit. Fraser, *The Six Wives of Henry VIII*, p.145
6. *L&P*, I, pt. I, p.351
7. *L&P*, I, nos.3355–6. This source states that Mademoiselle Boleyn went to France with Mary Tudor; French sources show this to be '*Marie Boleyn*'; Anne had probably not reached Paris in time for the wedding
8. Cit. Erickson, *Great Harry*, p.188
9. *L&P*, X, no.450
10. Cit. Ives, *Anne Boleyn*, p.24
11. *L&P*, X, no.450
12. *L&P*, III, pt. II, p.1539
13. *L&P*, III, nos.2074, 2297, 2993, 2994 and *L&P*, IV, nos.464, 1264, 202 and 2218
14. *L&P*, III, no.3358
15. *L&P*, X, no.450; *CSP, Spanish,* 1536–8, pp.39–40, 59
16. Cit. Baldwin Smith, *Catherine Howard: A Tudor Tragedy*, p.38

Chapter 5: Bastards of the King

1. *L&P*, VIII, no.567. His tomb inscription states that he died on 23 July 1596 in his seventy-second year, suggesting he was born in 1524
2. British Library, Harleian MS 252, f.26
3. *L&P*, VIII, no.565 (20th April 1535); *L&P*, VIII, no.862 (13 June 1535)
4. *L&P*, VIII, no.567
5. *Salisbury MSS*, 1.400; cit. Varlow, 'Katherine Knollys', *Oxford Dictionary of National Biography*
6. Hall, *Hall's Chronicle*, II, p.195
7. *CSP, Venetian*, II, 529
8. Mattingly, *Catherine of Aragon*, p.132
9. *CSP, Venetian*, III, 455
10. *CSP, Venetian*, 1520–26, no.1037
11. *L&P*, IV, pt. II, nos.1954 and 3135

12. Rogers (ed.), *The Correspondence of Sir Thomas More*, p.405; cit. James, *Kateryn Parr*, p.49

13. James, *Kateryn Parr*, pp.44–5

14. Cit. Hobden, *Tudor Bastard: King Henry VIII's Son, Henry Fitzroy, duke of Richmond and Somerset and His Mother*, Elizabeth Blount, p.18

15. *L&P*, IV, no.3051

16. Pollard, *Henry VIII*, p.147

17. *L&P*, VI, no.241

18. Genesis 20:12

19. *CSP, Spanish*, 1534–5, no.61 (6 June 1536)

20. Cit. Weir, *Henry VIII: King and Court*, p.125

21. Weir, *Henry VIII: King and Court*, p.125

22. Sander, *Rise and Growth of Anglican Schism*, p.8

23. Cit. Weir, *The Six Wives of Henry VIII*, p.274

24. Cit. Weir, *Henry VIII: King and Court*, p.385

25. Cit. Baldwin Smith, *Henry VIII: The Mask of Royalty*, p.66

26. Lancelot de Carles, lines 339–458. Anthony Browne came from a large family, and the Fitzwilliams were his half-siblings. However, there is nothing to link a sister of his to Henry

27. Byrne (ed.), *The Lisle Letters: An Abridgement*, iii. 703

28. *CSP, Domestic*, 1547–53, no.71

29. Cassell, *Perrot Notes, Some Account of the Various Branches of the Perrot Family*, p.40 (quote from Naunton)

30. Acheson, *Shakespeare's Lost Years in London*

Chapter 6: The Woman in the World That I Value the Most

1. Hall, *Hall's Chronicle*, p.707

2. Cit. Denny, *Anne Boleyn*, p.227

3. *CSP, Spanish*, IV, pt. II, p.487

4. Cit. Plowden, *Tudor Women*, p.67

5. McNalty, *Henry VIII: A Difficult Patient*, p.67

6. *Ibid.*

7. Cavendish, *The Life and Death of Cardinal Wolsey*, p.35; cit. Ives, *Anne Boleyn*, p.121

8. Ives, *Anne Boleyn*, p.4

9. Sander, *Rise and Growth of Anglican Schism*, pp.32–3

10. *L&P*, VI, no.923; VIII, nos.565, 567, *L&P*, XII, no.952

11. Paget, 'The Youth of Anne Boleyn', BIHR, 55, 1981, pp.163–4

12. Cit. Lindsey, *Divorced, Beheaded, Survived: A Feminist Reinterpretation of the Wives of Henry VIII*, p.50

13. Ascoli, *L'Opinion*, lines 37–42; cit. Ives, *Anne Boleyn*, p.34
14. Herbert of Cherbury, *Herbert's Autobiography and History of England under Henry VIII*, Ward, Lock and Co., 1881, p.157 and p.218
15. Cavendish, *The Life and Death of Cardinal Wolsey*, p.30
16. *CSP, Venetian*, IV, p.485
17. Plowden, *The Young Elizabeth*, p.25
18. De Carles, p.234; cit. Fraser, *The Six Wives of Henry VIII*, p.151
19. Sander, *Rise and Growth of Anglican Schism*, p.25
20. Fraser, *Love and Louis XIV*, p.30
21. George Wyatt, p.143
22. Cit. Carlton, *Royal Mistresses*, p.35
23. Gairdner and Motta, *The Draft Dispensation*, (EHR), p.544
24. Byrne (ed.), *The Letters of King Henry VIII*, p.75
25. Cavendish, *The Life and Death of Cardinal Wolsey*, p.35
26. Cit. Mattingly, *Catherine of Aragon*, p.191, (Du Bellay, French ambassador)
27. Byrne (ed.), *The Letters of King Henry VIII*, (June 1528), p.71
28. *L&P*, IV, no.4410

Chapter 7: The Lady is All-Powerful

1. Cit. Fraser, *The Six Wives of Henry VIII*, p.176
2. Cit. Weir, *Henry VIII: King and Court*, p.291
3. Cit. Wood, *Letters of Royal and Illustrious Ladies*, p.15; Anne Boleyn to Henry VIII
4. Hall, *Hall's Chronicle*, II, pp.145–7
5. Cit. Fraser, *The Six Wives of Henry VIII*, p.182
6. Cit. Lindsey, *Divorced, Beheaded, Survived: A Feminist Reinterpretation of the Wives of Henry VIII*, p.58
7. Cit. Byrne (ed.), *The Letters of King Henry VIII*, p.84
8. Ridley (ed.), *The Love Letters of Henry VIII*, p.511; circa June 1528
9. *Ibid.*, p.65
10. *Ibid.*, p.35 and p.43; written before 1527
11. *Ibid.*, p.37; Henry on Anne Boleyn, written before July 1527
12. British Library, King's MS 9, ff.66v, 231
13. Fraser, *The Six Wives of Henry VIII*, pp.69–70
14. *L&P*, I, pt. II, pp.419–20
15. Mattingly, *Catherine of Aragon*, p.190
16. *L&P*, IV, pt. III, no.2526; cit. Fraser, *The Six Wives of Henry VIII*, p.197
17. *CSP, Spanish*, IV, 349–52
18. *L&P*, VI, no.923. 'Mr. Daunsy' probably referring to Sir John Dauntesy, who was co-executor of Compton's will and can therefore be assumed to be someone Compton trusted

19. *L&P*, VI, no.924
20. *L&P*, V, no.1114
21. Ives, *Anne Boleyn*, p.200

Chapter 8: Grudge Who Will, But None Deny

1. Cit. Friedmann, *Anne Boleyn: A Chapter of English History 1527–36*, p.190
2. *L&P*, IV, pt. II, no.2210
3. *L&P*, VI, no.585
4. *L&P*, VIII, no.196
5. *L&P*, V, no.907
6. Cronica del Rey Enrico, p.17–18
7. *CSP, Venetian*, 1527–33, 912
8. Cit. Ives, *Anne Boleyn*, p.284
9. *L&P*, VI, no.241
10. Cit. Weir, *The Six Wives of Henry VIII*, p.274
11. *L&P*, VII, no.1193; Chapuys to Charles V; *CSP, Spanish*, 1534–35, no.90
12. *CSP, Spanish*, V, pt. I, p.264; *CSP, Spanish*, IV, pt. II, p.789
13. *CSP, Spanish*, 1534–35, no.88; *L&P*, VI, no.1054
14. *CSP, Spanish*, 1534–5, no.118
15. *L&P*, VI, no.556; Cromwell to Chapuys, 29th May 1533
16. Wood, *Letters of Royal and Illustrious Ladies*, pp.194–7; *L&P*, VII, no.1655
17. Friedmann, *Anne Boleyn: A Chapter of English History 1527–36*, II, p.13
18. *CSP, Spanish*, V, pt. I, p.376
19. *CSP, Spanish*, 1534–35, p.260–9
20. *L&P*, VIII, no.263
21. Heale, *Women and the Courtly Love Lyric: The Devonshire MS*
22. *CSP, Spanish*, 1536–38, no.29; Chapuys to Charles V
23. Cavendish (Singer, ed.), *The Life and Death of Cardinal Wolsey*, pp. 451–60
24. Cit. Froude, *The Divorce of Catherine of Aragon*, p.401
25. Cit. Wilson, *In the Lion's Court: Power, Ambition and Sudden Death in the Reign of Henry VIII*, p.428; John Hutton to Cromwell, December 1537
26. *Camden Miscellany*, 4th series, 39, pp.62–3
27. *L&P*, XXI, pt. I, no.1426
28. For more information on this, see Herman, *Rethinking the Henrician Era*, p.50
29. *L&P*, VI, no.923
30. *L&P*, XXI, pt. II, no.332
31. Cit. Remley, (Herman, ed.), *Rethinking the Henrician Era: Essays on Early Tudor Texts and Contexts*, p.45
32. *L&P*, XXI, pt. I, no.1426
33. *CSP, Spanish*, IV, pt. II, p.33

Chapter 9: The Year of Three Queens

1. Cit. Fraser, *The Six Wives of Henry VIII*, p.280
2. *L&P*, VII, no.1040
3. *CSP, Spanish*, 1536–38, no.21 and *L&P*, X, no.282; 17th February 1536
4. *L&P*, X, no.351
5. Vergil, *Anglica Historia*, p.337
6. Cit. Fraser, *The Six Wives of Henry VIII*, p.290
7. Cit. Martienssen, *Katherine Parr*, p.78
8. Strype, *Ecclesiastical Memorials of Henry VIII, Edward VI and Mary I*, I, ii, 304
9. *L&P*, X, p.245
10. Cit. Lindsey, *Divorced, Beheaded, Survived: A Feminist Reinterpretation of the Wives of Henry VIII*, p.119
11. Cavendish, (ed. Singer), *The Life and Death of Cardinal Wolsey*, p.452
12. *CSP, Spanish*, V, p.214; *L&P*, XII, no.48
13. Cavendish, (ed. Singer), *The Life and Death of Cardinal Wolsey*, p.453
14. *CSP, Spanish*, 1536–38, no.54; Chapuys to Granvelle, 18th May 1536
15. Cit. Fox, *Jane Boleyn*, p.202–3; Chapuys
16. *CSP, Spanish*, V, pt. II, p.28
17. Byrne (ed.), *The Letters of King Henry VIII*, p.171; letter from Henry to Norfolk
18. *CSP, Spanish*, IV, pt. II, p.84
19. *CSP, Spanish*, 1536–38, no.55
20. *Ibid.*; Chapuys to Charles V, 19th May 1536
21. *CSP, Spanish*, 1536–38, no.55
22. *CSP, Spanish*, V, pt. II, p.126; *L&P*, X, no.908
23. McNalty, *Henry VIII: A Difficult Patient*, p.16
24. *CSP, Spanish*, 1536–38, no.54; Chapuys to Granvelle, 18th May 1536
25. *Ibid.*
26. De Carles; cit. Fraser, *The Six Wives of Henry VIII*, p.315

Chapter 10: His 'True Wife'

1. Mattingly, *Catherine of Aragon*, p.161
2. Seymour, *Ordeal by Ambition*, p.36
3. Cit. Fraser, *The Six Wives of Henry VIII*, p.288
4. *L&P*, X, no.915
5. McNalty, *Henry VIII: A Difficult Patient*, pp.25–6 and p.28
6. *CSP, Spanish*, V, pt. II, p.125
7. *L&P*, XI, no.8; Chapuys to Granvelle, 1st July 1536
8. *L&P*, XII, p.254; Byrne (ed.), *The Lisle Letters: An Abridgement*, p.209
9. Cit. Baldwin Smith, *Henry VIII: The Mask of Royalty*, p.66

10. *Ibid.*
11. Castillon; cit. Baldwin Smith, *Henry VIII: The Mask of Royalty*, p.67
12. Cit. Byrne (ed.), *The Letters of King Henry VIII*, p.61
13. *L&P*, XII, pt. II, p.449
14. *L&P*, VIII, pp.142–6
15. Cit. Wilson, *In the Lion's Court: Power, Ambition and Sudden Death in the Reign of Henry VIII*, p.449
16. *L&P*, IX, no.24; John Hussey to Lord Lisle, 3rd January 1538
17. *L&P*, XIII, pt. I, no.795
18. Byrne (ed.), *The Lisle Letters: An Abridgement*, p.281

Chapter 11: 'I Like Her Not'

1. Cit. Fraser, *The Six Wives of Henry VIII*, p.373
2. *Ibid.*
3. *Ibid.*, p.367
4. Marillac; cit. Fraser, *The Six Wives of Henry VIII*, p.374; *CSP, Spanish*, VI, I
5. Cit. Fraser, *The Six Wives of Henry VIII*, p.378
6. *Ibid.*, p.379
7. *Ibid.*, p.380
8. Cit. Weir, *Henry VIII: King and Court*, p.404
9. Byrne (ed.), *The Lisle Letters: An Abridgement*, p.211
10. Cit. Fraser, *The Six Wives of Henry VIII*, pp.380–1
11. Strype, *Ecclesiastical Memorials of Henry VIII, Edward VI and Mary I*, I, II, pp.460–1
12. *Ibid.*, p.461; *L&P*, XV, no.823
13. Strype, *Ecclesiastical Memorials of Henry VIII, Edward VI and Mary I*, I, II, p.460
14. Cit. Wilson, *In the Lion's Court: Power, Ambition and Sudden Death in the Reign of Henry VIII*, p.461
15. Strype, *Ecclesiastical Memorials of Henry VIII, Edward VI and Mary I*, I, pt. II, p.462
16. Warnicke, 'Anne of Cleves', *Oxford Dictionary of National Biography*
17. Ives, 'Anne of Cleves', *Oxford Dictionary of National Biography*
18. *L&P*, XVI, p.655
19. *L&P*, XV, p.254
20. *L&P*, XVI, p.5
21. Cit. Baldwin Smith, *Catherine Howard: A Tudor Tragedy*, p.95
22. *L&P*, XV, no.901
23. Cit. Strickland, *Lives of the Queens of England, from the Norman Conquest: with Anecdotes of their Court*, III, p.122

24. *L&P*, XVI, no.1409
25. *L&P*, XVI, p.642

Chapter 12: Rose Without A Thorn

1. Cit. Loades, *The Politics of Marriage: Henry VIII and His Queens*, p.124; Thomas Cranmer's secretary, Ralph Morice, in a letter to his master, 1540
2. Marillac on Catherine Howard; cit. Fox, *Jane Boleyn*, p.271
3. Cit. Baldwin Smith, *Catherine Howard: A Tudor Tragedy*, p.192
4. Cit. Fraser, *The Six Wives of Henry VIII*, p.405
5. Chapuys to Charles V; *CSP, Spanish*, 1538–42, no.213
6. Cit. Baldwin Smith, *Catherine Howard: A Tudor Tragedy*, p.209
7. *L&P*, XVI, no.1320
8. Cit. Baldwin Smith, *Catherine Howard: A Tudor Tragedy*, p.50
9. Cit. Fraser, *The Six Wives of Henry VIII*, p.392
10. *Ibid.*, p.393
11. Norfolk to Thomas More; Rowse, (ed.), A Man of Singular Virtue: *A Life of Sir Thomas More by his son in law William Roper*, p.71; cit. Hume, *The Wives of Henry VIII*, p.162
12. Cit. Baldwin Smith, *Catherine Howard: A Tudor Tragedy*, p.156
13. *L&P*, XVI, pp.630–1
14. TNA SP.I, 167, 14
15. Cit. Plowden, *Tudor Women*, p.102
16. *CSP, Spanish*, VI, I, no.207
17. *L&P*, XVI, no.649
18. Cit. Baldwin Smith, *Catherine Howard: A Tudor Tragedy*, p.168
19. *L&P*, XVI, no.1426
20. *L&P*, XVI, pp.665–6
21. *L&P*, XVI, no.691
22. *L&P*, XVI, no.641
23. *L&P*, XVI, p.642
24. *CSP, Spanish*, 1538–42, no.228
25. Chapuys to Charles V; *CSP, Spanish*, 1538–42, no.230
26. Cit. Fraser, *The Six Wives of Henry VIII*, p.453
27. Harris, *The View from My Lady's Chamber: New Perspectives on the Early Tudor Monarchy*, 60, 3, English Political History, 1500–1640, p.240
28. Cit. Denny, *Katherine Howard*, p.108
29. Cit. Strickland, *Lives of the Queens of England, from the Norman Conquest: with Anecdotes of their Court*, III, pp.84–5; Weir, *The Six Wives of Henry VIII*, pp.465–6
30. Byrne (ed.), *The Lisle Letters: An Abridgement*, p.414

Chapter 13: How Many Wives Will He Have?

1. McNalty, *Henry VIII: A Difficult Patient*, p.167
2. Cit. James, *Kateryn Parr*, p.114
3. *L&P*, XVIII, pt. I, no.954; *L&P*, XX, pt. I, no.65; Chapuys to Charles V, 27th July 1543
4. Reverend Treadway Nash, 'Observations on the Time of Death and Place of Burial of Queen Katharine Parr', *Archaelogica*, IX (1789); James, *Kateryn Parr*, p.444
5. James, *Kateryn Parr*, p.11
6. Katheryn to her husband, Thomas Seymour, about her brother-in-law, the duke of Somerset; cit. Martienssen, p.232
7. James, *Kateryn Parr*, p.71
8. Cit. James, *Kateryn Parr*, p.76
9. *L&P*, XII, pt. II, no.14

Chapter 14: Queen Katherine the Fourth?

1. Cit. Weir, *The Six Wives of Henry VIII*, p.98
2. Cit. Fraser, *The Six Wives of Henry VIII*, p.462
3. *L&P*, XXI, pt. I, no.1027; by Francis van der Delft, imperial ambassador
4. Foxe, *Acts and Monuments of the Christian Church*, V, p.555; Henry VIII to Stephen Gardiner, bishop of Winchester
5. John Knox, *First Blast Against the Monstrous Regiment of Women*, p.3
6. Martienssen, *Katherine Parr*, p.215
7. *L&P*, XXI, pt. I, p.696; this is Foxe's version of events
8. *L&P*, XXI, pt. II, no.555
9. Heale, *Women and the Courtly Love Lyric: The Devonshire MS*, p.300
10. Richardson, Glenn, *Renaissance Monarchy: The Reigns of Henry VIII, Francis I and Charles V*, p.161
11. Cit. Fraser, *The Six Wives of Henry VIII*, pp.480–1
12. Cit. Weir, *Henry VIII: King and Court*, p.312
13. Cit. Fraser, *The Six Wives of Henry VIII*, p.481
14. *L&P*, XXI, pt. II, pp.320–1
15. Cit. James, *Kateryn Parr*, p.323

Conclusion

1. Cit. Baldwin Smith, *Henry VIII: King and Court*, p.18
2. Nicander Nucius, *Second Book of Travels*, p.16
3. Hall, *Hall's Chronicle*, p.356
4. Ecclesiastes 8:4
5. Cit. Fraser, *Love and Louis XIV*, xiv–xv

Bibliography

Primary Sources

Bruce, J. and Perowne, T.T. (ed.), *Correspondence of Matthew Parker*, Parker Society, 1853

Byrne, Muriel St. Clare (ed.), *The Letters of King Henry VIII*, Cassell and Company, 1936

Byrne (ed.), *The Lisle Letters: An Abridgement*, University of Chicago Press, 1983

Calendar of State Papers (CSP), Foreign, Elizabeth I

Calendar of State Papers (CSP), Spanish

Calendar of State Papers (CSP), Spanish, Elizabeth I

Calendar of State Papers (CSP), Venetian

Camden Miscellany, 4th series, 39, 1990, Royal Historical Society

Cavendish, George, (ed. Singer, Samuel Weller), *The Life and Death of Cardinal Wolsey*, Harding, Triphook and Lephard, 1825

Collection of State Papers ... Left by William Cecil, Lord Burghley, ed. Samuel Haynes, 1740

Collection of State Papers Relating to Affairs in the Reigns of Henry VIII, Edward VI, Queen Mary and Queen Elizabeth

Crawford, Anne (ed.), *Letters of the Queens of England*, Sutton Publishing, 2002

Ellis, Henry, *Original Letters, Illustrative of English History: Including Numerous Royal Letters*, Harding, Triphook and Lephard, 1824

Foxe, John, *Acts and Monuments of the Christian Church* (commonly referred to as 'Foxe's Book of Martyrs')

Gairdner, J. and Brodie, R.H., (ed.), *Letters and Papers, Foreign and Domestic, of the Reign of Henry VIII (L&P)*, 1862–1932

Giustiniani, Sebastiano, *The Court of Henry VIII*, 1854

Hall, Edward, *The Union of the Noble and Illustre Famelies of Lancastre and York* (commonly referred to as '*Hall's Chronicle*'), 1542

Herbert of Cherbury, Lord Edward, *Herbert's Autobiography and History of England under Henry VIII*, Ward, Lock & Co., 1881

Knox, John, *First Blast Against the Monstrous Regiment of Women*, Kessinger, 2004

Nucius, Nicander, *Second Book of Travels*, The Camden Society, 1841

Pasqualigo, *Four Years at the Court of Henry VIII*

Ridley, Jasper, *The Love Letters of Henry VIII*, Weidenfeld and Nicolson, 1988

Rogers, Elizabeth Frances (ed.), *The Correspondence of Sir Thomas More*, Princeton, 1947

Rye, William Brenchley, *England as Seen by Foreigners*, 1865

Sander, Nicolas, *Rise and Growth of Anglican Schism*, 1877

Strype, John, *Ecclesiastical Memorials of Henry VIII, Edward VI and Mary I*, 1822

Vergil, Polydore, *Anglica Historia*, J.B. Nichols, 1846

Wood, M.A.E., *Letters of Royal and Illustrious Ladies*, 1846

Secondary Sources

Acheson, *Shakespeare's Lost Years in London*, Kessinger Publishing Co., 2003

Baldwin Smith, Lacey, *Catherine Howard: A Tudor Tragedy*, Cape, 1961

——, *Henry VIII: Mask of Royalty*, Granada Publishing, 1971

Carlton, Charles, *Royal Mistresses*, Routledge, 1991

Denny, Joanna, *Anne Boleyn*, Piatkus Books, 2005

——, *Katherine Howard*, Portrait, 2007

Elton, G.R., *England Under the Tudors*, Routledge, 1992

Erickson, Carolly, *Great Harry*, Robson Books, 2004

Fox, Julia, *Jane Boleyn: the Infamous Lady Rochford*, Weidenfeld and Nicolson, 2007

Fraser, Antonia, *Love and Louis XIV*, Weidenfeld and Nicolson, 2006

——, *The Six Wives of Henry VIII*, Phoenix Press, 2003

Friedmann, Paul, *Anne Boleyn: A Chapter of English History 1527–36*, Ams Pr Inc, 1995

Froude, J.A., *The Divorce of Catherine of Aragon*, Longman, 1891

Gunn, S.J., *Charles Brandon*, Basil Blackwell Inc., 1988

Herman, Peter C. (ed.), *Rethinking the Henrician Era: Essays on Early Tudor Texts and Contexts* (Paul G. Remley, *Mary Shelton*), University of Illinois Press, 1994

Hobden, Heather, *Tudor Bastard: King Henry VIII's Son, Henry Fitzroy, duke of Richmond and Somerset and His Mother, Elizabeth Blount*

Hume, Martin, *The Wives of Henry VIII*, Eveleigh Nash, 1907

Ives, E.W., *Anne Boleyn*, Blackwell, 1998

Izon, John, *Sir Thomas Stucley c.1525–1578: Traitor Extraordinary*, Andrew Melrose Ltd, 1956

James, Susan E., *Kateryn Parr: the Making of a Queen*, Ashgate, 1999

Lindsey, Karen, *Divorced, Beheaded, Survived: A Feminist Reinterpretation of the Wives of Henry VIII*, Perseus, 1995

Loades, David, *Elizabeth I*, Hambledon and London, 2003

——, *The Politics of Marriage: Henry VIII and His Queens*, Sutton Publishing, 1994

——, *The Tudor Court*, The Davenant Press, 2003

Martienssen, Anthony, *Katherine Parr*, Cardinal, 1975

Mattingly, Garrett, *Catherine of Aragon*, Cape, 1963

McNalty, Sir A.S., *Henry VIII: A Difficult Patient*, Christopher Johnson, 1952

Miller, Helen, *Henry VIII and the English Nobility*, Basil Blackwell, 1986

Muir, Kenneth, *The Life and Letters of Sir Thomas Wyatt*, Liverpool University Press, 1963

Murphy, Beverley A., *Bastard Prince: Henry VIII's Lost Son*, Sutton Publishing, 2001

Plowden, Alison, *Tudor Women: Queens and Commoners*, Sutton Publishing, 2002

Pollard, A.F., *Henry VIII*, Longman, 1951

Richardson, Glenn, *Renaissance Monarchy: The Reigns of Henry VIII, Francis I and Charles V*, Hodder Arnold, 2002

Richardson, Walter, *Mary Tudor, the White Queen*, Peter Owen Ltd, 1970

Ridley, Jasper, *Henry VIII*, Constable and Company, 1984

Rowse, A.L. (ed.), *A Man of Singular Virtue: A Life of Sir Thomas More by his son in law William Roper*, Folio Society, 1980

Scarisbrick, J.J., *Henry VIII*, Pelican, 1968

Sessions, W.A., *Henry Howard, the Poet Earl of Surrey*, Oxford University Press, 2003

Seymour, William, *Ordeal by Ambition: An English Family in the Shadow of the Tudors*, Sidgwick & Jackson, 1972

Southall, Raymond, *The Devonshire Manuscript Collection of Early Tudor Poetry, 1532–41*, The Review of English Studies, 15, no.58, May, 1964, pp.142–50

Starkey, David, *The English Court from the Wars of the Roses to the Civil War*, Longman, 1992

Strickland, Agnes, *Lives of the Queens of England, from the Norman Conquest: with Anecdotes of their Courts*, James Miller, 1860

Thomson, Patricia (ed.), *Wyatt: The Critical Heritage*, Routledge & Keegan Paul Ltd, 1974

Weir, Alison, *Britain's Royal Family: A Complete Genealogy*, Pimlico, 2002

——, *Henry VIII: King and Court*, Pimlico, 2005

——, *The Six Wives of Henry VIII*, Pimlico, 1992

Wilson, Derek, *In the Lion's Court: Power, Ambition and Sudden Death in the Reign of Henry VIII*, Pimlico, 2002

Journal Articles

Bernard, G.W., *The Fall of Anne Boleyn*, The English Historical Review (EHR), 106, July 1991, p.420

Bernard, G., *The Rise of Sir William Compton*, EHR, 96, 1981, pp.754–77

Bindoff, S.T., *The History of Parliament: The House of Commons, 1509–1558*, 1982

Burke, Victor E. and Gibson, Jonathan, *Early Modern Women's Manuscript Writing: Selected Papers from the Trinity/Trent Colloquium*, Ashgate, 2004

Casady, Edwin, *A Reinterpretation of Surrey's Character and Actions*, MLA, 51, September 1936, p.626

Cassell, E. Barnwell, *Perrot Notes, Some Account of the Various Branches of the Perrot Family*, 1867

Duncan, J. and Derrett, M., *Henry Fitzroy and Henry VIII's 'Scruple of Conscience'*, Renaissance News, 16, Spring 1963, pp.1–9

Oxford Dictionary of National Biography

Fletcher, John, *A Portrait of William Carey and Lord Hunsdon's Long Gallery*, The Burlington Magazine, 123, no.938, May 1981, pp.304–5

Flugel, J.C., *The Character and Married Life of Henry VIII*, International Journal of Psychoanalysis, I, 1920

Gairdner, J., *Mary and Anne Boleyn*, The English Historical Review, 8, 29, (Jan. 1893), pp.53–60

Gairdner, J., and Motta, B., *The Draft Dispensation for Henry VIII's Marriage with Anne Boleyn*, The English Historical Review, 5, 19, July 1890, pp.544–50

Harris, Barbara J., *English Aristocratic Women, 1450–1550: Marriage and Family, Property and Careers*, 2002

———, *The View from My Lady's Chamber: New Perspectives on the Early Tudor Monarchy*, The Huntingdon Library Quarterly, 60, 3, English Political History, 1500–1640, 1997, pp.215–47

———, *Women and Politics in Early Tudor England*, The Historical Journal, 33, 2, June 1990, pp.259–81

Heale, Elizabeth, *Women and the Courtly Love Lyric: The Devonshire MS*, The Modern Language Review (MLR), 90, 2, April 1995, pp.296–313

Hodgkin, J. Eliot, *The Early Life of Anne Boleyn*, Notes and Queries, 1895, pp.141–2,

Hoskins, Anthony, *Mary Boleyn's Carey Children – Offspring of King Henry VIII?*, Genealogy Magazine

Ives, E.W., *The Fall of Anne Boleyn Reconsidered*, EHR, 107, no.424, July 1992, pp.651–64

Paget, Hugh, '*The Youth of Anne Boleyn*', Bulletin of the Institute of Historical
    Research, 55, 1981

Sir Thomas Nevill, 1503–82, Notes and Queries, 1906; s10–V: 2–4

Shrewsbury, J.F.D., '*Henry VIII: a Medical Study*', Journal of the History of
    Medicine

Siemens, R.G., *Thomas Wyatt, Anne Boleyn, and Henry VIII's Lyric 'Pastime with
    Good Company'*, Notes and Queries, 1997, 44: 26–27

Warnicke, Retha M., *Sexual Heresy at the Court of Henry VIII*, The Historical
    Journal, vol. 30, no.2, June 1987, pp.247–68

Welply, W. H., *The Date of Mary Boleyn's Death*, Notes and Queries, 1951

Whitaker, A.E., *The Shelton Family*, The William and Mary Quarterly, 2nd series,
    July 1929, pp.201–8

Index